The Changing Curriculum

Studies in the
Postmodern Theory of Education

Joe L. Kincheloe and Shirley R. Steinberg
General Editors

Vol. 18

PETER LANG
New York • Washington, D.C./Baltimore
Bern • Frankfurt am Main • Berlin • Vienna • Paris

Ivor F. Goodson

The Changing Curriculum

Studies in Social Construction

PETER LANG
New York • Washington, D.C./Baltimore
Bern • Frankfurt am Main • Berlin • Vienna • Paris

Library of Congress Cataloging-in-Publication Data

Goodson, Ivor.
The changing curriculum: studies in social construction/ Ivor F. Goodson.
p. cm. — (Counterpoints; v. 18)
1. Curriculum planning—Social aspects. 2. Curriculum change—Social
aspects. 3. Postmodernism and education. I. Title. II. Series: Counterpoints
(New York, N.Y.); vol. 18.
LB2806.15.G66   374'.001—dc21   96-50441
ISBN 0-8204-2609-1
ISSN 1058-1634

Die Deutsche Bibliothek-CIP-Einheitsaufnahme

Goodson, Ivor F.:
The changing curriculum: studies in social construction/
Ivor F. Goodson. –New York; Washington, D.C./Baltimore; Bern;
Frankfurt am Main; Berlin; Vienna; Paris: Lang.
(Counterpoints; Vol. 18)
ISBN 0-8204-2609-1
NE: GT

Cover design by Wendy Lee.

The paper in this book meets the guidelines for permanence and durability
of the Committee on Production Guidelines for Book Longevity
of the Council of Library Resources.

© 1997 Peter Lang Publishing, Inc., New York

Printed in the United States of America.

Contents

Introduction by Joe Kincheloe   ix

1   By Way of Introduction   1

2   Investigating Schooling:
    From the Personal to the Programmatic   7

3   "Chariots of Fire": Etymologies, Epistemologies,
    and the Emergence of Curriculum   23

4   Basil Bernstein and Aspects of the
    Sociology of the Curriculum   43

5   Curriculum History, Professionalization,
    and the Social Organization of Knowledge:
    ·An Extended Paradigm for the
    History of Education (with Ian Dowbiggan)   61

6   Docile Bodies: Commonalities in the
    History of Psychiatry and Schooling
    (with Ian Dowbiggan)   83

7   Curriculum Contests: Environmental
    Studies Versus Geography   113

8   Beyond the Subject Monolith:
    Traditions and Subcultures   139

9   Distinction and Destiny:
    The Importance of Curriculum Form in
    Elite American Private Schools (with Peter
    W. Cookson, Jr. and Caroline H. Persell)   163

10 On Curriculum Form: Notes Toward a
    Theory of Curriculum   181

Publications by the Author (1987-1997)   199

Index   207

Acknowledgements

"By Way of Introduction." Our thanks to D. Santor for the piece titled "A conversation with Ivor Goodson," which appeared in *Education News*, Vol. 5, No. 1, 1990, p. 2.

"Investigating Schooling: From the Personal to the Programmatic" appeared in *New Education*, Vol. 14, No. 1, 1992, pp. 21–30.

"'Chariots of Fire': Etymologies, Epistemologies, and the Emergence of Curriculum," appeared in *The Making of Curriculum: Collected Essays* 2d e. (1995). Thanks to Falmer Press for permission to print.

"Basil Bernstein and Aspects of the Sociology of the Curriculum" appeared in P. Atkinson, B. Davies, and S. Delamont, Eds., *Discourse and Reproduction*, Cresskill, New Jersey: Hampton Press, 1995, pp. 121–136.

"Curriculum History, Professionalization, and the Social Organization of Knowledge: An Extended Paradigm for the History of Education" appeared in *Curriculum and Teaching*, Vol. 12, No. 1-2, 1990, pp. 3–13.

"Docile Bodies: Commonalities in the History of Psychiatry and Schooling" first appeared in *Qualitative Studies in Education*, Vol. 2, No. 3, 1989, pp. 203–220.

"Curriculum Contests: Environmental Studies Versus Geography," will appear in *Environmental Education Research*, Vol. 2, No. 1, 1996, pp. 71–88.

"Beyond the Subject Monolith: Traditions and Sub-Cultures" appeared in A. Westoby, Ed., *Culture and Power in Educational Organizations*, Milton Keynes and Philadelphia: Open University Press, 1988, pp. 181–197. It also appeared in P. Harling, Ed., *New Directions in Educational Leadership*, London, New York, and Philadelphia: Falmer Press, 1984.

"Distinction and Destiny: The Importance of Curriculum Form in Elite American Private Schools" (with Peter W. Cookson, Jr., and Caroline H. Persell). Appeared in *Discourse* Vol. 18, No. 2, 1997.

Thanks to Falmer Press, Philadelphia, for allowing us to use "On Curriculum Form," which first appeared in "On Curriculum Form: Notes Towards a Theory of Curriculum" in *Sociology of Education*, Vol. 65, No. 1, January 1992, pp. 66–75.

My thanks to Carol Brookbanks, particularly for her help on this manuscript and, more generally, for her help in my office administration.

Introduction

Joe L. Kincheloe

Ivor Goodson is one of a kind—indeed, only a unique constellation of circumstances could have converged to produce this character. Like many other educational scholars I know, I am an Ivor-watcher. I enjoy watching him present a speech to a conference, work a crowded room, procure a book contract from a publisher, or tell a story to an appreciative congregation. In these contexts Ivor operates within a symbiotic dialectic constructed by a keen academic insight and a razor sharp sense of irony. Ever ready to raise an eyebrow at the posturings of the bourgeoisie, Ivor sees the universe from an angle that never fails to inform and entertain me. Bound by our romance with the burlesque of pomposity, Ivor and I walk into the academy with a similar outsider's "take" on the circus unfolding around us. For these and many other reasons I am honored by Ivor's request for me to write an introduction to *The Changing Curriculum*. My purpose in this effort involves the delineation of a few of the main themes of Ivor's work in the process situating it in relation to the advances in U.S. curriculum studies over the last quarter century. Hopefully, this volume will grant U.S. curriculum scholars unfamiliar with Ivor's brilliance an *entrée* to his *oeuvre*.

Etymologies

Goodson's work is predicated on the belief that a curriculum scholar's task involves the development of more profound understandings of the curriculum. Eschewing the technical call for the formulation of formulas and cookbook strategies for course development and pedagogy, he explores the nature of interpretation and its relation to the remaking of experience.

Grounded in the paradigmatic upheavals of the 1960s and their intuitive rejection of hypothetico-deductive pursuit of objective facts about the world at large and education in particular, Ivor was influenced by the efforts sociologists of knowledge to make sense of the subjective perceptions of human beings, people's constructions of reality. Reading Weber, Mead, Schutz, Goffman, and Berger and Luckman, Goodson began to seek out that knowledge which allowed one to understand the forms of meaning making on which the social order is grounded. Like William Pinar and the Reconceptualist movement in curriculum studies in the U.S., Goodson appreciated that the future of the field would revolve around understanding not technical curriculum development.

By the early 1970s the new sociology of knowledge had precipitated the rise of a new sociology of education in England. Questions surrounding the ways that a culture selects, classifies, distributes, transmits, and evaluates curricular knowledge were driving a new body of scholarship. With its concern for the distinctions between high-status and low-status knowledge and the role of power in the production of knowledge, this new scholarship helped Goodson lay out the initial parameters for his study of schooling and the curriculum. Paying close attention to the new sociologists of education's critique of mainstream educational theory and practice and their exposé of its false claim to political objectivity, Ivor took to heart their rejection of an epistemology that reduced both scholarship and pedagogy to procedural fidelity rather than to careful analysis and contextual insight. Knowledge, he quickly came to understand, is not simply something to pass along uncritically to students; rather, it is a social construction that reflects status patterns and social hierarchies existing in the larger society.

Working with Brian Davies, Michael Young, and Basil Bernstein at the Institute of Education in London, Goodson was fascinated by the power of their lectures. After having studied Irish immigrants in Victorian England at the London School of Economics, he was amazed by the study of working class educational and cultural experiences—experiences so much like his own. Davies and Bernstein's tutorial were exciting, if for no other reason, than that they proved that learning did not have to be painful, disconnected from life, and alienating. One senses Ivor's revivification, his renewed sense of possibility in light of his experiences at the Institute. In this exciting context Ivor eagerly read the papers on knowledge, power, and education being pushed at him by his professors—essays that would lay the foundation for much of the political work that would emerge over the next two decades in the paradigmatic shift in curriculum studies. Schools, Davies, Young, and Bernstein argued, are political and cultural domains that can serve as sites of social control. Knowledge production, they continued, is never sweet and innocent and is always connected on some level to political needs and machinations. And of special interest to Ivor, his professors maintained that subordinate cultures and subjugated ways of seeing were significant and merited serious study. So much of Ivor's (and later my own) pedagogical foundations were developed during his time at the Institute in the late 1960s and early 1970s.

So many politically-oriented curriculum scholars found sustenance in this work—Henry Giroux, Michael Apple, Jo Anne Pagano, Jean Anyon, Philip Wexler, and Peter McLaren to name but a few. All of these curricularists would come to maintain that any critical analysis of curriculum would: question what the curriculum *excluded* as well as what it included; make connections between the curriculum and larger cultural processes involving the validation of racial, class-based, and gendered social formations; view the curriculum as part of a larger cultural learning process inseparable from questions of privilege and oppression. As British cultural studies from Birmingham began to exert more of an impact on political curriculum studies, questions of representation and signification would come to play a more important role in such analysis. Wherever political work takes us, the Institute exerted an influence that still informs the study of schooling and curriculum.

Social/Historical Constructionism

Emerging from the Institute in the early 1970s, Goodson began to carve out his niche in the effort to move beyond the search for scientifically-based universals to a historically and socially constructionist mode of examining curriculum. It is in this context that we can begin to make sense of Ivor's work and its relationship to similar work in the U.S. When Pinar spoke of the reconceptualization of curriculum studies, Ivor was interpreting the paradigmatic shift as a move to a more multi-dimensional analysis of the spheres and levels where curriculum is produced and negotiated. Ivor's particular form of multi-dimensional analysis combines the analysis of the lives of individuals who directly experience curricula with the antecedent structures that lay the foundations for the development of curricula—a so-called "middle ground" methodology (Hargreaves, 1994). Such a method moves beyond the effort to develop models of idealized practice that tend to remove the curriculum from the context that produced it. Goodson contends that any curriculum scholar needs to be able to explain how particular knowledge forms are canonized, the ways that power reifies and calcifies. As Peter McLaren (1993) observes, one of the central themes that appears and reappears in Ivor's work involves the way that disciplinary subjects are better understood as "continually changing subgroups of information" rather than sacred bodies of knowledge. With this concept in mind Goodson maintains that a socially and historically constructed, ever-mutating curriculum simply cannot be taught as an incontestable fixity.

Those who fail to understand the social and historical construction of the curriculum cannot understand there is simply no truth that exists beyond culture. Ivor is especially critical of those who refuse to recognize this observation, maintaining that trans-historical curriculum theories often misrepresent reality, often fail to appreciate the unexamined cultural assumptions underlying such theories. Operating without such insight curriculum developers are unable to move beyond the status quo, often retreating to the comfort of popular mystifications about what every student "has to cover." No matter what ideological background one brings to the negotiation, Goodson insists, the failure to understand the reasons why present structures exist will undermine reform efforts. In periods of great upheaval and social change curriculum reformers notoriously tend to reject established procedures and content. Supported by a knowledge of the social and historical construction of the extant curriculum, reformers are far better equipped to make long-term changes that accomplish goals of social justice, democracy, and pedagogical excellence.

The Reconceptualization

Before the Reconceptualization of the U.S. curriculum field in the 1970s the discipline was perceived as conceptually underdeveloped. Since that time curriculum studies has emerged as a vibrant field, replete with excitement, creative energy, and a body of theoretically informed scholarship. William Pinar, as a central catalyst of the Reconceptualization, characterized the field in the early 1970s as populated by three distinct groups: 1) the Tylerian traditionalists with their emphasis on a linear delineation of objectives and models; 2) the conceptual-empiricists with their positivistic grounding in the theory and practice of contemporary social science; and 3) the Reconceptualists with their emphasis on understanding curriculum and its context in a historical, philosophical, and literary sense. From the outside the Reconceptualization was often viewed as a radical insurgency dedicated to moving curriculum studies away from its "proper" concern with curriculum development and evaluation in school settings. Phillip Jackson, an outsider, described the movement as characterized by three main features: 1) a rejection of Tylerianism; 2) the use of diverse theoretical traditions to study curriculum such as psychoanalysis, phenomenology, and existentialism; and 3) a leftist politics grounded upon Marxist and neo-Marxist theory.

Pinar quickly recognized that there were as many differences between those identified with the Reconceptualization as there were similarities. The movement's success with the delegitimization of the traditionalists' ahistorical and atheoretical approach led to the dissolution of any strong sense of solidarity. With the advent of autobiographical studies, critical pedagogy, feminist theory, and poststructuralism and the expansion of existential and phenomenological approaches, the Reconceptualization as a movement collapsed. The work in sociology of knowledge at the London Institute of Education and the scholarship emerging in the 1960s and 1970s in cultural studies in Birmingham are inseparable from the theoretical and political dynamics at work in the U.S. Reconceptualization. Many of the same debates occurred in the U.S., Canada, and England during the period. In the U.S., for example, Joseph Schwab's call for a return to the practical school-based role of curriculum specialists is echoed in England at the Centre for Applied Research in Education (CARE) at the University of East Anglia (Interestingly, Goodson moved to a Chair of Education at the University of East Anglia in 1997). Both Schwab and the curricularists at CARE were ambivalent about the role of the theoretical and the relation between theory and practice. In both nations scholars in the field struggled with they might deal with such questions.

As Pinar explored the etymology of the word, curriculum, in the U.S., Goodson pursued his own etymological analysis in England. In Pinar's reconceptually-related effort to analyze educational experience, he connected his understanding of phenomenology, psychoanalysis, and aesthetics to the etymology of curriculum to produce a unique analytical form. *Currere*, the Latin root of the word, curriculum, in Pinar's context concerns the investigation of the nature of the individual experience of the public. In Latin, Pinar maintained, *currere* means running the race course—a verb. Traditional understandings in the field of curriculum have reduced the word to its noun form, the track—i.e., the course of study. In this context Pinar's student Patrick Slattery (1995) argues that mainstream educators forget that curriculum is an active process; it is not simply the lesson plan, the district guidebook, the standardized test, the goals and milestones, or the textbook. The curriculum, Slattery continues, is a holistic life experience, the journey of becoming a self-aware subject capable of shaping his or her life path. As a perpetual struggle, the curriculum in Pinar's *currere* is never a finished product that can be finally mastered and passed along to an awaiting new generation. If Pinar examined *currere* in a phenomenological, psychoanalytical, and aesthetic context, Goodson's etymological analysis was historical. Following the term's linguistic history, Goodson displayed his ability to historically contextualize the evolution of curricular change, illustrating in the process its social construction. As examples of the paradigm shift in curriculum studies on both sides of the Atlantic, Pinar's and Goodson's work is fascinating in its complementarity.

Goodson's Uniqueness As A Scholar

While there is theoretical and methodological overlap between Goodson and Pinar's reconceptualization of curriculum studies, one can also find connections between Ivor's scholarship and many other U.S. curricularists such as Herbert Kliebard, Lois Weis, Henry Giroux, Peter McLaren, and Philip Wexler to name only a few. Still, Goodson has carved a unique notch in the larger paradigm shift within the field as the consummate foundations of curriculum scholar. In this role he draws upon history, sociology, and philosophy to make sense of subject development. As a foundations of curriculum scholar, Goodson becomes a rogue contextualizer who repairs the epistemological damage of technical modes of knowledge production. As he challenges these discourses of inquiry, Goodson uses his foundational tools to develop a more textured and complex sense of the ways curriculum is constructed. In my own work on the nature of power and how it works to produce and transmit knowledge, shape identity, and construct values, Goodson has offered important insight.

Understanding the propensity of political students of curriculum to focus on general cultural dynamics (macro-theories) to explain educational inequality and the tendency of phenomenologically-based students to privilege the particularistic domain of classroom interaction (micro-theories), Goodson early on recognized the need to analyze the interrelation of the two spheres of activity. Goodson's friend and colleague, Andy Hargreaves (1994) recognizes this dynamic and points to Ivor's bridging of the chasm via his analyses of subject traditions. In this context Goodson has brought together the theoretical (macro) and the empirical (micro), attacking directly the complexity of lived experience and its refusal to fit "too neatly" into any theoretical category. In doing so he provides us with a more detailed and usable corpus of work than scholars who would opt for simplistic explanations of power's ability to maintain its privilege. In this manner Goodson places himself on the middle ground between the theoretical and the particular—a location that provides him unique insight into the messy process of power's confrontation with curriculum.

Convinced that any successful reconceptualization of curriculum as study and practice must make use of historical data to inform our analysis of the relationship binding power, curriculum, and schooling, Ivor focuses on the evolution of curriculum. Such a focus allows Goodson to generate theoretical frameworks that are intimately connected to empirical evidence. Synchronic analysis—snapshots of complex processes at a particular moment—cannot compensate for extended analysis over time. Indeed, such snapshots, Goodson contends, may actually mislead curriculum scholars attempting to trace the evolutionary process. Only through a careful historical analysis can explanation be developed. Theoretical explanation should not drive historical scholarship, Ivor admonishes, but the identification of the recurrence of historical events can elucidate theoretical explanation. Goodson's subtle understanding of these historiographical and social theoretical dynamics is instructive for curriculum scholars and well as students of history and sociology.

The Centrality of Class

As many observers have noted, Goodson's working class origins have played a major role in the formulation of his academic work. Like many of us, Ivor's gaze on schooling is shaped by his humble roots, his living around poor people. The curriculum was not only alien and uninteresting to him as a student, but often unintelligible, a second language, a form of cultural displacement. Reflecting W. E. B. DuBois's notion of the double consciousness of the oppressed, Ivor's marginality allowed him to see the curriculum from an angle more privileged observers might miss. Goodson the scholar recognizes the importance of the everyday experiences of ordinary students, the ways educational policy makers ignore the needs of basic and general level kids, and the centrality of keeping students in school who typically drop out. As a teacher, Goodson watched this process play itself out as the curriculum "broke the will" of most of his working class students. Such students were victimized by a devil's bargain that agreed to teach them specific facts in a mechanical manner. Students were not taught to generalize across contexts with such data and were thus rendered increasingly passive in the school setting.

Ivor's concern with issues of socio-economic class shaped his fascination with Basil Bernstein's analysis of the everyday experiences of ordinary students and people in general. Such concerns have shaped the work of many critical scholars around the world, myself included. Taking our cue from the same sources as Goodson, we have focused on subjugated knowledges—ways of seeing the world by marginalized peoples that have been dismissed or suppressed and information that has been disqualified by social and academic gatekeepers. We believe that through the cultivation of low ranking knowledges alternate democratic visions of society, education and cognition are possible. Teachers who take subjugated knowledges seriously become transformative agents who alert the community to its own dangerous memory, in the process of helping individuals name their oppression or possibly understand their complicity in oppression. Such a naming process allows students, teachers, and community members to reflect on the construction of their lived worlds. With such reflection individuals develop the ability to become subjects of their own lives.

Thus, critical teachers work to uncover dangerous memories that involve the remembrance of how the consciousness of various groups and individuals has come to be constructed. Such an awareness frees students, teachers, and community members to claim an identity apart from the one that was forced on them. Indeed, identity is constructed when memories are aroused—in other words, confrontation with dangerous memory changes our perceptions of the forces that shape us, which in turn moves us to redefine our world views, our way of seeing. The social forces that shape us have formed the identities of both the powerful and the marginalized. Without Goodson's type of historical analysis of this process, it will never be clear why students succeed or fail in schools. We will forever be blind to the tacit ideological forces that construct student perceptions of school and the impact such perceptions have on their school experience. Such blindness restricts our view of our own and our student's perception of their place in history and in the web of reality. Historical decontextualization renders us vulnerable to the myths employed to perpetuate social domination.

Thus, Goodson explores the dangerous memories of curriculum, uncovering the ways class bias undermines opportunity even in contexts ostensibly designed to address such prejudice. In this context Goodson's exploration of comprehensive schools in England exposes the duplicity of the claim that such institutions were developed to unify educational experience and address the socio-economic class segregation of the grammar schools and the secondary modern schools. Pointing out that the new comprehensive schools retained the curricular form and content and the accompanying class segregation of the previous schools, Goodson justifies the importance of curriculum history in the effort to delineate the actual effects of school reform as opposed to merely its stated intentions. The same class conscious lenses are used in Goodson's analysis of Canadian commercial and technical education. Viewing such curricula as specialized training for a particular class of people, he classifies commercial and technical education as narrowly utilitarian courses of study that consistently fail to earn high status for students who take them. If such studies do nothing else, Goodson concludes, they remove working class students from the high-status academic courses that are necessary for socio-economic mobility.

One area where Ivor's work on class specifically intersects with my own studies revolves around questions of socio-economic class and cognition. Goodson's historical analysis of curriculum has revealed that school reformers developed a class-specific cognitive theory that delineated different orders of intelligence or "mentalities" for different class groupings. Indeed, the manual/mental division of labor found analogous expression in curriculum and cognitive tracks. Students with "lower order" mentalities from the subordinate classes would take technical and commercial courses that would not call attention to their cognitive "inadequacies." Goodson outlines what he calls three dichotomies of thought that emerge from this cognitive theory: 1) lower-order mentalities were characterized by sensual and concrete thinking while higher-order mentalities were grounded on intellectual, verbal, and abstract qualities. Goodson conceptualizes this dichotomy in Calvinistic terms, viewing the academic "elect" as those students who possess a facility for academic subjects. Their election, he tells us is manifested by their "ascension" to higher education where they continue to study the disciplines.

2) Lower-order mentalities were capable of simplistic thinking while higher-order students were capable of complexity and sophistication. In this context Goodson repositions Adam

Smith in cognitive theory as well as an economic theory, as the father of the dismal science viewed laborers as "stupid and ignorant" and managers as more complex and sophisticated thinkers who must daily confront extremely complicated issues; and 3) lower-order mentalities were passive in their response to experience and knowledge while the upper-order was active and engaged, ready to make connections between disparate ideas and apply such thinking to a wide variety of contexts. Such unexamined cognitive assumptions, Ivor tells us, were used to build curricular foundations, thus reifying the construction of the alleged mentalities and, concurrently, the class structure itself. Thus, even though unified and common schools were developed, the self-validating division of mentalities were used to justify class divisions.

Shirley Steinberg and my notion of post-formal thinking is grounded on the recognition of the socio-historical division of class mentalities that Goodson documents. Using such cognitive demarcations educators in both Europe and North America attributed differences in student performances to individual differences in ability. Without a sensitivity to class and other forms of marginalization, educators and cognitive psychologists failed to dig deeper, to discover abilities hidden in the school context, to explore the impact of the student's lived culture on his or her perceptions or actions. With our interest in understanding the way socio-economic class shapes both student performance in school and educator perception of students, Goodson, Steinberg, and myself have found that some innate form of intellectual ability has relatively little to do with one's academic success or failure. We have discovered that even *measured* differences in intelligence make little difference in worker productivity in the workplace or in occupational achievement. Both educational scholars and practitioners have, unfortunately, been oblivious to the way power interests have produced curricular formats, systems of instruction, methods of evaluation, and definitions of teacher and student success. The way, we argue, that such power interests interact with personal behavior is that school leaders induce students to believe that such class-based divisions of students are natural and necessary.

As Steinberg and I take into account the higher/lower mentalities identified by Goodson and connect them to class dynamics of student academic performance, we move cognitive theory to a post-formal perspective. Such a vantage point overtly politicizes cognition, as it attempts to free students marginalized by class, race, or gender factors from socio-interpersonal norms and ideological expectations. The post-formal concern with questions of curricular formation, meaning making, emancipation via ideological awareness, and attention to the process of self-production moves beyond traditional concerns cognitive theory. Post-formalism, like Goodson's scholarship, grapples with purpose, devoting attention to issues of human dignity, freedom, authority, and social responsibility. A critical post-formalism grounded on a concern with social justice initiates a reflective dialogue that is always concerned with the expansion of an awareness of power's complicity in the production of subjectivity, never certain of the definition of emancipation, and perpetually reconceptualizing the structure of the curriculum in light of social, economic, political, and communicational changes.

Drawing upon Goodson's historical insights, post-formal cognitive theory attempts to remove working class students from their placement in a psychological discourse that views them as Lockean individuals, isolated entities. Critical studies (McLaren, 1986; McLeod, 1987) have long maintained that children come to school with disparate amounts of cultural capital that can be traded for advantage in the school microcosm. Knowledge of white middle-class language, concern with academic success, and the ability to deport oneself in what the upper- middle-class considers a courteous manner all contribute to one's advantage at school. Metaphorical constructs and meaning-making frameworks brought to school by working class students are often dismissed as developmentally arrested. Because traditional forms of psychological developmentalism fail to ground themselves within a constructivist understanding of power relationships of dominant and subordinate cultures, they have often privileged white middle-class notions of meaning and success. Critical outcomes are far from the consciousness of many curriculum makers who ground their work in the discourse of child development.

Obviously, the study of curriculum cannot be separated from questions of class and its impact on knowledge forms. Yet in the reconceptualization of curriculum studies class analysis declined in importance, as race and gender studies became more and more popular. One important factor that induced the decline of class analysis involved the failure of so-called reproduction theory. This theory viewed schools as mechanisms that unproblematically taught the values, social practices and skills required for the dominant corporate order. The curriculum from the perspective of reproduction theory provides students from different social backgrounds with knowledge and skills that both validate the dominant social order and track young people into a workforce stratified by race, gender, and class dynamics. There is little we can do to subvert this process, reproduction theorists contended, short of abandoning schools altogether. Developing no theory that delineated alternatives, reproduction theorists offered a pessimistic vision of the future of schooling. As the preeminent critic of reproduction theory, Henry Giroux (1988) argued that we must understand schools as sites of struggle between dominant and subordinate forms of power that always hold within them latent possibilities for democratic change. No chance of reform exists, he contended, unless we gain an awareness of the ways students and teachers create spaces for empowerment within the everyday life of schools. Such a perspective, Giroux concluded, refuses the nihilism of reproduction theory, as it recognizes the multiple voices and power dynamics that interact on the terrain of schooling.

Among politically-grounded scholars of curriculum the debate about the role of class-analysis in the field continues. Scholars such as Goodson, Giroux, Aronowitz, McLaren, Apple, Weis, and Wexler have discussed how we engage class and curriculum in a post-socialist, postmodern era where the political struggle has been ensnared in the realm of the symbolic. Given the information bombardment and representational politics (the ability of powerful groups to use the media to portray themselves positively and those who might threaten their interests negatively) of the postmodern condition to help students make meanings, political scholars have to expand the venue of their analysis to include the workings of hyperreal, media-propelled power formulations. Both Lois Weis and Philip Wexler have addressed this point, maintaining the processes of signification must be explored in the context of how it produces the identities of students and citizens in ways that render them complicit and/or resistant to the needs of the power bloc. Goodson's scholarship in the context of this work is extremely important, as he historically grounds the discussion of class-bias in relation to the curriculum in particular and pedagogical concerns in general.

Power and Justice: The Politics of Curriculum

The logical extension of Goodson's sensitivity to questions of class is his concern with social justice, his moral assertion that schools should attempt to deal with students from all different backgrounds equally. Accomplishing such a goal, however, is not a matter of simply "doing the right thing." Indeed, the ways schools fail to travel the path of justice is an extremely complex, often irrational process that is idiosyncratic and covert. Ivor is acutely aware of the way this drama works and traces the convoluted footprints of power to corporations, businesses, universities, subject discipline organizations, and other unlikely curriculum developers. The way school policy and curricular decisions are made is not made on the basis of what's best for children—especially poor children. Such determinations are first and foremost political acts, marked by the power plays of material and ideological interests that may ostensibly have little to do with school or its students. The truth is that such struggles have everything to do with the school and its students and the social roles they play. The power struggle over curriculum shapes our views of ourselves and our visions for a better and more just world.

In studying the politics of curriculum Goodson understands that power is a dialectical force that works both on and through people—it em*powers* and dis*empowers*. Ivor's work on the complexity of power in education along with the work of his professor, Basil Bernstein, have laid an important conceptual foundation on which many political curriculum analysts, including myself, have drawn in our attempt to understand this hydra-like entity. A highly contested subject of analysis, power, many have come to maintain, is a basic dynamic in human existence. Consensus, however, dissolves at this point with various scholars running like quail in diverse theoretical directions. Students from both the symbolic interactionist and the cultural studies traditions accept the fundamental-constituent-of-reality thesis, as they contend that power is embedded in the social frameworks of race, class, gender, schooling, occupations, and everyday interaction and communication. Poststructuralists such as Foucault agree, maintaining that power is present in all human relationships be they lovers, students-teacher, business partners, or researchers and the researched. Indeed, Foucault concluded that like the capillaries in the circulatory system, power is inseparable from the social domain. As to the form of this ubiquitous social dynamic, Foucault never offered a definition more specific than the exercise of power is a way in which particular actions modify others or guide their possible conduct. Since power is everywhere, therefore, it is not something that can be easily dispensed with or overthrown. Simplistic politics, pedagogies, or curriculum theories that propose to put an end to power relations, do not understand its relation to the web of socio-political reality (Musolf, 1992; McCarthy, 1992; Cooper, 1994).

Social constructivists like Goodson understand, of course, that there is nothing simple about the workings of power. They appreciate that power is not simply the changing exercise of a binary relationship: A exercises its power over B and B responds by formulating acts of resistance against A. In its complexity and ambiguity power is deployed by both dominant and subordinate individuals and groups—it is not the province of one group and not the other. Thus, conceptions of power that depict it as a one-dimensional, unified force with standardized outcomes miss important aspects of its nature. For example, when advocates of a free market capitalism argue that the market works to satisfy consumer needs—i.e., that consumer power flows in one direction toward the producers of goods to shape their production decisions—they fail to understand the two way (and more) flow of power in the circumstance. Consumer power is not sufficient to thwart producer ability to hide information concerning safety, environmental aspects of production, exploitation of labor in the production of particular goods, etc. . . that would drastically change the behavior of many consumers. Thus, power flows in a variety of directions often behind the curtain of surface appearances (Rorty, 1992; Keat, 1994).

Concerned with contributing to the understanding of how power *dominates* via the curriculum, Goodson analyzes curriculum as a form of socio-economic exclusion. Acting on his appreciation of power's complexity, he questions the processes by which curricula seem to internalize the social division of labor. Curriculum analysis is extremely important in the larger critical project of exposing and understanding the nature of power relations, Ivor argues, as it specifically highlights the ways social interests are internalized within what is referred to as disinterested, objective knowledge. In this manner the fingerprints of power are erased, as the covert internalization process camouflages power's preferential process of privileging the already privileged. To appreciate such a covert process Goodson insists that we must look inside the curriculum, transcending the reliance or banal generalizations that emerge from grand social theories. It is only in this specific scholarly work in the trenches that the political interests behind bureaucratic proclamations of curricular neutrality can be revealed. In this context Goodson's analysis of the curricula of elite American private schools can be understood. As such institutions teach the classical curriculum, the "best of Western Civilization," the "quintessence of what it means to be civilized," students learn knowledge that is beyond reproach, above social conflict. Students who internalize the socio-political *accouterments* of the elite private school curriculum, learn that their privilege is also beyond reproach. While adolescents gain knowledge that helps shape identity from a plethora of experiences outside the classroom, Goodson cautions, privileged students in such institutions find much in the curriculum to justify the social hierarchy on which they sit atop.

Turning to Foucault to help him theorize how the curriculum and its socially approved structures of knowledge helped discipline self, body, emotions, intellect, and behavior, Goodson explores Foucauldian theories of domination. Disciplinary power can both punish and transform individuals into subjects, Foucault maintained, through the disciplines of the human sciences—e.g., medicine, education, psychiatry, penology, criminology, and the various social sciences. Foucault contends that the power of these disciplines has created a normalized culture through the use of discourses of expertise at particular social sites—hospitals, schools, asylums, prisons, etc. . . .While accepting Foucault's general premise that knowledge disciplines exert the power to normalize, Goodson critiques what he calls the one-dimensionally of Foucault's interpretation of the influence of professional knowledge. Foucault fails to consider the idiosyncratic, context-specific ways schools and other institutions practice domination and enforce docility, Goodson charges. Knowledge in disciplines, he continues, shapes not only the perspectives of the clientele (students and patients) professionals serve, but such knowledge also shapes the professionals themselves. We see evidence of the latter dynamic at work when professionals are moved to operate on the basis of career motivations, not on the needs of the client—needs that tend to conflict with career interests.

Anticipating the work of power theorists in critical pedagogy and cultural studies, Goodson understands that the disciplinary bodies of knowledge formulated to regulate the public never quite complete their task. Targeted individuals and groups are never rendered as docile as power wielders might hope or as political analysts once theorized. Goodson appreciates that while all oppositional behavior is not emancipatory, the process of domination and the ways it elicits both compliance and resistance is a domain that demands serious study in the coming years. Indeed, the attempt to create democratic schooling and vibrant democracies may hinge on our ability to appreciate the multidimensional nature of power, domination, compliance, and resistance in a way that informs our effort to reconstruct the public sphere in Western societies. It is at this point that Goodson's and my own political and pedagogical concerns intersect. Upon Ivor's shoulders I attempt to extend his analysis of power and curriculum, moving many directions at once. The direction I will explore here involves the expansion of Goodson's important recognition that the power of knowledge disciplines never renders students and other targets as docile as expected.

Despite the work of previous generations of critical scholars, no one theory of power or domination can work for all
places and all times. Power is by nature context specific, socially embedded, and historically situated—trying, for example,
to impose Gramscian hegemony theory on an explanation of
the L. A. uprising of 1992 may be quite misleading. The L. A.
police were not attempting to "win the consent" of Rodney
King and other South Central residents; a more naked form of
domination by force might better explain the workings of power
in this context. Even when hegemonic consent is sought, as
Goodson well knows, many individuals refuse to accept it—so
many, in fact, that the effort may fail. My point here is that
power theory is leaky, that power relations cannot explain all
human behavior. People do not occupy their everyday realities
like small cogs in a larger social machine; their lives are not
totalized by the conveyance of power upon and through them.
Human beings are active agents that bring to disciplinary sites
the identities and abilities they have constructed in their own
life histories often outside of regulatory contexts. Thus, power
blocs do not possess the ability to homogenize the cultural
landscape and consolidate its interests in some seamless sort
of way. With such understandings we are far better theoretically prepared to examine the disciplinary process. We are vigi-
lant not to abandon all we have learned and assume that the
possibility of freedom from domination is easy and all possess
an equal potential to achieve it—such is simply not the case,
for oppression exists. The point is that macro-processes must
be analyzed at the level of the particular.

If power is not a unitary force with unitary effects or unidi-
rectional hierarchy, then we can be alert to different ways oppressed people elude control. If we are all empowered by our
particular capacities and skills and we are all unempowered by
our in ability either to satisfy our wants and needs or express
our living spirit, we begin to understand that power is exercised by both dominant and subordinate forces. Even though
subordinated people have little access to any larger social,
political, economic, or educational *system* of power, they do
possess their own types of power. The nature of this power
can be viewed from a variety of perspectives including everything from the oppressed's depth and nobility of character to

what has been termed manifest and latent power. The manifest power of subordinates involves the skills and resources they exhibit in their work for themselves and for their managers; their latent power involves the power to resist, the ability to reorient their consciousness in a way that refuses to see themselves as subordinate. An important aspect of this latent power involves the poor's ability to present themselves as a potential menace to "polite" society. W. E. B. DuBois understood this dynamic decades ago, as he spoke of African American boycotts of particular consumer goods. Black leaders have subsequently picked up the DuBoisian strategy, arguing that African Americans should consume as a block in order to undermine white domination in black communities. Crowds always hold a latent power as an army of chaos—a reality not lost on power wielders.

John Fiske (1993) uses the term, imperializing power, to describe strong, top-down forms of power; he uses the term, localizing power, to label weak, bottom-up forms of power. Imperializing power attempts to spread its influence as far as possible—from outer space to inner consciousness. Localizing power, on the other hand, tries to control the immediate space around it, including an individual's thoughts, feelings, identity, and interpersonal relationships—dynamics subordinate individuals often feel under threat from imperializing powers. Thus, localizing powers always find themselves in a conflictual relationship with imperializing power, as they attempt self-determination in face of the imperializing power of, for example, the dominant economic classes, patriarchy, and white supremacy. In the context of Goodson's work in subject histories, the imperializing power of the subject discipline attempts to colonize the localizing power of secondary teachers and their students to make the subject relevant to their everyday lives.

In this context we can understand the importance of power theory in Goodson and other critical curriculum scholars' attempt to understand the social construction of the curriculum. Using Fiske's concept of imperializing and localizing power, students of curriculum are able to focus on power as a *productive* social dynamic, i.e., the power to. . . . Making use of feminist theory, we begin to understand that power is not merely a zero-sum competitive struggle or an equation in search of balancing. Neither is power simply a form of repression. In this context the Latin derivation of power, *potere*, meaning to be able, is relevant. As a productive force, power in this sense denotes "potential" or "capacity,"—e.g., the capacity for moral judgment or action. At this point in the conceptual mapping of power, Foucault's role in the theorization process is clarified. Always presupposing the importance of power to . . ., he points to power's inescapability—a claim if received outside the productive concept of *potere* is often mistakenly translated as a neo-conservative expression of nihilism. Thus, from a curricular perspective the purpose of pedagogy, as W. E. B. DuBois (1973) put it decades ago, is the development of power. Like the critical educators who would follow him, DuBois envisaged a pedagogy of empowerment that would enable students to conceive and take action.

From this theoretical vantage point we can see the importance of Goodson's work. Ivor knows that, for example, working class students (Fiske would argue that they are exerting localizing power) often reject the ways of knowing and the discipline of school. As with Willis' lads, such a refusal tacitly references the recognition of social inequality and marginalized individuals' ability (power) to confront representatives of power with their view of this injustice. Such recognitions should be validated and used as a conceptual infrastructure for making sense of one's educational experiences—indeed, Goodson is himself a model for such a process. Ivor's success is a testimony to the strength and potential of localizing power. Underestimated by many, localizing power does more than defensively protect the boundaries separating individuals from the oppression of imperializing power. Localizing power is a social resource that always challenges the influence of power wielders and produces alternative spaces for self-production. Such a power, whether it draws upon racial, gender, or class-based counter-knowledge, creates an epistemology that informs both a way of seeing the world and of engaging in social relationships in everyday life. It is exactly this type of localizing power that students of curriculum can draw upon to build a more democratic education (for further information on power theory see Nelson, Treichler, and Grossburg, 1992; Kellner, 1990; Wartenberg, 1992; Fiske, 1993; Rorty, 1992; Cooper,

1994; Airaksinen, 1992; DuBois, 1973; Miller, 1990; Patton, 1989).

I agree with Peter McLaren's (1993) observation that Goodson's work on academic discourses and curriculum provides profound insights into the way knowledge is produced and validated by power in a variety of circumstances including the out-of-school cultural pedagogical landscape of contemporary Western societies. With the conflation of various knowledge forms by the electronic media in hyperreality, a new cultural curriculum is emerging that shapes individuals' perspectives of self and world. While the interactions between individuals and culture are idiosyncratic and contradictory, still an overall conservative effect can be detected. The right-wing, as Goodson tells us, in Great Britain and North America has successfully produced both centralized written curricula and an out-of-school cultural curriculum. The cultural curriculum has fostered a set of issues that subsume other concerns. For example, the war on drugs and addiction in the 1980s and 1990s removed attention from poverty and alienation and even the economic and political interests that sustain the drug traffic. These issues take a backburner in relation to the curriculum's depiction of the evil of drugs—values central to the democratic tradition such as civil liberties are pushed aside in the search for offenders. The family is another issue used to politicize the popular, the everyday. The cultural curriculum in this context reduces all problems to the absence of the family. Portraying the nation-state as a union of families, the right-wing cultural curriculum can attack any egalitarian, democratic, or social justice-oriented tradition as long as it is justified in the name of family values.

Goodson understands the political power of such actions, especially when viewed in relation to right-wing school curricula that reassert the value of fragmented and socially decontextualized synopses of traditional academic subject matter. Despite a rhetoric of teacher empowerment, right-wing groups have tended to see teachers as mere technicians who pass along a body of unproblematized traditional "facts." Under the banner of teaching as the transmission of the best of our cultural heritage, the superiority of laissez-faire economics, and the unquestionable wisdom of our patriarchal fathers, curriculum has been politicized to an unprecedented level and teachers have been deskilled and deprofessionalized. In this context the "safe" curriculum of the Western tradition can be transmitted and then scientifically assessed to make sure that teachers are performing their tasks "properly." With these concerns in mind, Goodson contends that educators who are concerned with establishing a socially just curriculum must constantly assert the necessity for an ongoing dialogue around the reconstruction of knowledge. Understanding the specifics of the socio-historical construction of the curriculum, he knows that the content and form of an institution's course of study tacitly privileges a particular constellation of political relations and social hierarchy.

Where the Hell Did This Thing Come From?
Historical and Historiographical Considerations

As delineated previously, the starting point for Goodson's scholarship involves his search for the origins of the social construction of school subjects. Where the hell did the curriculum come from, Ivor asked in frustration after witnessing the irrationality and hurtfulness of schooling—a question that reveals both the subject and the spirit of Goodson's valuable work. As Goodson began to explore the historical question, he found to his surprise little academic investigation of the area. Without such analysis, he reasoned, too much curricular and educational theory and practice will leave intact a set of priorities and unstated assumptions that are inscribed with dominant power. Left unchallenged, such priorities and assumptions will thwart efforts for democratic educational reform. Historical myopia undermines efforts to garner an appreciation of the complexities of classroom life necessary to successful critical interventions. In his critique of educational scholarship Goodson singles out those scholars who have neglected historical contextualization. Theories of curriculum prescription devoid of historical insights, he charges, can be misleading in their neglect of the web of interests at work in the maintenance of the status quo. It was these etymological concerns that induced Goodson to initiate his Falmer Press book series on the history of school subjects . The studies emerging from the series, Ivor concludes, not only provide insight into curriculum development and classroom practice but grant a unique look at the wider educational and political culture of a country. Goodson's encouragement of needed scholarship in this and other domains is an important aspect of his multidimensional contribution to the field of education.

In the context of his leadership in educational and curricular studies, Goodson has been a major figure in the rise of curriculum history and its recently achieved status as a central component of contemporary curriculum scholarship. Every curriculum and instruction department should have at least one curriculum historian, William Pinar, William Reynolds, Patrick Slattery, and Peter Taubman (1995) argue in their tome on the curriculum field. If one aspect of the pre-reconceptualized curriculum field was its ahistorical nature, the authors continue, then one important dynamic of the reconceptualized field in the late 1990s is that it is "profoundly historical." An important reason for this transformation has involved the historical consciousness of Ivor Goodson. Such a consciousness recognized that historical studies in curriculum enable scholars to elucidate the role disciplines occupy in the social construction of knowledge. Such inquiries have helped educationists to appreciate the ways teachers are induced to think of their subject knowledge in abstract, decontextualized, formal, and scholarly terms so it can be traded in the academic marketplace for status, validation, turf control, and accreditation. More information is needed about this historical process, Goodson insists, because it provides so much illumination of contemporary curriculum development.

With a sophisticated socio-political macro-view intact, Goodson is that rare scholar who connects it to the study of the micro-world, the particularistic realm of curriculum. I look *inside* the curriculum, he says, in the process smoking out the specific internal workings of stabilizing and destabilizing forces. To accomplish such a task Ivor has led the discipline into the teacher life-history domain. Such particularistic explorations when considered in larger socio-political and pedagogical contexts provide a unique insight into the curriculum. Using the analysis of a teacher or a group of teachers' life experiences and backgrounds, in-school and outside-school lifestyles, life cycles, career stages, critical life instances, and perceptions and practices, Goodson's work raises new questions about teaching. Using such life histories in tandem with his understanding that curriculum is made in a variety of venues and at a variety of levels, Goodson rejects thin reductionistic scholarship that demotes curriculum study to an outside observation of a black box described on one extreme by reproduction theory and on the other by a functionalist construct. When life histories are connected with a cognizance of curriculum as a written text and curriculum as a classroom activity, scholars can avoid the various forms of abstractions, reductionisms, overdeterminisms that pass for curriculum studies. From Ivor's perspective any reconceptualization of curriculum must take these points into account—a project that will necessitate a large cadre of scholarly archaeologists (in the Foucauldian sense) digging at various sites, both preactive and interactive. Such archeologists will demand new research methodologies and knowledge production strategies including textual analyses, semiotics, psychoanalysis, and discourse analysis to name only a few possibilities. Creative, multi-dimensional, and methodologically innovative studies of this type would provide cognitive maps for scholars of curriculum and teachers seeking innovation.

Such methods when used with critical historical strategies of inquiry help with the complex task of recovering the patterns of power that influence knowledge production and transmission. Unlike many other historians, Goodson uses his research tools to analyze historical curricular structures and their ambiguous relationship to national and local curriculum debates and the professional survival struggles individual practitioners must negotiate around them. Power patterns in this context can be viewed as hegemonic processes, as established high-status disciplines interact with evolving disciplines in battles for academic prestige and control of knowledge production. These battles between subject groups or scholarly disciplines provide sobering enlightenment about the "nobility" of academic discourse, as Goodson's research depicts much curricular debate as simply a naked power struggle—a Texas Death Match over who gets the power, prestige, and financial rewards. The outcomes of such turf wars help shape relation-

ships between professionals and clients, the nature of the social regulation particular disciplines inflict, and the form disciplinary knowledge takes.

In this way Goodson fills in the blanks left by Foucault's
declaration that power produces knowledge and knowledge
produces discipline. Goodson wants to know how this general
process works—much of his scholarship is structured around
this important question. As he researches and formulates his
answers, Goodson notices the similarities of development between, say, psychiatry and education. In both discplines knowledge enhanced the power of licensed professionals to replace
experienced amateurs in institutional practice and to pursue
governmental agendas of classifying and regulating targeted
marginalized groups. The flexibility and freedom of the amateurs disappeared, as state certified public schools and asylums developed. Teachers, Ivor points out, were increasingly
controlled by examinations, supervisory inspections, required
textbooks, and teacher training. In this regulatory context practitioners lost much of their power to define their practice, as
specialists and administrators far removed from the setting of
practice increasingly dictated their new role. Until such power
patterns are widely understood, Goodson argues, the disciplin-
ary/regulatory processes that pass for schooling will never allow for a truly emancipatory and vibrant *education* to develop.

Goodson's is not mainstream version of educational history.
Concerned with issues of class, power, social regulation, macro-
micro level interaction, and contemporary educational practice, Ivor presents both a transgressive history and historiography. Well aware of the chronicles of revisionist
historiography, he understands that the appeal of 1960s and
1970s New Left educational historical revisionism is fading.
Finding this a mixed blessing, Goodson does not dismiss the
important questions such revisionists raised about power, social regulation, racism, sexism, and class bias; Goodson's critique of the revisionists centers more around their tendency
(not unlike mainstream historians of education) to focus their
research on the political and administrative aspects of schooling that take place outside the school. The critical histories
produced by scholars such as Michael Katz (1968, 1971), Joel
Spring (1972), Colin Greer (1972), and Clarence Karier (1975),

and many others have been viewed by mainstream historians as simple extensions of leftist politics. The politics of the present, not rigorous historical data gathering, formed the basis for their histories, critics maintained. These New Left revisionists, Diane Ravitch (1978) charged, simply selected passages that supported their ideological perspective, reducing complex history to mere ideological chiche.

In retrospect, the hindsight of the late 1990s, both Goodson and myself recognize many of the flaws of the revisionists. With the political agenda on the front burner, revisionist educational history over-simplified the ambiguities, the incompleteness, and the irrationality of historical events. The radical revisionist story of imposition was too sparse: the power bloc coerced the masses into accepting a system of schooling that was not in the best interest of the proletariat. Questions were left unanswered: how did it happen?; who made the decisions?; what were the long-term effects of such policies?; what was the role of teachers in the process?; how did such puposes shape the everyday classroom? A more sophisticated educational history was needed to address such micro-level questions. No history or historiography can assume that educational actions can be inferred directly from structural factors. We understand now that the revisionists at times reduced the complexity of human behavior to an identification of factors they believed shaped certain behaviors—factors typically involving economic interests. Of course, economic factors are important, but the point to be made here involves the recognition that the way historical actors fit themselves into the cultural forms and institutions created by economic structures is complex and is in itself a unique form of self-production. The way subjectivity is constructed is a central element of study for historians and other scholars concerned with the process by which power influences educational activity and consciousness formation. Mainstream critics of the revisionists missed this point when they argued that power and class analysis are not useful in America because of the lack of class divisions and class consciousness in this society. They also missed the point when they argued that their mainstream historiography was objective and the revisionist work was subjective and politicized.

As Goodson has focused his history of curriculum on the *internal* patterns of social regulation and schooling, he has participated in the construction of a new paradigm in educational historiography. The new paradigm treasures the New Left revisionists' concern with power, social regulation, and schooling, as it penetrates the aspects of schooling historians have tended to overlook: the internal, everyday processes of schooling (the black box) in which micro-level practices intersect with macro-level socio-political ideologies and structures. Such history, of course, focuses on how school subjects, tracking policies, and teacher subjectivity have created ways of differentiating and regulating students. As Ivor puts it, such a history examines the ambiguous connections between school and society that both reflect and refract the culture's definitions of high-status knowledge and its political impact on students in particular and the social world in general. New paradigmatic educational/curriculum history understands that social regulation and domination are always contextually contingent and how disciplined individuals can inhabit contradictory ideological positions. Such an understanding opens new windows through which to view the contradictory roles and effects of schooling throughout Western history. The reproduction theory that tacitly inhabited the work of many of the radical revisionists allowed little room for a contradictory ideological production of subjectivity. Indeed, as Goodson well understands, ideology and power-inscribed institutions can never "reproduce" human beings as passive, predictable subjects ready and willing to be inserted into specific social roles in relation to the demands of capital.

Goodson's historiography, Andy Hargreaves (1994) argues, uses micro-analysis of the curriculum to reinstate the past within the frame of the present. It also, Hargreaves continues "recreates the present within the remembrace of the past" (p. 10). Indeed, Goodson's new paradigmatic educational historiography directly confronts traditional history's concern with disinterested scholarship. Pure scholarship, objectivist historians argue, is best served by a consistent resistance to the attempt to compare historical events to the present. Uncomfortable with the alleged distortion of a *histoire engage*, such historians sever the umbilical chord connecting past and present and urge colleagues to understand the past on its own ground. On one hand, objectivist historians are correct when they reference the often dishonorable heritage that has attempted to appropriate the past for some desirable end. In many hands history has become little more than a repository of relevant anecdotes, moralist admonitions, and precedents to be invoked at will by jurists and politicians. The intent of Goodson's new paradigmatic historiography is not to reduce the project of history to some *immediate* political utility—immediate in the sense that specific lessons for educational reform can be drawn from historical scholarship. Reagan, Bush, Dole, Thatcher, Major and the New Right serve as excellent examples of how the conception of immediate utility eventuates in the abuse of history. The new historiographical paradigm attempts to move the dialogue between past and present to a more subtle level—a realm where admittedly history is used, but the use involves the acquisition of critical insight into existing situations and a sensitivity to the values historically embedded within these present realities.

Among mainstream educational historians the subtlety of Goodson's dialogue between past and present will be missed. Inevitably charges of presentism will surface. The admonition to avoid presentist history is at best a negative injunction, failing even to bestow insight into the attempt to ascertain what a particular segment of the past was like. It does not recognize the fact that the historian's knowledge and experience of the present is necessary to his or her understanding of the past. The appreciation of an historical form rests on the interplay between past and present. Indeed, the past can be understood only insofar as it has continued to live in the present. Goodson as curriculum historian, for example, is not interested merely in the documentation of past educational information for passive consumption only by other educational historians. Historical knowledge is necessary to the critical attempt to appreciate the workings of social, political, psychological, and educational processes and their subtle interrelationships. Our postmodern unconsciousness of history does not free us from the past, but to the contrary, traps us in the snare of an unconscious destiny. When the past is forgotten, its power over the present is hidden from view. In education especially we are victimized by an amnesia that makes "what is" seem as if "it had to be." Contrary to what objectivist historians might argue, historians will be judged by the contributions they make in putting their knowledge of the past to work in the attempt to understand the present and to shape the future. The point is so obvious that it might not be worth stressing, except for the fact that many historians have worked so diligently to deny it.

Goodson's new educational paradigm grasps the multi-dimensionality of the relationship between past and present curricular practice. In this context he recognizes the ties between history, education, and politics. In this particular interplay Goodson realizes that the way one makes sense of the past is necessary in the determination of what political and educational perspectives one will view as realistic or socially responsible. Indeed, one could argue that all political or policymaking deliberation is grounded on either an overt or a tacit historical understanding. Goodson's and my opinion of a new paradigmatic critical historiography asserts that when historians maintain a "*disinterested* interest" in the past, they serve the powers that maintain the status quo. Historical knowledge that presents itself as apolitical and a mere attempt to tell the truth about the past will rub shoulders with power bloc. This type of "objectivity" is a luxury only dominant groups can afford. For subordinate groups the admonition that they view history with objectivity and dispassion can only come across as another example of the ideology they feel compelled to oppose. On the other hand, the kind of educational politics that is based on a social vision of an egalitarian practice of schooling can elict support only by contrasting its sense of possibility with an oppressive past. One can never insist that things should be otherwise without an understanding and rejection of the conditions that are to be superceded. Thus, Goodson recognizes the deception inherent in the call for a snow white, politically untouched curriculum history (for further information on this theme see Frisch, 1986; Kocka, 1980; Lucas, 1985; Kaye, 1987; Allison, 1995; White, 1987; Popular Memory Group, 1982).

Goodson's prominence as a curriculum scholar is no doubt related to the consistency and innovation of his scholarship, his theoretical sophistication vis-a-vis his sensitivity to the particularistic. Though germinated in separate gardens, Goodson's scholarship is quite compatible with the diverse work of the North American Reconceptualization—at times extending it, especially in the realm of curriculum history and teacher life history. I sincerely hope that *The Changing Curriculum* will introduce Ivor's work to U.S. students of curriculum unlucky enough to not have already encountered it. Pushing the envelop of critical scholarship, Goodson's studies will provide new vantage points on the ways the social, political, and pedagogical intersect. Appreciative to Ivor for all he has taught me, I welcome him to Shirley Steinberg's and my Counterpoints: Studies in the Postmodern Theory of Education series with Peter Lang Publishers. His presence in this series honors all of us connected with it.

References

Airaksiren, T. (1992). "The rhetoric of domination." In T. Wartenberg (Ed.), *Rethinking power*. Albany, NY: SUNY Press.

Allison, C. (1995). *Present and past: Essays for teachers in the history of education*. New York, NY: Peter Lang.

Cooper, D. (1994). "Productive, relational, and everywhere? Conceptualizing power and resistance within Foucauldian feminism." *Sociology, 28*(2), 435–454.

DuBois, W. (1973). *The education of black people: Ten critiques, 1906-1960*. Edited by H. Apthinker. New York: Monthly Review Press.

Fiske, J. (1993). *Power plays, power works*. New York: Verso.

Frisch, M. (1986). "The memory is history." In S. Benson, S. Brier, & R. Rosenzweig (Eds.), *Presenting the past: Essays on history and the public*. Philadelphia, PA: Temple University Press.

Giroux, H. (1988). *Teachers as intellectuals: Toward a critical pedagogy of learning*. Granby, MA: Bergin and Garvey.

Greer, C. (1972). *The great school legend: A revisionist interpretation of American public education*. New York: Viking.

Hargreaves, A. (1994). "Critical introduction." In I. Goodson, *Studying Curriculum*. Buckingham, England: University Press.

Karier, C. (1975). *Shaping the American educational state: 1890 to the present*. New York, NY: Free Press.

Katz, M. (1968). *The irony of early school reform: Educational innovation in mid-nineteenth century Massachusetts*. Boston, MA: Beacon.

Katz, M. (1971). *Class, bureaucracy, and schools: The illusion of educational change in America*. New York, NY: Praeger.

Kaye, H. (1987). "The use and abuse of the past: The new right and the crisis of history." *Socialist Register*, 332–65.

Keat, R. (1994). "Scepticism, authority, and the market." In R. Keat, N. Whiteley, & N. Abercrombie (Eds.), *The Authority of the Consumer*. New York, NY: Routledge.

Kellner, D. (1990). *Television and the crisis of democracy*. Boulder, CO: Westview Press.

Kocka, J. (1980). "Theory and social history: Recent developments in West Germany." *Social Research, 47*(3), 426–57.

Lucas, C. (1985). "Toward a pedagogy of the useful past for teacher preparation." *Journal of Thought, 20,* 19–33.

McCarthy, T. (1992). "The critique of impure reason: Foucault and the Frankfurt School." In T. Wartenberg (Ed.), *Rethinking Power.* Albany, NY: SUNY Press.

McLaren, P. (1986). *Schooling as ritual performance: Toward a political economy of educational symbols and gestures.* London, England: Routledge and Kegan Paul.

McLaren, P. (1993). "Foreward to the Third Edition." In I. Goodson, *School subjects and curriculum change: Studies in curriculum history.* (3rd Ed). London, England: Falmer Press.

MacLeod, J. (1987). *"Ain't no makin' it" Leveled aspirations in a low-income neighborhood.* Boulder, CO: Westview Press.

Miller, J. (1990). "Carnivals of atrocity: Foucault, Nietzsche, Cruelty." *Political Theory, 18*(3), 470–91.

Nelson, C., Treichler, P., & Grossberg, L. (1992). "Cultural studies: An introduction." In C. Nelson, P. Treichler, & L. Grossberg (Eds.), *Cultural Studies.* New York, NY: Routledge.

Patton, P. (1989). "Taylor and Foucault on power and freedom." *Political Studies, 37,* 260–76.

Pinar, W., Reynolds, W., Slattery, P., & Taubman, P. (Eds.). (1995). *Understanding Curriculum.* New York, NY: Peter Lang.

Popular Memory Group (1982). "Popular memory: Theory, politics, and method." In Centre for Contemporary Cultural Studies. *Making histories: Studies in history-writing and politics.* Minneapolis, MN: University of Minnesota Press.

Rawitch, D. (1978). *The revisionists revised.* New York, NY: Basic Books.

Rorty, A. (1992). "Power and powers: A dialogue between Buff and Rebuff." In T. Wartenberg (Ed.), *Rethinking Power.* Albany, NY: SUNY Press.

Spring, J. (1992). *Education and the rise of the corporate state.* Boston, MA: Beacon.

Wartenberg, T. (1992). "Introduction." In T. Wartenberg (Ed.), *Rethinking Power.* Albany, NY: SUNY Press.

White, H. (1987). *The content of the form.* Baltimore, MD: Johns Hopkins University Press.

1

By Way of Introduction

An Interview with Ivor Goodson by Don Santor

Don: Looking back to your seven years as a school teacher, what did you find most personally satisfying?

Ivor: Retrospectively, I have a somewhat idealized view of it. What I did as a beginning teacher in England was to pioneer with others a series of what we called "O" level exams (equivalent to the OACs here) in different subjects like community studies, urban studies, and environmental studies. I had the job in the early stages of actually writing up these exams and leading my kids through the exams on the O level. And we kept a significant number of the children, who normally left go into factories, go onto what we call the sixth form, and from there on to university. So it was a way of keeping the kids who normally dropped out and went to work in factories. I viewed that, and still view that, as perhaps the major challenge for schooling.

Don: Why, after seven years in the comprehensive school, did you return to higher education?

Ivor: I had spent a lot of time working up these new subjects which, I thought, appealed to a wide group of children. They seemed to appeal to the kinds of children I'd grown up with. I was a working-class child myself, and so I was very excited by the way that we were able to develop new subjects which had mass educational appeal. At that time, I think I was a relatively sheltered, conservative man. Having developed these new "subjects" that clearly were motivating all sorts of children, I was astonished that the powers that be in England refused to let any of them go forward as "proper subjects." It seemed to me that there was no point in giving children a meaningful education when they were not allowed to get the proper recognition and credentials. So I decided I would return to university on what was called an environmental education project (initially just a two-year project), to study what the impediments were to giving proper educational credentials to ordinary children. It seemed to me that there was a basic blockage in the system that only a more penetrating period of research and reflection would allow me to understand.

Don: Ivor, you've written and edited sixteen books. How would you summarize your main interest in education as far as those books are concerned?

Ivor: I suppose, in a way, Don, they're consistent in growing out of my experiences as a practicing teacher, which were happy experiences. But I also experienced the limitations of what you can do, as a teacher, if the examination bodies and the other bodies controlling education refuse to take seriously the demands of basic- and general-level kids. And so, the books are an attempt to provide what you might call *cognitive maps* for teachers and administrators who want to provide real education for all children. They examine how we set about getting rid of some of those blocks, how we analyze some of the interest groups that cause education to be a very selective enterprise, and how we give back some sort of knowledge to the practicing teachers who do have concerns and aspirations to resolve those blockages.

Don: What activities are you engaged in now?

Ivor: At the moment I am finishing off three books: on teachers' lives, on schooling and curriculum, and on curriculum history. This work all feeds into my graduate courses and, of course, into my supervision of graduate dissertations, as do the various research projects that I run. These include the Computer Project, Studying Computer Use in Schools; the Community College section of the Teacher Development Project; and a new Social Science and Humanities Research Council Grant to study the history of vocational schooling.

Don: Let's go back to your books. Are you saying that the teacher is the key player in the educational process?

Ivor: I'm saying there are a number of key players in the educational process, but the most neglected is the teacher. Teachers' opinions have not been sought and their counsel has not been used in research. I think that teachers are clearly an absolutely central agent, and it is regrettable that this potential is not reflected in the educational-policy process.

Don: Earlier in your career you had difficulty in getting environmental studies adopted as a school subject. What does your research tell you about how subjects become part of the curriculum?

Ivor: I suppose it tells me that you have to have a fairly fine sense of who's in control of the curriculum, of which interest groups have a voice. You need a *cognitive map* of who's defining subjects. You have to have some sense of the organization of subject groups, of how universities have influence, and of how other interest groups, business and otherwise, have influence. The bringing of subjects into schooling is not a dispassionate, rational decision on those things that are judged to be of interest to pupils. It is a much more broadly conceived political act where all interest groups, quite rightly in a democracy, have a say; but it is a misconception to think of it as a detached rational exercise. It is an eminently political exercise, and it is my view that we need to have some understanding of that process.

Don: You talk a lot about teachers' lives. How has your own childhood and adolescence affected the kind of teacher that you have become?

Ivor: I grew up in a very tight, happy, well-organized working class community with its own values, which I still think were fine values, and a better bunch of people I've never met in my life. I came from a community that I was deeply proud of and had to leave that community to go quite some way away to a grammar school. I was the only child in the village to go to that grammar school. So from an early age I felt a sense of detachment from my roots and community, since there was only a small group of children like me in the school, and we were pretty identifiable. And, as a result, I didn't like school very much, although I was very excited by some of the ideas that were around. But I couldn't wait to join all my friends at work. So I left the school as soon as I could, which was at the age of fifteen, to go to work in a factory. It was only by chance that I returned to school. My favorite teacher at the grammar school, a history teacher, actually came to the factory, talked to me over a lunch break, and urged me to come back. When I returned, I began to perform a little better and subsequently went to university. But, even when I went to university, I didn't leave my own community. I stayed at home and traveled up to London. When I finally went into school teaching, it was directly from my home community and with a strong sense of the values and aspirations of my home group, which I still hold dear.

Don: Ivor, what critique do you bring to education?

Ivor: I suppose it's that critique, isn't it? It's the critique that schooling ought to try to deal equally with all the different groups, whether they be stratified by social processes, or gender, or race. I'm much encouraged by Canadian schooling. It seems to be more equal here than in many places I've been, certainly more than in Britain. It is an attempt to deal equally with all groups, to cater to their needs, and to try to make sure that all children are educated. I would always hold that to be my main desire, that all children get a fair kick at the can in those early years. I'm always opposed, and always will be, I think, to the notion that some children deserve better than others . . . that you can buy better things for some and the others can go hang themselves. I think if we take democracy seriously, or indeed just basic morality seriously, then all children deserve a chance to become the best that they can become.

Santor, Don (January 1990) A Conversation with Ivor Goodson. *Education News*, Vol. 5, No. 1, p. 2.

Chapter 2

Investigating Schooling:
From the Personal to the Programmatic

In this chapter, I provide an initial exploration of the personal origins of scholarly inquiry and a brief introduction to the field of study pursued. It is always difficult to question the relationship between self and scholarship, not least because of the difficulty of retrospective reconstruction. I think, however, that it is important we try, for scholarship is not a process of dispassionate inquiry. It is a socially and politically grounded enterprise and we should do well to remember this. I am much reminded of J. G. Farrell's description of academics in *The Singapore Grip*:

> He sensed that what distressed him was a gap which had opened up between thought and feeling, the remoteness, the impartiality of his friends to the subjects they were teaching or studying. Objectivity, he had to agree with them, was important obviously. But what was required he had declared . . . was 'a passionate objectivity (whatever that might be)'.

Personal Points of Entry

Ever since my own experience as a school pupil in England in the immediate postwar period, I have been deeply interested in the process of "schooling." My own parents viewed the achievement of "their" Labour government after the war as most clearly demonstrated by the new schooling that was offered to me and to other working people's children. Here, I was told, was the chance to learn, a chance to start to understand the world in which I was growing up.

Yet, from the beginning I experienced odd contradictions, for while I was supposed to learn, most of the questions for which I inarticulately and tentatively sought answers were not on the school's agenda. They were, it is true, mainly childish questions, but they turned on my understanding of the world at the time. They were things that we talked about at home: Why did my father work so hard? Why did I not see him in the mornings, or until late in the evening? Why did my mother go to work to "support me"? Why were all the fields I played in being developed by more and larger "council estates"? Why did we have to walk (or later, ride) more than three miles to school? Why was the school in a "posh" village and not in my village? Why were the children from my village treated differently to the children from the immediate school locality?

These then were aspects of my world; but why did we never talk about them, let alone learn about them at school?

My concerns about schooling increased when I went to secondary school. I passed the "11-plus" and was sent off to a grammar school (again, miles away from my village). All my friends now went to *our* village's school: a secondary modern. The long ride to the grammar school through the council estates wearing a blue "venetian" blazer and a hat with a yellow tassel cemented an incurable fascination with schooling. (The fascination lasted longer than the blazer and hat which I took to packing in my bike saddlebag and putting on in the school's bike shed.)

At the grammar school the curriculum made my sense of dichotomy at the primary school seem churlish. Here, not only was the content alien and dull but the very form of transmission and structure (the discursive formation no less) utterly bewildering. I experienced schooling as one learning a second language. A major factor in this cultural displacement was the school's curriculum.

At the school I languished: taking nine O-level exams and failing eight. By the age of fifteen I was at work in a potato-chip factory. Later, however (through the intervention of one teacher), I returned to school and, though still burdened with a sense of alienation from the subject matter, began to perform the tests of rote learning and memory that were rewarded with exam passes.

A degree (in economic history) and a period of doctoral work (Irish immigrants in Victorian England) followed, but in 1968 the continuing sense of dichotomy between "life" and "study" led me to abandon all thought of an academic career. The starting points were two articles, one by Basil Bernstein in *New Society*, "Open Schools, Open Society," the other by Barry Sugarman on secondary-school-pupil cultures (*British Journal of Sociology*, 1967).

These articles showed me that there were modes of academic study where the everyday experiences of ordinary pupils and people might be investigated. In short, modes where my experience of life and my intellectual questions about that experience might be finally reconnected. But, just as before, I had to abandon my intellectual interests to pass examinations; now once again, I had to forgo an academic career so that self and study might be reinvested with some degree of authenticity.

At the heart of the academic examinations and the academic career that had followed were the same alien and seemingly redundant bodies of knowledge. Was it merely a personal pathology that made me reject them? Some species of infantilism? Some battle with the "father figure"? Something worse? Was this a problem of *individual* response?

The decision to abandon my academic career was essentially a positive redirection. Once I had identified the kind of work epitomized in Bernstein and Sugarman, I saw the newly organizing comprehensive schools as the place where I wanted to work. Here, my own class background and experience might engage with that of my pupils in a "common language" of dialogue between teacher and taught. For the new generation of pupils from working-class homes there might be something beyond the pervasive alienation I had experienced at school.

These, then, were the hopes I set off with as I left my working-class home in a Berkshire village to settle in another village in Leicestershire and begin teaching in a comprehensive school. The school was new, very well equipped, and highly innovative. The environment at the school was extremely liberal and friendly. There were no uniforms, no punishments and very little compulsion, no regimentation, no bells, no school teams. The school staff were highly gifted and deeply dedicated:

> Hence, most of the normal 'stumbling blocks' or coercive and repressive devices which we hold culpable in our accounts of schooling were absent. The relationships with our (predominantly) working class clients were quite simply, wonderful (this is not idealised retrospection, there is much supportive evidence). Yet the educational endeavour still proved highly problematic. One feature assaulted me with its intractability of form and irrelevance of content: the curriculum, especially the curriculum for examination.

> I remember sitting one night after a day of utter frustration saying to myself again and again, 'where the hell, where on earth did this thing come from (i.e. the curriculum)?'[1]

The comprehensive school had been devised to unify educational experience for all children. Before, schools had been organized mainly into grammar schools (predominantly for the middle class) and secondary modern schools (essentially for the working class). The grammar schools were given preferential staffing, the best teachers, the most resources. Any notion of equality or democracy made it difficult to defend such deliberate sponsorship of privilege for particular social groups.

But the comprehensive schools, reorganized into schools for all, supposedly to give opportunity for all, had retained much of the form and content of curriculum from the previous patterning of schooling. Particularly in the "high ground" of O- and A-level examinations, the curriculum derived mainly from the grammar school curriculum I had experienced.

I had, as we saw, loathed the irrelevance and pedantry of that curriculum. But was this individual pathology? As I watched year after year as a teacher at the comprehensive school, this curriculum, with its continuities to the old grammar schools, broke the will and interests of virtually all my working-class students. Truly if there was a heart to the problem of mass education, it was here. Far from being individual pathology, rejection of the curriculum that was offered was collective unanimity. The most consistent and unanimous rejection was reserved for the examination subjects, the so-called "traditional" subjects. The establishment of these traditional subjects as the heartland of comprehensive schooling represents at once a renunciation of certain groups and a privileging of other groups. It would seem that the divisive internal patterns once reinforced by separate types of schools were now reinforced *within* the ostensibly comprehensive school. The continuation of differential success for different class groups was related to the continuation of internal curriculum patterns of differentiation.

Developing a Program of Study

Following my experiences of schooling in Britain, to pursue an understanding of the problems and possibilities of mass schooling would then require a sustained and systematic project of enquiry into school subjects. A field of study that made school subjects the central artifacts of investigation would need to evolve. The starting point would be to look for the origins of the social construction that is schooling and to analyze reasons for the emergence and subsequent institutionalization of school subjects.[2]

In our studies of schooling, curriculum is a "keyword" in the full sense of Raymond Williams's definition. The use of such a word and its place in our discourse on schooling needs to be fully examined because "like any other social reproduction it is the arena of all sorts of shifts and interests and relations of dominance." Curriculum is a keyword with substantial potential for scholarly exhumation, examination, and analysis, for the "moral panics" over meaning are often carried out in a most public manner. As Williams comments:

> Certain crises around certain experiences will occur, which are registered in language in often surprising ways. The result is a notation of language as not merely the creation of arbitrary signs which are then reproduced within groups, which is the structuralist model, but of signs which take on the changeable and often reversed social relations of a given society, so that what enters into them is the contradictory and conflict-ridden social history of the people who speak the language, including all the variations between signs at any given time.[3]

In such a manner the conflicts over the definition of the written curriculum offer visible, public, and documentary evidence of the continuing struggle over the aspirations and intentions of schooling. For this reason alone it is important to develop our understandings of this king of curriculum conflict. But conflict over the written curriculum has both "symbolic significance" and practical significance—by publicly signifying which aspirations and intentions are to be enshrined in written curriculum, criteria are established for the evaluation and public estimation of schooling. In this sense, "ground rules" are publicly established by which practice is evaluated or to which it is related. Financial and resource allocation is similarly linked to these ground rules of curriculum criteria.

The establishment of rules and criteria has significance even if practice then seeks to contradict or transcend this preactive definition. We are therefore bound by previous forms of reproduction as we become creators of new ones.

This relationship between antecedent definitions and present potential is of enormous significance in the study of curriculum. Jackson has characterized the two elements (although in some senses this is falsely dichotomous) as *preactive* definition of curriculum and *interactive* realization of curriculum.[4] Maxine Greene has developed a dual notion of curriculum that furthers our understanding of the distinction. She describes the dominant view of curriculum as "a structure of socially presented knowledge, external to the knower, there to be mastered."[5] This is to present preactive definition *as* curriculum, but against this she juxtaposes a notion of curriculum as "a possibility for the learner as an existing person mainly concerned with making sense of his own life world." M. F. D. Young has used this distinction to develop two views of curriculum. The first he calls " curriculum as fact." He suggests that

> the 'curriculum as fact' needs to be seen as more than mere illusion, a superficial veneer on teachers' and pupils' classroom practice, but as a historically specific social reality expressing particular production relations among men. It is mystifying in the way it presents the curriculum as having a life of its own, and obscures the human relations in which it, as any conception of knowledge, is embedded, leaving education as neither understandable nor controllable by men.

He goes on to argue that the notion of "curriculum as practice" can equally mystify to the degree that

> It reduces the social reality of 'curriculum' to the subjective interventions and actions of teachers and pupils. This limits us from understanding and historical emergence and persistence of particular conceptions, of knowledge and particular conventions (school subjects for example). In that we are limited from being able to situatise the problems of contemporary education historically we are again limited from understanding and control.[6]

Seen in this manner one can grasp some of the range of debate and conflict that is likely to surround the word curriculum. In a certain sense promoting the notion of curriculum as fact is liable to give priority to the past intellectual and political "settlement" as enshrined in the written curriculum. Curriculum as practice rather gives precedence to contemporary action, and allows for contradictory or transcendent action in relation to preactive definition. This has often led reformists to seek to ignore preactive definitions, viewing them as a legacy of the past, and to try to spontaneously create new ground rules for action.

Curriculum as Social Conflict

Central to the project of the pervasive reconceptualization of curriculum studies is the range of arenas and levels where curriculum is produced, negotiated, and reproduced. A move toward a more historical and social constructionist view of curriculum work would have to work across the full range of these arenas and levels. Plainly this is an undertaking for a whole cohort of scholars, and at the moment one can only provide or point to a few parts of the mosaic of such a reconceptualized undertaking.

Curriculum, then, is made in a variety of arenas and at a variety of levels. Central to this variety, however, is the distinction between the written curriculum and the curriculum as classroom activity. The dangers of only studying the written curriculum are manifest, for as Rudolph has warned us: "The best way to misread or misunderstand a curriculum is from a catalogue. It is such a lifeless thing, so disembodied, so unconnected, sometimes intentionally misleading."[7]

As we have noted, this misreading often leads on to the assertion or implication that the written curriculum is in a real sense irrelevant to practice: that the dichotomy between espoused curriculum as written and the active curriculum as lived and experienced is complete and inevitable. There are a number of versions of the complete dichotomy thesis. Some versions of "conspiracy theory" would argue that since schooling, particularly state schooling, is intimately related to economic and social reproduction, and is compulsory and underresourced, certain intractable features of classroom practice and life are virtually inevitable (true) and that, therefore, written curriculum "rhetoric" is basically irrelevant (unproven). More common would be the "worldly wise" view. This is typified by Cuban's commentary on U.S. schooling:

> In examining how various forces shaped the curriculum and their consequences for classrooms over the last century, I used the metaphor of a hurricane to distinguish between curriculum theory, courses of study, materials and classroom instruction. Hurricane winds sweep across the sea tossing up twenty foot waves, a fathom below the surface turbulent waters swirl, while on the ocean floor there is unruffled clam.[8]

Of course Cuban's ocean analogy does resonate with a good deal of our understanding and experience of curriculum reform attempts. Yet even within his exemplary study of how teachers taught, data emerge that hint at conflicts over "what counts as curriculum," at how certain apparent "givens" in the situation were constructed.

This implies that there may have been a prior debate about what passes as curriculum (and as curriculum theory) that was resolved in one way that is now presented as a *fait accompli*, as a once and for all given. Hence, while Cuban stresses the constancy of classroom practice, the parameters of that practice with regard to different versions of curricula remain unanalyzed. This leads him to statements such as:

> We have a lot of work. The curriculum is overloaded and we have so many assessments to do. So much paperwork. Yet I teach Spanish in the first grade. That's not in the curriculum. Every other Friday, we cook. That's not in the curriculum. But I feel that they need these extras.[9]

Hence such a research view of practice, albeit a historical view, leaves major questions unanalyzed as to what counts as curriculum and as to the manner in which other potential curriculum areas simply become "extra." Constancy in classroom practice there may be, but is not the historical conflict over these precursors to practice, the construction and reconstruction of these parameters, part of that story? Even if there is a contradiction between written curriculum, curriculum theory, and practice, is not that contradiction part of an ongoing context, a situation that is in a sense "achieved" rather than inevitable?

Certainly histories of the relationship between theory and practice point to wide differentials in the gap between the two. This dichotomy far from being wide and intractable seems to be, at least partially, tractable and highly variable over time. Simon examined the relationship between theory and practice in three periods: 1880–1900, 1920–1940, and 1940–1960. In the first and last periods he found "a close relation between theory and practice".[10] For instance in the period of 1880–1900:

> For a whole concatenation of reasons, and from a variety of motives, it was thought that the masses should be educated, or at least schooled—and they were. This whole enterprise was, as it were, powered by an ideology—or theoretical stance—which emphasized the educability of the normal child, a view underpinned by advances in the field of psychology and physiology relating to human learning.[10]

The point is that the potential for close relationship—or at the other extreme, no relationship—between theory and practice or between written curriculum and active curriculum depends on the preactive construction of curricula statements, syllabus, and theory as well as the interactive realization of curriculum in the classroom.

As currently constituted our understandings of preactive construction are so minimal as to make any thoroughgoing study of the relationships, between preactives and practices, virtually unachievable. The precursor then to any study of this kind is to begin to analyze the social construction of curricula. Social constructionist study has the intrinsic value of allowing insights into the assumptions and interests involved in the making of curriculum; by furthering our understanding of the manner in which some of the parameters to practice are negotiated, such work should facilitate subsequent studies of relationships between preactive construction and interactive realization.

This is not of course to suggest a direct or easily discernible link between the preactive and the interactive, nor that on occasions the interactive might not subvert or transcend the preactive. But it is to argue that preactive construction may set important and significant parameters for interactive realization in the classroom. Therefore, unless we analyze the making of curriculum, the temptation will be to accept it as a given and look for variables inside the classroom or at least within the individual school domain. We would be accepting as "traditional" and "given" versions of curricula that on closer inspection can be seen as the culmination of long and continuing conflict.

Two final instances will substantiate this point and I hope illustrate the potential significance of analyzing the making of curriculum. Vulliamy has studied the origins of "what counts as school music." He concludes that the definition of school music as a curriculum subject that focuses on "serious music" involves a clear set of social and political priorities that inevitably effect pedagogic orientation and potential realization within the classroom. The making of curriculum in this case plainly sets parameters for practice:

> My analysis of the subject perspective of music teaching suggests that with music we have a rigid stratification of knowledge and perhaps the clearest example in the school curriculum of a rigid distinction between subject-based knowledge ('serious music') which is the musical culture of the school, and everyday knowledge ('pop music') which is the musical culture of most of the school pupils.[11]

Curriculum theory for the training of music teachers has often reinforced this dichotomy. Brocklehurst, for example, is quoted as arguing that

> The primary purpose of musical appreciation is to inculcate a love and understanding of good music. It is surely the duty of teachers to do all they can to prevent young people falling ready prey to the purveyors of commercialised popular music.[12]

In the making of the music curriculum the conflict between serious and popular music has then resulted in a clear victory for the former. We have insights into a conflict not only about the intrinsics of curriculum but about the purposes and potentials of curriculum. What sort of mass education is being pursued when that which is popular is not merely ignored but positively disvalued? Is it advisable to analyze classroom practice without consideration of this critical antecedent struggle over curriculum definition and construction? If investigation is limited to immediate realization of subject knowledge, is there not grave danger of perpetrating a classroom myopia that inevitably obscures and mystifies a central component in the complexities of classroom life?

A further historical example might suggest an answer. In *Science for the People*, David Layton describes a movement in the initial development of the school science curriculum called the "Science of Common Things."[13] In this curriculum the pupils' experiences of the natural world, of their homes, daily lives, and work, formed the basis of their enquiries in school science (almost by analogy, like teaching music through the pupils' experience of popular music rather than through their nonexperience of serious music). But the curriculum was limited to elementary schools with a predominantly working-class clientele. There is clear evidence provided by Layton and in contemporary government reports that the science of common things allowed considerable practical success in classrooms. We would be wrong, however, to assume that the problem was therefore solved and that the science of common things provided the basis for the definition of school science. Far from it. Other definitions of school science were being advocated by powerful interests. Lord Wrottesley chaired a parliamentary committee of the British Association for the Advancement of Science on the most appropriate type of science education for the upper classes. Hodson argues that the report

> reflected a growing awareness of a serious problem: that science education at the elementary level was proving highly successful, particularly as far as the development of thinking skills was concerned, and the social hierarchy was under threat because there was not corresponding development for the higher orders.[14]

Wrottesley gave an instance that confirmed his worst fears:

> a poor boy hobbled forth to give a reply; he was lame and humpbacked, and his wan emaciated face told only too clearly the tale of poverty and its consequences . . . but he gave forthwith so lucid and intelligent a reply to the question put to him that there arose a feeling of admiration for the child's talents combined with a sense of shame that more information should be found in some of the lowest of our lower classes on matters of general interest than in those far above them in the world by station.

He concluded:

> It would be an unwholesome and vicious state of society in which those who are comparatively unblessed with nature's gifts should be

generally superior in intellectual attainments to those above them in station.[15]

Soon after, Wrottesley's comments on 1860 science were removed from the elementary curriculum. When science eventually reappeared in the curriculum of the elementary schools some twenty years later, it was in a very different form from the science of common things. A watered-down version of pure laboratory science had become accepted as the *correct* view of science, a view that has persisted, largely unchallenged, to the present day. Science as a school subject was powerfully redefined to become similar in form to so much else in the secondary curriculum—pure, abstract, a body of knowledge enshrined in syllabuses of textbooks.

To begin any analysis of schooling by accepting without question a form and content of curriculum that was fought for and achieved at a particular historical point on the basis of certain social and political priorities—to take that curriculum as a given—is to forgo a whole range of understandings and insights into features of the control and operation of the school and the classroom. It is to take over the mystifications of previous episodes of governance as unchallengeable givens. We are, let us be clear, talking about the systematic "invention of tradition" in an arena of social production and reproduction, the school curriculum, where political and social priorities are paramount.

Histories of other aspects of social life have begun to systematically scrutinize this process. Hobsbawm argues that the term "invented tradition"

> includes both traditions actually invented, constructed and formally instituted and those emerging in a less traceable manner within a brief and dateable period—a matter of a few years perhaps—and establishing themselves with great rapidity.

Hobsbawm defines the matter this way:

> Invented tradition is taken to mean a set of practices, normally governed by overtly or tacitly accepted rules and of a ritual or symbolic nature which seek to circulate certain values and norms of behaviour by repetition, which automatically implies continuity with the past. In fact, where possible, they normally attempt to establish continuity with a suitable historic past.[16]

In this sense the making of curriculum can be seen as a process of inventing tradition. In fact, this language is often used when the "traditional disciplines" or "traditional subjects" are juxtaposed against some new fangled innovation of integrated or child-centered topics. The point, however, is that the written curriculum is a supreme example of the invention of tradition, but as with all tradition, it is not a once-and-for-all given, it is a given that has to be defended, where the mystifications have to be constructed and reconstructed over time. Plainly if curriculum theories, historians, and sociologists of education substantially ignore the history and social construction of curriculum, such mystification and reproduction of "traditional" curriculum form and content becomes easier.

In such a situation it is quite possible to develop an ideology, as in current times, where our gaze is directed to individual classrooms and schools, since they are thought to have "autonomy"; the search is on for efficient teaching (i.e., teacher appraisal or "incompetent teachers") for "school effectiveness" or "better schools." The researcher is guided toward the individual classroom or school in a quest for the ingredients of the more successful practice. The differentials of success become paramount: that is, why is one classroom better than another? why do parents choose one school rather than another? This all restores attention to the individual practice of school and classroom.

Conversely our gaze is directed away from the parameters of practice, from the commonalities of success and failure in schooling, from the historical analysis of the social construction of the curriculum. Yet this is part of the story of the "good" classroom or the "better" school; for this is the story of how this particular range of goals was established and enshrined. In short there has been an antecedent struggle to achieve a belief that one particular version of school should be viewed as "good."

As the episode of the "science of common things" makes clear, it is also the story of how other goals and values were defeated. In taking the current parameters as given and searching for better classrooms and schools of the established sort, we would be foreclosing any analysis of fundamental alternatives. But research that accepts major variables as *fait accompli* is undeserving of that title: we are in the business of "fine-tuning" or, to pursue the car analogy, "maintenance." The struggle over the definition of curriculum is a matter of social and political priorities as well as intellectual discourse. The history of past curriculum conflicts therefore needs to be recovered. Otherwise our studies of schooling will leave unquestioned and unanalyzed a set of inherited priorities and assumptions that should be at the heart of our intellectual understanding and practical operation of schooling.

Notes

1. Goodson, I. F. (1988) "Introduction." In I. F. Goodson (ed.) *International Perspectives in Curriculum History*, London and New York: Routledge, pp. 2-3.

2. The following section derives from a paper presented to the American Educational Research Association Conference, Washington, DC, Easter 1987, entitled "Studying Schooling: The Struggle for the Written Curriculum." Parts of the paper appeared in Goodson, I. F. (1988) *The Making of Curriculum: Collected Essays*, London, New York, and Philadelphia: Falmer Press.

3. Williams, R. (1974) *Politics and Letters*, London: New Left Books, p. 176.

4. Jackson, P. (1968) *Life in Classrooms*, New York: Holt Rinehart & Winston, pp. 151-152.

5. Greene, M. (1971) "Curriculum and Consciousness," Teachers College Record, Vol. 73, No. 2, pp. 253-269.

6. Young, M., and G. Whitty. (1977) *Society, State and Schooling*, Lewes, England: Falmer.

7. Rudolph, F. (1977) *Curriculum: A History of the American Undergraduate Course of Study Since 1636*, San Francisco: Jossey Bass, p. 6.

8. Cuban, L. (1984) *How Teachers Taught Constancy and Change in American Classrooms 1890-1980*, New York: Longman, p. 2.

9. Ibid., 255.

10. Simon, B. (1985) *Does Education Matter?* London: Lawrence and Wisehart, p. 49.

11. Vulliamy, G. (1976) "What Counts as School Music." In G. Whitty and M. Young (eds.) *Explorations in the Politics of School Knowledge*, Driffield, England: Nafferton, pp. 24-25.

12. Brocklehurst, J. B. (1962) *Music in Schools*, London: Routledge & Kegan Paul, p. 55.

13. Layton, D. (1973) *Science for the People*, London: Allen & Unwin.

14. Hodson, D. (1987) "Science Curriculum Change in Victorian England: A Case Study of the Science of Common Things." In I. F. Goodson (ed.) *International Perspectives in Curriculum History*, London: Croom Helm, p. 36.

15. Ibid., 36-37.

16. Hobsbawm, E., and T. Ranger (eds.) (1985) *The Invention of Tradition*, Cambridge, England: Cambridge University Press, p. 1.

Chapter 3

"Chariots of Fire"
Etymologies, Epistemologies, and the Emergence of Curriculum

I believe part of the problem of reconceptualizing our study of schooling can be illustrated in the basic etymology of curriculum. The word *curriculum* derives from the Latin word *currere*, which means to run, and refers to a course (or a racing-chariot). The implications of etymology are that curriculum is thereby socially constructed and defined as a course to be followed, or most significantly, presented. As Barrow notes "as far as etymology goes, therefore the curriculum should be understood to be 'the presented content' for study."[1] Social context and construction by this view is relatively unproblematic for by etymological implication the power of "reality-definition" is placed firmly in the hands of those who draw up and define the course. The bond between curriculum and sequential prescription, then, was forged early; it has survived and grown stronger over time. Part of the strengthening of this bond has been the emergence of sequential patterns of learning to follow and operationalize the curriculum as prescribed.

From these Latin origins it is important to trace the emergence of curriculum as a concept to be employed in schooling. According to Gibbons and Hamilton "the words class and curriculum seem to have entered educational discourse at a time when schooling was being transformed into a mass activity."[2] But the origins of the class/curriculum juxtaposition can be found earlier and at the higher education level. From Mir's analysis of the origins of "classes" as first described in the statutes of the College of Montaign, we learn:

> It is in the 1509 programme of Montaign that one finds for the first time in Paris a precise and clear division of students into *classes* . . . That is, divisions graduated by stages or levels of increasing complexity according to the age and knowledge required by students.[3]

Mir argues that the College of Montaign actually inaugurated the Renaissance class system. The vital connection to establish, however, is the way in which organization in classes became associated with a curriculum prescribed, and also sequenced, for stages or levels.

The *Oxford English Dictionary* locates the earliest source of "curriculum" as 1663 in Glasgow, Scotland. The annexation of the Latin term for a race-course may be related to the emergence of sequencing in schooling, but the question "Why Glasgow?" remains. Hamilton believes that "the sense of discipline or structural order that was absorbed into curriculum came not so much from classical sources as from the ideas of John Calvin (1509-1564)."

As Calvin's followers gained political as well as theological ascendancy in late sixteenth-century Switzerland, Scotland, and Holland, the idea of discipline—"the very essence of Calvinism"—began to denote the internal principles and external machinery of civil government and personal conduct. From this perspective there is a homologous relationship between curriculum and discipline: curriculum was to Calvinist educational practice as discipline was to Calvinist social practice.[4]

We have, then, an early instance, if these speculations carry weight, of the relationship between knowledge and control. This works at two levels with regard to curriculum definition. First there is the social context in which knowledge is conceived and produced. Second there is the manner that such knowledge is "translated" for use in a particular educational milieu. In this case classes but later classrooms. The social context of curriculum construction must take account of both levels.

The evidence of Paris and Glasgow in the sixteenth and seventeenth centuries can be summarized as follows and makes a fairly clear statement of the interlinked nature of the emerging mode of curriculum and patterns of social organization and control:

> the notion of classes came into prominence with the rise of sequential programmes of study which, in turn, resonated with various Re-

naissance and Reformation sentiments of upward mobility. In Calvinist countries (such as Scotland) these views found their expression
theologically in the doctrine of predestination (the belief that only a
preordained minority could attain spiritual salvation) and, educationally, in the emergence of national but bipartite education systems
where the 'elect' (i.e. predominantly those with the ability to pay)
were offered the prospect of advanced schooling, while the remainder (predominantly the rural poor) were fitted to a more conservative curriculum (the appreciation of religious knowledge and secular
virtue).[5]

This quote sets up the unique significance of curriculum as
it developed. For soon after, as its power to designate what
should go on in the classroom was realized, a further power
was discovered. Alongside the power to *designate* was the power
to *differentiate*. This meant that even children who went to the
same school could be given access to what amounted to different "worlds" through the curriculum they were taught.

It has been argued that "the 'class' pedagogies pioneered at
Glasgow University had a direct influence on those adopted
in the elementary schools of the 19th century."[6] The general
connection between class pedagogies and a curriculum based
on contemporary sequence and prescription should be clear,
but to move toward the more contemporary duality of pedagogy and curriculum involves the transition from class to classroom system.

In analyzing the historical transition from class to classroom
system the shift in the initial stages of the Industrial Revolution in the late eighteenth and early nineteenth centuries "was
as important to the administration of schooling as the concur-
rent shift from domestic to factory production was to the management of industry." Indeed, as Smelser has shown, the two
were intimately related. In the "domestic-putter out" system
the family unit remained home and education, albeit rather
more in the guise of training and apprenticeship, could take
place at home. With the triumph of the factory system the
associated breakup of the family opened up these roles to subsequent penetration by state schooling and to their replacement by the sort of classroom system where large groups could
be adequately supervised and controlled. Hence "the change
from class to classroom reflected a more general upheaval in
schooling-the ultimate victory of group-based pedagogies over
the more individualized forms of teaching and learning."[7]

At this stage in the development of schooling the intersection of pedagogy and curriculum begins to resemble "modern" patterns. As Bernstein has argued pedagogy, curriculum, and evaluation considered together constitute a modern epistemology. In the 1850s the third prong was pioneered with the founding of the first university examination boards. The centennial report of the University of Cambridge Local Examinations Syndicate says:

> The establishment of these examinations was the universities' response to petitions that they should help in the development of 'schools for the middle classes'.[8]

Also at this time the features of curriculum mentioned earlier, the power to differentiate, was being institutionalized. The birth of secondary *examinations* and the institutionalization of curriculum *differentiation* were then almost exactly contemporaneous. For instance the Taunton Report in 1868 classified secondary schooling into three grades, depending on the time spent at school. Taunton asserted:

> The difference in time assigned makes some difference in the very nature of education itself; if a boy cannot remain at school beyond the age of 14 it is useless to begin teaching him such subjects as require a longer time for their proper study; if he can continue till 18 or 19, it may be expedient to postpone some studies that would otherwise be commenced earlier.

Taunton noted that "these instructions correspond roughly but by no means exactly to the gradations of society." (This statement could, as we shall see, be equally well applied to the Norwood Report nearly a century later.) In 1868 schooling till 18 or 19 was for the sons of men with considerable incomes independent of their own exertions, or professional men, and men in business whose profits put them on the same level. These received a mainly classical curriculum. The second grade up to 16 was for sons of the "mercantile classes." Their curriculum was less classical in orientation and had a certain practical orientation. The third grade till 14 was for the sons of "the smaller tenant farmer, the small tradesmen (and) the superior artisans." Their curriculum was based on the three Rs but carried out to a very good level. This, then, covers secondary schooling. Meanwhile most of the working class remained in elementary schools where they were taught rudimentary skills in the three Rs. By this time the curriculum had achieved a major role as a mechanism for social differentiation. This power to designate and differentiate established a conclusive place for curriculum in the epistemology of schooling.

At the turn of the century the epistemology, with which we are familiar, was emerging. Thus:

> By the 20th Century, the batch production rhetoric of the 'classroom system' (for example lessons, subjects, timetables, grading, standardisation, streaming) had become so pervasive that it successfully achieved a normative status—creating the standards against which all subsequent educational innovations came to be judged.[9]

The dominant epistemology that characterized state schooling by the beginning of the twentieth century combined the trilogy of pedagogy, curriculum, and evaluation. The last of the pieces in the trilogy was the establishment of university examination boards, and here the side effects on curriculum were to be both pervasive and long-lasting. As we have seen, the classroom system inaugurated a world of timetables and compartmentalized lessons—the curriculum manifestation of this systematic change was the school subject. If "class and curriculum" entered educational discourse when schooling was transformed into a mass activity "classroom system and school subject" were linked at the stage at which that mass activity became a state-subsidised system. And in spite of the many alternative ways of conceptualizing and organizing curriculum, the convention of the subject retains its supremacy. In the modern era we are essentially dealing with the *curriculum as subject*.

While this pattern was inaugurated in the 1850s, it was established on the present footing with the definition of the Secondary Regulations in 1904, which list the main subjects followed by the establishment of a subject-based School Certificate, in 1917. From this date curriculum conflict began to resemble the existing situation in focusing on the definition and evaluation of *examinable* knowledge. Hence the School Certificate subjects rapidly became the overriding concern of grammar schools and the academic subjects it examined soon established ascendancy on these schools' timetables. In 1941 Norwood reported that:

> a certain sameness in the curriculum of schools resulted from the double necessity of finding a place for the many subjects competing for time in the curriculum and the need to teach these subjects in such a way and to such a standard as will ensure success in the School Certificate examination.

The normative character of the system is apparent and as a result of "these necessities" the curriculum had "settled down into an uneasy equilibrium, the demands of specialists and subjects being easily adjusted and compensated."[10] The extent to which university examination boards thereby influenced the curriculum through examination subjects is evident. The academic subject-centered curriculum was in fact strengthened in the period following the 1944 Education Act. In 1951 the introduction of the General Certificate of Education allowed subjects to be taken separately at O level (in the School Certificate blocks of "main" subjects had to be passed), and the introduction of A level increased subject specialization and enhanced the link between "academic" examinations and university "disciplines." The academic subjects that dominated O- and especially A-level examinations were then closely linked to university definitions, but even more crucially, they were linked to patterns of resource allocation. Academic subjects claiming close connections to university disciplines were for the "able" students. From the beginning it was assumed that such students required "more staff, more highly paid staff and more money for equipment and books."[11] The crucial and sustained link between academic subjects and preferential resources and status was therefore established.

But if this system was predominant with regard to staffing and resources in grammar schools, the implications for the other schools (and styles of curriculum) should not be forgotten. Echoing Taunton, Norwood had discovered that schooling had "thrown up certain groups each of which can and must be treated in a way appropriate to itself." This time the social and class basis of differentiation remained the same, except for the rationale, and mechanism for differentiation was significantly different. Now the emphasis was on different "mentalities," each recognizing a different curriculum. First the pupil who is interested in learning for its own sake, who can grasp an argument or follow a piece of connected reasoning. Such pupils "educated by the curriculum commonly associated with grammar schools have entered the learned professions or have taken up higher administrative or business posts!" The second group, whose interests lie in the field of applied science or applied arts, were to go to technical schools (which never developed very far). Third the pupils who deal "more easily with concrete things than with ideas." The curriculum would "make a direct appeal to interests, which it would awaken by practical touch with affairs." A practical curriculum, then, for a manual occupational future.

We see here the emergence of a definite pattern of *prioritizing* of pupils through curriculum; what emerged I have called elsewhere "the triple alliance between academic subjects, academic examinations and able pupils." Working through patterns of resource allocation this means that a process of pervasive "academic drift" afflicts subgroups promoting school subjects. Hence proponents of subjects as diverse as woodwork and metalwork, physical education, art, technical studies, bookkeeping, needlework, and domestic science have pursued status improvement by arguing for enhanced academic examinations and qualifications. In a way the evolution of each subject reflects in microcosm a struggle over alternatives over time that is not dissimilar to the overall pattern discerned as state schooling. Hence Layton sees the initial stage as one where "the learners are attracted to the subject because of its bearing on matters of concern to them." At this point the teachers are seldom trained as subject specialists but do "bring the missionary enthusiasms of pioneers to their task." Significantly at this stage "the dominant criterion is relevance to the needs and interests of the learners." However, as the subject "progresses" (a subject at any point in time resembling a coalition that overlays a subset of warring factions) the role of the universities becomes more and more important. This is not least because subject groups employ a *discourse* where they argue increasingly for their subject to be viewed as an "academic discipline" (thereby claiming the financial resources and career opportunities that accrue). The corollary of this claim is that the university scholars must be given control over defining the "discipline" (the aspiration to the rhetoric of the disci-

pline is related to acceptance of this hierarchical pattern of
definition, so in this sense the discursive formation is critical). Jenkins and Shipman have noted that "one detects a certain embarrassment in teachers who not unnaturally feel the
difference between forms, disciplines and subjects are in part
differences of status."[12] In effect the differences are over *who*
can define disciplines—essentially this is presented as the characteristic activity of university scholars.

The progressive refinement of an epistemology suited to state
schooling then embraces the trilogy of pedagogy, curriculum,
and examination. Until recently a triple alliance of academic
subjects, academic examinations, and able students have been
able to enjoy a clear hierarchy of status and resources. Thus
our understanding of curriculum has to focus mainly on analyzing the dominant convention of the school subject and the
associated examination by university boards. The linking of
resources to academic subjects places a priority on subjects
that can be presented as academic disciplines, and this places
further power in the hands of the universities. Not that the
power of the universities over curriculum is unchallenged; the
challenges are recurrent. Reid has noted that a major area of
conflict is "between the external constraints arising from university requirements and the internal pressures which have their
origins in the school. Schools are, however, poorly equipped
to resist university pressures. To a large extent they allow the
legitimacy of the university demands, and have evolved an
authority structure which is linked to them."[13]

Such recurrent conflict is, of course, likely as the school
subjects "progress" away from Layton's early stage where "the
dominant criterion is relevance to the needs and interests of
the learners." But as we have seen an epistemology has been
institutionalized and resourced that places the academic discipline at the top of the curriculum apex. It is not surprising,
therefore, that the culminating stage in the establishment of
an academic subject celebrates the power of scholars to define
the discipline's field. In the last stage "the selection of subject
matter is determined in large measure by the judgements and
practices of the specialist scholars who lead enquiries in the
field. Students are initiated into a tradition, their attitudes
approaching passivity and resignation, a prelude to disenchantment."[14]

The final stage of Layton's model summarizes (and comments upon) the kind of political "settlement" with regard to curriculum, pedagogy, and evaluation currently in operation. Plainly, however, there are recurrent conflicts, and the "achievement" of this settlement has been a painstaking and deeply contested process. It is important when assessing the contribution of scholars of education to establish how their work resonates with the contested nature of education generally and curriculum specifically. As always there is a danger of accepting that which is worked for and achieved as a *fait accompli*, a given. Nothing could be further from the truth.

Antecedents and Alternatives

The epistemology and institutionalized system of state schooling briefly described in the preceding section was in sharp contrast to antecedent forms of education. Rothblatt, for instance, describes education in Georgian England as follows:

> The State was not interested in 'national education'—indeed the idea had not yet occurred. The Church, which was interested in education, because of its continuing rivalry with Dissent, still did not have a firm policy and left the direction of studies to local or personal initiatives, or to the forces of the market. The demand for education and the demand for particular levels of education varied radically from period to period and from group to group, depending upon social and economic circumstances, occupational distributions, and cultural values. Countless persons, lay as well as clerical, opened schools, tried out various educational experiments and programmes in an effort to retain a fickle or uncertain clientele. And home tuition, where adjustments in curricula could be made quickly and easily according to the learning ability of the pupil, certainly remained one of the most important means of elementary and secondary education throughout the nineteenth century.[15]

Such a personal and local mode of educating could well have allowed response to the experience and culture of the pupils even in situations less ideal than home tuition "where adjustments could be made quickly and easily according to the learning ability of the pupil." But among working-class groups, certainly in the sphere of adult education, such respect for life experience in curriculum was a feature at this time and later. This contribution can be summarized as "the students' choice of subject. The relation of disciplines to actual contemporary living and the parity of general discussion with expert instruction."[16] Above all there is the idea of curriculum as a two-way *conversation* rather than a one-way *transmission.*

Likewise with the working-class private school, which turned in the first half of the nineteenth century and confirmed with the second half in many places even after the 1870 act. Harrison has described these schools and the views of the state held of them:

Government inspection and middle-class reformers condemned such schools as mere baby-minding establishments. They noted with strong disapproval the absence of settled or regular attendance. The pupils came and went at all times during the day. School hours were nominal and adjusted to family needs; hence the number of two- and three-year olds who were sent to be "out of the way" or "kept safe." The accommodation was overcrowded and sometimes stuffy, dirty, and unsanitary. The pupils were not divided into classes, and the teacher was a workingman or -woman . . .

As well as not being arranged in classes, the curriculum was often individualized rather than sequential. Harrison describes "Old Betty W's School" where "on five days the little forms were taken outside her cottage and placed under the window. The children had their books, or their knitting and the old lady, knitting herself incessantly marched backwards and forwards hearing lessons and watching work. . . ."

These working-class schools were effectively driven out by the version of state schooling that followed the 1870 act.

Thompson has argued that the watershed for such styles—certainly styles of working-class education-was fears engendered by the French Revolution. From now on the state played an increasing role in the organization of schooling and of curriculum:

attitudes towards social class, popular culture and education became 'set' in the aftermath of the French Revolution. For a century and more most middle class educationalists could not distinguish the work of education from that of social control: and this entailed too often, a repression or a denial of the life experience of their pupils as expressed in uncouth dialect or in traditional cultural forms. Hence education and received experience were at odds with each other. And those working men who by their own efforts broke into the educated culture found themselves at once in the same place of tension, in which education brought with it the danger of rejection of their fellows and self-distrust. The tension of course continues.[17]

The disjuncture then between common cultural experience and curriculum can be estimated for working-class clienteles, as developing after the moral panics associated with the French Revolution. From this date on the school curriculum was often overlaid by social control concerns for the ordinary working populace.

For other classes at the time this overlay of closely structured, sequenced, and presented curriculum was not deemed necessary. We learn that the public schools "followed no common pattern of education," though they agreed on the taking of Latin and Greek as the main component of the curriculum. Each evolved its own unique forms of organization with idiosyncratic vocabularies to describe them![18] In so far as the curriculum depended on a learning of texts it was not judged essential that the teacher taught the text—a highly individualized form of curriculum. Moreover "where students were divided into 'forms' (a term referring originally to the benches on which they sat) this was done in a rough and ready manner for the convenience of teaching and not with the idea of establishing a hierarchy of ability or a sequence of learning."[19]

Hence coherent alternative forms of education and curriculum developed in a wide range of schools for all classes prior to the Industrial Revolution, and even after industrial transformation these forms were retained in the public schools for the "better classes" (and indeed for the working class were retained and defended in pockets such as "adult education"). The model of curriculum and epistemology associated with state schooling progressively colonized all educational milieu and established itself as the dominant pattern some time in the late nineteenth century. The subsequent linking of this epistemology to the distribution of resources and the associated attribution of status and careers stands at the center of the consolidation of this pattern. The assumption that the curriculum should be primarily academic and associated with university disciplines has been painstakingly worked and paid for. We should beware of any accounts that present such a situation of "normal" or "given."

In many ways such a hierarchical system denies the dialectic of education, the notion of dialogue and flexibility that might be viewed as central to the way we learn. If "subject matter is in large measure defined by the judgements and practice of the specialist scholars" and "students are initiated into a tradition," their attitudes approach passivity and "resignation" and this mutuality is deliberately denied. The rhetoric of the "discipline" and the academic subject might therefore be seen as characterizing a particular mode of social relations.

Educationists concerned with establishing a more egalitarian practice and curriculum are then driven to constantly assert the need for dialogue and mutuality and with it to argue for "reconstruction of knowledge and curriculum." For if the opinions cited are right the very fabric and form of curriculum (as well as the content) assumes and establishes a particular mode of social relations and social hierarchy. Seen in this way to argue only for changing the teaching method or the school organization is to accept a central mystification of hierarchical structure through curriculum that would actively contradict other aspirations and ideals. Hence where pockets of alternative practice exist they present a similar case for egalitarian practice: in liberal adult education the following argument is presented:

> All education which is worth the name involves a relationship of mutuality, a dialectic: and no worthwhile educationalist conceives of his [sic, and as follows] material as a class of inert recipients of instruction—and no class is likely to stay the course with him—if he is under the misapprehension that the role of the class is passive. What is different about the adult student is the experience which he brings to the relationship. This experience modifies, sometimes subtly, and sometimes more radically, the entire educational process: it influences teaching methods, the selection and maturation of tutors, the syllabus: it may even disclose weak places or vacancies in received academic disciplines and lead on to the elaboration of new areas of study.[20]

By this view then the disciplines cannot be taught as final "distillations" of knowledge unchallengeable and unchanging, and should not be taught as incontestable and fundamental structures and texts. This would provide a deeply flawed epistemology, pedagogically unsound and intellectually dubious, for in human scholarship "final distillations" and "fundamental" truths are elusive concepts. We are back with the dual face of socially contexted knowledge—both because knowledge and curriculum are pedagogically realized in a social context and are originally conceived of and constructed in such a context.

The alternatives to such a dominant view continue to surface. In the contemporary debate we find certain radical teachers taking the comprehensive ideal seriously and arguing that in such a milieu knowledge and curricula must be presented as provisional and *liable to reconstruction*. Armstrong writes that his "contention is that the process of education should imply a dynamic relationship between teacher, pupil and task out of which knowledge is reconstructed, for both teacher and pupil, in the light of shared experience."[21] He likens this in some way to the philosopher R. S. Peters's writing about conversation: Conversation is not structured like a discussion group in terms of one form of thought or toward the solution of a problem. In a conversation lecturing to others is bad form; so is using the remarks of others as springboards for self-display. The point is to create a common world to which all bring their distinctive contributions. By participating in such a shared experience much is learned, though no one sets out to teach anyone anything. And one of the things that is learned is to see the world from the viewpoint of another whose perspective is very different. different.[22] Armstrong then comments: "Unfortunately, but not unexpectedly, Peters assumes that conversation is possible only between people who are already 'well-educated'. A large part of the contemporary philosophy of education rests on this mistake."[23]

A Brief Excursion into Philosophy of Education in Britain

In the preceding section we traced the emergence of the epistemologies related to state schooling. In the contemporary "settlement" the school subject stands as the main manifestation of curriculum, and the philosophy of education has provided a range of insights and comments on the status and origins of subjects, disciplines and forms, and fields of knowledge. I do not here want to intrude too far on the debate between the philosophical absolutionists and social relativists: plainly a dialogue of the deaf. My concern is rather to characterize the implicit *posture* of much of the "philosophy of education" that is institutionalized and taught with regard to the school curriculum. At its heart, philosophy of education seems to hold itself well above the fray of curriculum as it exists and as it is currently realized. The core of this aloofness is a commitment to rational and logical pursuit. But the other side of the coin is a resistance to the force of social influence. It is as if the philosopher searches for truths *beyond* social interference. This is true even of more liberal philosophers. Take Hirst, for instance: objective knowledge he says "is a form of education knowing no limits other than those necessarily imposed by the nature of rational knowledge and thereby developing in man [sic] the final court of appeal in all human affairs." [24] Or Pring: "Forms of knowledge therefore are fundamental structures picked out by characteristic concepts and characteristic tests of truth. They are not options open to us; they constitute what it *means* to think and they characterise all our particular judgements." [25]

Whatever the carefully constructed "let out" clauses, that is, the philosophical discourse, the likely implication to be drawn is that the "philosopher king" knows only "truth"; there are no options for they have access to a truth beyond culture and beyond history. The static, ahistorical "givenness" of the position is shown when Hirst asserts "to acquire knowledge is to become aware of experience as structured, organised and made meaningful in some quite specific way." [26] "Quite specific" indeed and quite possibly a misrepresentation of reality. No matter, we are invited to embrace the *fait accompli*.

At a certain level of discourse this may well be a sustainable position. But facing the process of teaching forms of knowledge, we are still in a position where "they are not options open to us": on this point some of the philosophers show signs of almost human ambivalence. Others, however, have the strength of their convictions. Phenix, for instance, deliberately equates the disciplines with teachability: "My theme has been that the curriculum should consist entirely of knowledge which comes from the disciplines, for the reason that the disciplines reveal knowledge in its teachable forms." [27]

The "disciplines" then are imposed by the nature of rational knowledge; they are "fundamental structures," not options open to us. Clearly such fundamental distillations should be used as the basis of teaching.

Phenix's statement reveals, I think, the likely policy outcome of the more recently dominant mode of theorizing in philosophy of education. Whatever the qualifications, whatever the studied detachment, the likely effect of the posture will be a prescriptive curriculum. From a certainty that "there are no options" it is clear that prescriptive objectives for schooling will be both the expectation and the culmination.

The extent to which philosophy has in fact contributed in this way can be seen in a wide range of curriculum books from specialists of all kinds, the work of Bruner and Phenix in the United States through to Lawton and Peters in the United Kingdom. Lawton is a particularly useful example of how an experienced curriculum specialist receives the messages of the philosopher. In assessing Hirst's view, Lawton argues: "the theory seems to me to run as follows: the first principle is that we should be clear about our educational goals. The second is that 'the central objectives of education are developments of the mind'." He adds later:

> I have included Hirst's viewpoint here as an example of curriculum planning which is largely 'non-cultural' in the sense of being transcultural. This is because Hirst sees the curriculum largely in terms of knowledge, and the structure and organisation of knowledge is, by his analysis, universal rather than culturally based.[28]

Philosophy then leads us beyond culture, and above all leads to curriculum theories that allow us to "be clear about our educational goals" that relate to "developments of the mind." The emphasis on *the mind* confirms the fundamental preeminence of the "disciplines."

However, the believers in educational goals based on theories about the fixed nature of the disciplines have ultimately to face the sad truth that the world of schooling as it currently exists is played on a soccer field where scoring goals is difficult and where the goalposts are not always relevant. There is a tearful little section in Lawton headed "Disciplines but not Subjects." Here the confrontation between philosophies and prescriptive truth and classroom reality leads to peculiar paroxysms to escape culpability for the prescription's failures. Hence Lawton writes:

> there is no reason why a curriculum based on disciplines should not be related to the children's own experience and interests. The fact

that so much so-called academic teaching of subjects does tend to
neglect children's everyday knowledge . . . is a condemnation of traditional pedagogy or teaching-method rather than disciplines themselves as a basis of the curriculum.[29]

One wonders what a philosopher would make of the logic
of culpability here? (Are the disciplines beyond logic as well
as culture?)

But this is to do less than justice to Lawton or Hirst. Both of
these writers have, of course, shown considerable sensitivity
to the problems of curriculum change and implementation. I
have really pursued the point to show that even more sophisticated theorists are on the horns of a dilemma when working
with the prescriptive mode. Hirst has pronounced at length
on the dilemma in his article "The Forms of Knowledge Revis-
ited":

The importance of the disciplines, in the various senses distinguished,
for school education, must not be minimised. What matters in this
discussion is that the logical priority of intellectual objectives be
recognised even if in terms of wider human values they are sometimes judged secondary. Equally their logical structure cannot be denied if they are ever to be attained. The concerns of the universities
mean that their organisations of teaching and research necessarily
embody these concerns to a high degree. But schools are not universities and their teaching functions are significantly different. These
need to be seen in their own right for what they are. And if once that
is done then not only do the disciplines matter, but many other things
matter as well, things of major psychological and social concern which
must not be overlooked.

This leads to a final epilogue for the forms of knowledge as
prescriptions:

Education is a complex business and philosophical analysis can contribute to our planning of it in a limited way. What it can do is alert us
to the danger of too easy decisions and the issue of the place of the
disciplines in more than a philosophical affair. What more there is to
it I must, however, leave to others.[30]

The humility of this epilogue is both appealing and a clear
statement of how limited the aspirations of the philosopher
have become. But several logical steps are still missing before
we arrive at this denouement. It is all very well to leave it to
others. But who? It is all very well to alert us to the danger of

easy decision. But what if philosophy has led us to the very dangers of prescriptive simplicities to which we have drawn attention? To go even further back, if schools and teaching need to be seen in their own right for what they are, why does the analysis not start there? Perhaps after all we do not need theories of curriculum prescription but studies and eventually theories of curriculum production and realization.

Conclusion

In this chapter some of the origins of curriculum have been analyzed. In particular we have seen that the notion of curriculum as structured sequence or "discipline" derived a good deal from the political ascendancy of Calvinism. From these early origins there was a "homologous relationship between curriculum and discipline." Curriculum as discipline was allied to a social order where the "elect" were offered the prospect of advanced schooling and the remainder a more conservative curriculum. Out of these origins we have seen how this concept of curriculum became appended to a new notion of discipline: this time (so we are to believe) "fundamental" disciplines of "the mind." The juxtaposition of curriculum with (newly defined) discipline intersects with a remarkably similar social configuration. This time the elect are recruited by their capacity to display a facility for those academic subjects allied to the disciplines; their election is signified by going on to study the disciplines in the universities where they are defined and institutionalized.

Notes

1. Barrow, R. (1984) *Giving Teaching Back to Teachers: A Critical Introduction to Curriculum Theory*, London, Ont., Canada: Althouse Press, p. 3.

2. Hamilton, D., and M. Gibbons (1986) "Notes on the Origins of the Educational Terms, Class and Curriculum." Paper presented at the Annual Conference of the American Educational Research Association, Boston, p. 15.

3. Hamilton and Gibbons, "Origins," p. 7.

4. Hamilton and Gibbons, "Origins," p. 14.

5. Hamilton, D. (1980) "Adam Smith and the Moral Economy of the Classroom System." *Journal of Curriculum Studies*, Vol. 12, No. 4, p. 286.

6. Hamilton, "Moral Economy," p. 282.

7. Ibid.

8. University of Cambridge Local Examinations Syndicate (May 29, 1958) *One Hundredth Annual Report to University*.

9. Hamilton, "Moral Economy," p. 282.

10. Committee of the Secondary School Examinations Council (1943). The Norwood Report *Curriculum and Examinations in Secondary Schools*. Report of the Committee appointed by the President of the Board of Education in 1941, London: His Majesty's Stationery Office, p. 61.

11. Byrne, E. M. (1974) *Planning and Educational Inequality*, Slough, England: National Foundation for Educational Research, p. 29.

12. Jenkins, D., and M. Shipman (1976) *Curriculum: An Introduction*, London: Open Books, p. 106.

13. Reid, W. A. (1972) *The University and the Sixth Form Curriculum*, London: Macmillan, p. 106.

14. Layton, D. (1972) "Science as General Education." *Trends in Education*. England.

15. Rothblatt, S. (1976) *Tradition and Change in English Liberal Education: An Essay in History and Culture*, London: Faber & Faber, p. 45.

16. Williams, R. (1975) *The Long Revolution*, London: Penguin, p. 165.

17. Morrison, J. F. C. (1986) *The Common People*, London: Flamingo, p. 292.

18. Thompson, E. P. (1968) *Education and Experience*. Fifth Mansbridge Memorial Lecture, Leeds, England: Leeds University Press, p. 16.

19. Reid, W. A. (1985) "Curriculum Change and the Evolution of Educational Constituencies: the English Sixth Form in the Nineteenth Century." In I. F. Goodson (ed.) *Social Histories of the Secondary Curriculum: Subjects for Study*, London, New York, and Philadelphia: Falmer Press, p. 296.

20. Ibid.

21. Thompson, *Education and Experience,* p. 9.

22. Armstrong, M. (1977) "Reconstructing Knowledge: An Example." In J. Watts (ed.) *The Countesthorpe Experience*, London: Allen & Unwin, p. 86.

23. Peters, R. S. (1967) "What Is an Educational Process?" In R. S. Peters (ed.) *The Concept of Education*, London: Routledge & Kegan Paul, p. 2.

24. Hirst, P. M. (1965) "Liberal Education and the Nature of Knowledge." In R. D. Archambault (Ed.) *Philosophical Analysis and Education*. London: Routledge & Kegan Paul, p. 127.

25. Pring, R. (1972) "Focus of Knowledge and General Education. *General Education*, Vol. 19, p. 27.

26. Hirst, "Liberal Education."

27. Phenix, P. M. (1968) "The Disciplines as Curriculum Content." In E. C. Short and C. D. Marconnit (eds.) *Contemporary Thought on Public School Curriculum: Readings*. Dubuque, Iowa: W. C. Brown, p. 133.

28. Lawton, D. (1975) *Class, Culture and the Curriculum*. London: Routledge & Kegan Paul, p. 18.

29. Ibid., p. 85.

30. Hirst, P.M. (1974) *Knowledge and the Curriculum*. London: Routledge & Kegan Paul, p. 99.

Chapter 4

Basil Bernstein and Aspects of the Sociology of the Curriculum

In this chapter, I relate some personal comments about the significance of Basil Bernstein to my own notions of curriculum study. I then move on to comment on the kind of program of study that have developed, partly due to his influence. In short, I move from the personal to the programmatic. In doing so, I shall not try to cover all of Bernstein's influences upon, or theories about, the school curriculum. I shall confine myself to issues of personal significance and to the terrain of curriculum studies with which I have been involved. In providing a personal introduction, the intention is to ground a discussion of academic discourses in some understanding, albeit limited, of social structure and lived experience.

Some Biographical Background

I was born in England in 1943. My father was a gas fitter; my mother worked in a wartime munitions factory. My father was the youngest of thirteen children (he was lucky enough to be preceded by twelve sisters); his father was an unskilled laborer, mostly unemployed, his mother took in laundry. My mother was one of six children and had two sisters and three brothers. Her father and mother ran a workingman's cafe in Reading, England. (It was while serving breakfast one morning in 1929 that she met my Dad.)

My parents married in 1932 and went to live in a working-class suburb of Reading, called Woodley. I was born during the war. My Dad was involved with the Gas Fitters Union and in 1945 both my parents voted for a Labour government committed to bringing a better deal for working people and their children. This government was to substantially affect my schooling. In 1949, I went to a school attached to the Church of England; it was very ill-resourced, having no textbooks, or qualified teacher, or separate classrooms (just one huge room with curtains across). I can still vividly recall the "earth closets" that passed as toilets. At the time I could not read or write. But the new Labour government had initiated a vigorous campaign to build new "county primary schools." So in 1950, I left the earth closets behind, to go to Loddon County Primary School. At the time I still could not read but, given the ready supply of books and the qualified teachers, soon learned. Three years later I passed the "11-plus" examination.

The grammar school to which I was directed was a long way from my village, and I had to travel by bus and train or, in summer, undertake a long bicycle ride. This was only the beginning of a process that seemed calculated to take me away from my family and my culture. Within the school many features jarred with my cultural experiences. I was a ten-year-old child adrift in a very alien world. In retrospect, the major vehicle of alienation was the school curriculum—Latin, Greek, ancient history, grammar, English literature, physics, chemistry, and so on. A classical curriculum utterly divorced from my experience of the world. Like so many of my social class—as was well documented by Jackson and Marsden, Lacey and David Hargreaves—I settled near the bottom of my grade. In 1959, I took nine O-level examinations and passed . . . one subject (history). That summer, I went to work in a potato chip factory with three of my friends from Woodley.

My history teacher must have been pleased with his singular success at teaching me something (compared with the other eight subject teachers), for he arrived at the factory in September and announced that I should return to school. Shouting above the noise of the factory I said I might do just that. School had begun to look desirable.

So I worked hard, passed a few O levels that year, and joined the sixth form. In due course, I passed my A-level examinations and went off to London University (London was, in fact, the only place I could go because, at that time, all other universities required Latin or Greek). I did an Economics Degree and, doing quite well in the final examinations, was offered a research studentship at the London School of Economics. For four years I fumbled away at a doctorate on Irish immigrants in Victorian England, and in my final year became a lecturer at what is now Kingston University.

But throughout this period, I was spending increasing amounts of time back home in Woodley (which was an hour from London). This still felt like home. This was where my friends and family were. Moreover, the grammar schools were being replaced by comprehensive schools, and the word in the pubs and clubs of Woodley was that this would offer an education to my class of people that would be of more interest and relevance than Latin, Greek, and ancient history. My friends spent a lot of time talking about all this as a political strategy of hope.

So I began to read more about education. In the summer of 1967, I came across an article titled "Open Schools, Open Society," by Basil Bernstein, first published in *New Society*:

> we are moving from secondary schools where the teaching roles were insulated from each other, where the teacher had an assigned area of authority and autonomy, to secondary schools where the teaching role is less autonomous and where it is a shared or co-operative role. There has been a shift from a teaching role which is, so to speak, 'given' (in the sense that one steps into assigned duties), to a role which has to be *achieved* in relation with other teachers. It is a role which is no longer made but *has to be made*. The teacher is no longer isolated from other teachers, as where the principle of integration is the relation of his subject to a public examination. The teacher is now in a complementary relation with other teachers at the level of his day-by-day teaching.[1]

More or less, there and then I decided to stop wasting my time studying Victorian England and lecturing in higher education to the "sons and daughters of gentlefolk" and to get involved in teaching in comprehensive schools. I applied to the Institute of Education in London to train as a teacher.

The Institute of Education, circa 1969

In 1969, the Institute of Education was scattered through many buildings clustered around Senate House in Malet Street, WC1, London. On Taviton Street a number of terraced houses were grouped together to form the Sociology Department. It was here that my tutors, Brian Davies and Basil Bernstein, held their seminars and occasional personal tutorials.

I attended a range of "methods" courses, but some of my time was spent completing a term project on "working-class students in the new comprehensive schools." As a result, I got a lot of papers pushed my way that Brian Davies, Michael Young, and Basil Bernstein were writing: I still have the papers and, of course, they were early drafts of work that later appeared in *Knowledge and Control*[2] and *Class, Codes and Control*.[3]

It is difficult to describe the liberating power of tutorials at the Institute at this time. After fifteen years of schooling and university being taught by people from another social class about subjects utterly disconnected from anything I had experienced, suddenly everything changed. The tutors were mostly from a similar background and the subject was essentially *our* experience of education and culture. The sociology department in 1969 was in a real sense like coming home (with all the tensions and ambivalences carried therein). And it was to know, for perhaps the first time, that learning did not have to be alienating, that connectedness was possible. It was also to likewise learn that disconnectedness was often socially constructed.

To experience what "could be" in terms of social science scholarship was also then to learn what was "not allowed to be." To learn what could be in terms of pedagogic discourse and relationships was to be shown with unforgettable clarity how curriculum, culture, and class were irrevocably enmeshed. For a few years (in the social democratic moment that followed 1968), in the sociology department a "contradictory gap" was opened up. During that time work on *Knowledge and Control* proceeded not only at the scholarly level but also at the level of the lived experience for those who clustered around the tables of Taviton Street and of the local pubs. Many conversations have stayed with me since. One I remember was between me, Rob Walker (who was finishing a research degree with Basil Bernstein), and Basil. It started in Taviton Street with a long argument about styles of pedagogy and the comprehensive school. It then moved along the street to the Marlborough pub, where it went on for five hours. A good deal of the discussion turned on Basil's use of the term transmission in some of his work.[4] This we argued was to use the language of dominant pedagogies while speaking of other visions. By the end of the evening we were, it has to be said, all absolutely drunk.

In the cold light of day, though, I found myself nagging away at what had been said. Through the mists of the Marlborough a program of study began to tentatively emerge, and it was clear that the "agent provocateur" in all this was Bernstein himself.

As I recounted in Chapter 2, Bernstein's work in particular helped confirm that there were forms of academic discourse and study whereby the everyday experiences of ordinary pupils and people might be represented. To explore this, let me now switch discourses from this personal introduction to programmatic exploration.

From the Personal to the Programmatic

So move from the personal to the programmatic. In doing so, I shall also be switching voices, codes, and discourses. For the rest of this chapter, I will adopt the disembodied voice of scholasticism. In this sense the chapter moves between the two "worlds" of my experience.

In his essay "On the Classification and Framing of Educational Knowledge," Bernstein wrote that

> How a society selects, classifies, distributes, transmits and evaluates the educational knowledge it considers to be public, reflects both the distribution of power and the principles of social control. From this point of view, differences within and change in the organization, transmission and evaluation of educational knowledge should be a major area of sociological interest.[5]

He extended this idea later in the chapter in a very suggestive paragraph

> We can look at the question of the framing of knowledge in the pedagogical relationship from another point of view. In a sense, educational knowledge is uncommonsense knowledge. It is knowledge freed from the particular, the local, through the various languages of the sciences or forms of reflexiveness of the arts which make possible either the creation or the discovery of new realities. Now this immediately raises the question of the relationship between the

uncommonsense knowledge of the school and the *commonsense* knowledge, everyday community knowledge, of the pupil, his family and his peer group. This formulation invites us to ask how strong are the frames of educational knowledge in relation to experiential, community-based non-school knowledge? I suggest that the frames of the collection code, very early in the child's life, socialize him into knowledge frames which discourage connections with everyday realities, or that there is a highly selective screening of the connection. Through such socialization, the pupil soon learns what of the outside may be brought into the pedagogical frame. Such framing also makes of educational knowledge something not ordinary or mundane, but something esoteric which gives a special significance to those who possess it. I suggest that when this frame is relaxed to include everyday realities, it is often and sometimes validly, not simply for the transmission of educational knowledge, but for purposes of social control of forms of deviancy. The weakening of this frame occurs usually with the less 'able' children whom we have given up educating.[6]

Bernstein's work on the school curriculum then exhorts us to investigate how a society selects, classifies, distributes, and transmits its educational knowledge and to relate this to issues of power and social control. In Britain, the major vehicle for educational knowledge, certainly at the secondary-school level, has been the school subject. Moves toward a different pattern of social relations and reproduction have often focused on the attempts at "reforming" or "integrating" the subject-centered curriculum. A program of study focuses on school subjects, thereby offered some promise in furthering a project of social enquiry.

Programs for Studying School Subjects

With the growth of the state systems of education the school subject became the major focus of schooling for increasing numbers of pupils. As a result scholarship began looking into the origins of school subjects. Foster Watson, a pioneer in this field, was clear that "owing to the rapid development of a system of County and Municipal Secondary Schools in England and Wales, at the present time, a special interest is centred on the place and function of the 'modern' subjects in the secondary schools."[7] This rationale anticipates in some manner the later exhortations of sociologists of knowledge, for he argued that "it is high time that the historical facts with regard to the beginnings of the teaching of modern subjects in England were known, and known in connection with the history of the social forces which brought them into the educational curriculum."[8] In the fifty-year period following 1909 few scholars followed Watson and sought to relate school subjects to the "social forces which brought them into the educational curriculum" in any general way.

In the 1960s, however, a new impetus to scholarship on school subjects came from sociologists like Bernstein. Writing in 1968, Frank Musgrove exhorted educational researchers to "examine subjects both within the school and the nation at large as social systems sustained by communication networks, material endowments, and ideologies."[9] In the 'communication networks" Esland later argued that research should focus, in part, on the subject perspective of the teacher:

> The knowledge which a teacher thinks 'fills up' his subject is held in common with members of a supporting community who collectively approach its paradigms and utility criteria, as they are legitimated in training courses and 'official' statements. It would seem that teachers, because of the dispersed nature of their epistemic communities, experience the conceptual precariousness which comes from the lack of significant others who can confirm plausibility. They are, therefore, heavily dependent on journals, and, to a lesser extent, conferences, for their reality confirmation.[10]

He, together with Dale, later developed this focus on teachers within subject communities:

> Teachers, as spokesmen for subject communities are involved in an elaborate organization of knowledge. The community has a history, and, through it, a body of respected knowledge. It has rules for recognizing 'unwelcome' or 'spurious' matter, and ways of avoiding cognitive contamination. It will have a philosophy and a set of authorities, all of which give strong legitimation to the activities which are acceptable to the community. Some members are accredited with the power to make 'official statements'—for instance, editors of journals, presidents, chief examiners and inspectors. These are important as 'significant others' who provide models to new or wavering members of appropriate belief and conduct.[11]

In particular, Esland was concerned that we developed scholarship that illuminated the role of professional groups in the social construction of school subjects. These groups can be seen as mediators of the 'social forces' to which Watson had eluded:

> The subject associations of the teaching profession may be theoretically represented as segments and social movements involved in the negotiation of new alliances and rationales, as collectively held reality constructions became transformed. Thus, applied to the professional identities of teachers within a school, it would be possible to reveal the conceptual regularities and changes which are generated through membership of particular subject communities, as they were manifested in textbooks, syllabi, journals, conference reports, etc.

In the light of the importance of historical perspectives, Esland added that "Subjects can be shown to have 'careers' which are dependent on the social-structural and social-psychological correlates of membership of epistemic communities."[12]

The relationship between the content of schooling, "what counts as education and issues of power and control" has been elucidated by Raymond Williams in the *Long Revolution*. He noted:

> It is not only that the way in which education is organized can be seen to express consciously and unconsciously, the wider organization of a culture and a society so that what has been thought of a single distribution is in fact an actual shaping to particular social ends. It is also that the content of education which is subject to great historical agnation, again expresses, again both consciously and unconsciously, certain basic elements in the culture. What is thought of as 'an education' being in fact a particular set of emphases and omissions.[13]

One might add to Williams's notion of "the content of education." For I have noted elsewhere that the battle over the *content* of the curriculum, while often more visible, is in many senses less important than the control over the underlying *forms*.[14]

Michael F. D. Young sought to follow up the relationship between school knowledge and social control and to do so in a manner that focused on content and form. He argued following Bernstein that: "those in positions of power will attempt to define what is to be taken as knowledge, how accessible to different groups any knowledge is, and what are the accepted relationships between different knowledge areas, and between those who have access to them and make them available."[15]

His concern with the form of high-status school subjects focused on the "organizing principles" that he discerned as underlying the academic curriculum:

> These are literacy, or an emphasis on written as opposed to oral presentation, individualism (or avoidance of group work or cooperativeness) which focused on how academic work is assessed and is a characteristic of both the 'process' of learning and the way the 'product' is presented; abstractness of the knowledge and its structuring and compartmentalizing independently of the knowledge of the learner; finally and linked to the former is what I have called the unrelatedness of academic curricula, which refers to the extent to which they are 'at odds' with daily life and experience.[16]

This emphasis on the form of school knowledge should not, however, exclude concerns like that of Williams with the social construction of *particular contents*. The crucial point to grasp is that it is the interrelated force of form *and* content that should be at the center of our study of school subjects. The study of subject form and content should moreover be placed in an historical perspective.

In fact, in his later work Young came to acknowledge the somewhat static determination of his writing in *Knowledge and Control* and to argue that historical work should be an essential ingredient of the study of school knowledge. He wrote of the need to understand the "historical emergence and persistence of particular conventions (school subjects, for example)." When we are limited from being able to situate the problems of contemporary education historically, we are again limited from understanding issues of politics and control. He concluded that "one crucial way of reformulating and transcending the limits within which we work is to see . . . how such limits are not given or fixed but produced through the conflicting actions and interests of men in history."[17]

Studying the Social History of School Subjects

The important work by sociologists of knowledge such as Bernstein in defining research programs for studies of school knowledge led on, then, to an acknowledgment by some of them that historical study might complement and extend their project. In studying school subjects we have arrived at a new stage. Initial work in the early twentieth century has provided some important precursors to our work; the sociologists of knowledge have subsequently played a vital role in rescuing and reasserting the validity of this intellectual project; in the process, however, some of the necessary focus on historical and empirical circumstances has been lost. The task now being undertaken is to reexamine the role of historical methods in the study of curriculum and to rearticulate a mode of study for carrying further our understanding of the social history of the school curriculum and, in this work, particularly school subjects.

In *School Subjects and Curriculum Change*, first published in 1983, I looked at the history of three subjects; geography, biology, and environmental studies.[18] Each of the subjects followed a similar evolutionary profile, and this initial work allowed a series of hypotheses to be developed about the way that status and resources, the structuration of school subjects, push school-subject knowledge in particular directions: toward the embrace of what I call the "academic tradition." Following this work a new series *Studies in Curriculum History* was launched. In the first volume, *Social Histories of the Secondary Curriculum,*[19] work is collected together on a wide range of subjects: classics (Stray, English) or science (Waring, who earlier had written the seminal study on Nuffield science), domestic subjects (Purvis), religious education (Bell), social studies (Franklin and Whitty), and modern languages (Radford). These studies reflect a growing interest in the history of curriculum and, besides elucidating the symbolic drift of school knowledge toward the academic tradition, raise central questions about past and current explanations of school subjects, whether they be sociological or philosophical. Another work in the series *Studies in Curriculum History* has looked in detail at particular subjects-in 1985 McCulloch, Layton, and Jenkins produced *Technological Revolution?*[20] This book examines the politics of school science and technology curriculum in England and Wales since the Second World War. Subsequent work by Brian Woolnough has looked at the history of physics teaching in schools in the period 1960 to 1985.[21] Another area of emerging work is the history of school mathematics: Cooper's book *Renegotiating Secondary School Mathematics* looks at the fate of a number of traditions within mathematics and articulates a model for the redefinition of school-subject knowledge;[22] Bob Moon's book, *The 'New Maths' Curriculum Controversy*, meanwhile looked at the relationship between maths in England and America, and has some very interesting work on the dissemination of textbooks.[23]

Emerging work in America has also begun to focus on the evolution of the school curriculum studied in an historical manner. H. M. Kliebard's seminal *The Struggle for the American Curriculum 1893-1958* discerns a number of the dominant traditions within the school curriculum.[24] The book also comes to the intriguing conclusion that by the end of the period covered the traditional school subject remained "an impregnable fortress." But Kliebard's work does not take us into the detail of school life. In this respect Barry Franklin's book, *Building the American Community*, provides us with some valuable insights in a case study of Minneapolis, Minnesota.[25] Here we see the vital negotiation from curriculum ideas, the terrain of Kliebard's work, toward implementation as school practice. In addition a collection of papers put together by Tom Popkewitz looks at the historical aspects of a range of subjects: early education (Bloch), art (Freedman), reading and writing (Monagha and Saul), biology (Rosenthal and Bybee), mathematics (Stanic), social studies (Lyburger), special education (Franklin and Sleeter), socialist curriculum (Teitelbaum), and a study of Ruggs's textbook by Kliebard and Wegner.[26]

In Canada curriculum history has been launched as a field, most notably by George Tomkins' pioneering work *A Common Countenance*.[27] This studies the patterns of curriculum stability and change in a range of school subjects throughout Canada over the past two centuries. The book has stimulated a wide range of important new work of curriculum history. For instance, Rowell and Gaskell's very generative study of the history of school physics.[28] The Rowell and Gaskell piece provides one important case study in a new book *International Perspectives in Curriculum History* that seeks to bring together some of the more important work emerging in different countries on curriculum history.[29] Besides some of the work already noted by Stanic, Moon, Franklin, McCulloch, Ball and Gaskell, there are important articles on Victorian school science by

Hodson, on science education by Louis Smith, on English in the Norwegian common school by Gundem, and on the development of senior school geography in West Australia by Marsh.[30]

Other work has begun to look beyond traditional school subjects to examine broader topics. For example, Peter Cunningham's book looks at the curriculum change in the primary school in Britain since 1945.[31] P. W. Musgrave's book, *Whose Knowledge?* is a case study of the Victoria University Examinations Board 1964 to 1979.[32] Here historical work begins to elucidate the change from curriculum content to examinable content that is such an important part of understanding the way that status and resources are apportioned within the school.

Recent work has begun to explore gender patterns in curriculum history. Jane Bernard Powers excellent study *The Girl Question in Education* is a pioneering work in this regard.[33] Likewise, work is beginning on the modernist construction of curriculum as a world movement. The work of John Meyer et al., *School Knowledge for the Masses,* provides a path-breaking study of national primary curricula categories in the twentieth century throughout the world.[34]

In many countries curriculum history is now being systematically analyzed and promoted. In the last couple of years educational journals in Brasil, Australia, Scandinavia, and Spain have provided special editions on curriculum history (Goodson, 1990a, 1990b, 1990c, 1991a, 1991b; Goodson and Dowbiggin, 1991) and new books are planned in Germany, Portugal, Italy, and South Africa.[35]

Future directions for the study of school subjects and curriculum will require a broadened approach. The baseline of the work just reported is only a precursor to more elaborate work. In particular this work will have to move into examining the relationship between school-subject content and form, and issues of school practice and process. In addition, more broadly conceived notions of curriculum will have to be explored: the hidden curriculum, the curriculum conceived of as topics and activities, and most important of all the primary and preschool curricula. As we begin to explore the way in which school-subject content relates to the parameters of practice, we shall begin to see in a more grounded way how the world of schooling is structured. In addition more work must be undertaken on comparative studies of the school curriculum.

It is now vital to also redirect this work to an exploration and critique of the National Curriculum, for the resonances at the level of class, gender, and race to previous patterns are overwhelming. The comparison between Bernstein's work on the curriculum and the current state of the art of curriculum analysis in the United Kingdom is a salutary reminder of the changes in political climate and responses within the academy. There could be no clearer indicator of the general climate of withdrawal and deference within the academy. Because the National Curriculum cries out for the kind of social analysis epitomized by Bernstein and first called for by Watson.[36] To paraphrase: "It is high time that the historical facts with regard to the National Curriculum were known, and known in connection with the social forces which brought them into the educational curriculum."

In terms of the Bernstein legacy and what I have called social constructionist study of the curriculum, this lacuna in studying the National Curriculum is little short of astounding.[37] As I have detailed, work on the history of school subjects has been sustained, particularly in Britain, itself for over a decade of intensive scholarship. We now know a great deal about the class, gender, and racial biases of school subjects. Yet in recent years, scholars close to these developments, with a few dignified exceptions, have virtually ignored this legacy in their work on the National Curriculum. The effect is to conspire with the Thatcherite view that the National Curriculum is a new and compelling revolution in educational provision. In fact, curriculum history indicates that nothing could be further from the truth. As I have argued elsewhere,[38] government policy and pronouncements have encouraged this amnesia (and a failure to present academic challenges has the same effect): "The obsessive presentism of many of the current government initiatives has successfully obscured this deeply-embedded connectedness which is of course relevant to the present and future of the UK as a class society."[39]

Curriculum histories then should provide a systematic analysis of these ongoing social constructions and selections that form the school curriculum, pointing up continuities and discontinuities of social purpose over time. It is important to note that the prevailing paradigm, of curriculum study focusing on implementation, is devoid of such sociohistorical perspective, but more importantly so too is the more "radical" focus on curriculum that studies school-based "resistance" to new national directives. Not only is such work without sociohistorical range but it focuses only on the reaction. As Frederick Jameson recently noted in a conversation at The University of Western Ontario's Centre for Theory and Criticism, "The violence of the riposte says little about the terms of the engagement." So it is with school resistance to the National Curriculum. The latter sets the terms of the engagement and does so in ways that link to a history of social purposes. Curriculum histories should seek to elucidate and analyze this ongoing process. These histories provide a new terrain of study where the school subject might again be employed as an entry point for social analysis. It is an entry point, though, that can be clearly traced back to Basil Bernstein and his work at the Institute of Education in London.

Notes

1. Bernstein, B. (1975) *Class, Codes and Control*, Vol. 3, *Towards a Theory of Educational Transmissions*, 2d ed., London: Routledge & Kegan Paul, p. 71.

2. Young, M. F. D. (1971) (ed.) *Knowledge and Control: New Directions for the Sociology of Education*, London: Collier-Macmillan.

3. Bernstein, *Class, Codes and Control*.

4. See Bernstein, B. (1971) "On the Classification and Framing of Educational Knowledge." In Young, *Knowledge and Control*, p. 47.

5. Bernstein, "Classification and Framing," p. 47.

6. Ibid., p. 58.

7. Watson, F. (1909) *The Beginning of the Teaching of the Modern Subjects in England*, London: Pitman, p. vii.

8. Ibid., p. viii.

9. Musgrove, F. (1968) "The Contribution of Sociology to the Study of the Curriculum." In J. F. Kerr (ed.) *Changing the Curriculum*, London: University of London Press, p. 101.

10. Esland, G. M. (1971) "Teaching and Learning as the Organization of Knowledge." In Young, *Knowledge and Control*, p. 79.

11. Esland, G. M. and R. Dale (eds.) (1973) *School and Society*, Course E282, Unit 2, Milton Keynes, England: Open University Press, pp 70-71.

12. Esland, G. M. (1971) "Teaching and Learning as the Organization of Knowledge." In Young, *Knowledge and Control*, p. 107.

13. Williams, R. (1975) *The Long Revolution*, London: Penguin, p. 146.

14. Goodson, I. F. (1992) "On Curriculum Form" *Sociology of Education*, Vol. 65, No. 1, pp. 66-75.

15. Young, *Knowledge and Control*, p. 52

16. Ibid., p. 38.

17. Young, M.F.D. (1977) "Curriculum Change: Limits and Possibilities." In M. F. D. Young and G. Whitty (eds.) *Society, State and Schooling*, Lewes, England: Falmer Press, pp. 248-249.

18. Goodson, I. F. (1993) *School Subjects and Curriculum Change*, 3d ed., London, New York, and Philadelphia: Falmer Press.

19. Goodson, I. F. (ed.) (1985) *Social Histories of the Secondary Curriculum*, London and Philadelphia: Falmer Press.

20 McCulloch, G., E. Jenkins, and D. Layton (1985) *Technological Revolution?*, London and Philadelphia: Falmer Press.

21 Woolnough, B. E. (1988) *Physics Teaching in Schools 1960-85: Of People, Policy and Power*, London, New York, and Philadelphia: Falmer Press.

22 Cooper, B. (1985) *Renegotiating Secondary School Mathematics*, London and Philadelphia: Falmer Press.

23. Moon, B. (1986) *The 'New Maths' Curriculum Controversy*, London, New York, and Philadelphia: Falmer Press.

24 Kliebard, H. M. (1986) *The Struggle for the American Curriculum 1893-1953*, London: Routledge & Kegan Paul.

25 Franklin, B. (1986) *Building the American Community*, London, New York, and Philadelphia: Falmer Press.

26 Popkewitz, T. S. (1987) *The Formation of School Subjects: The Struggle for Creating an American Institution*, London, New York, and Philadelphia: Falmer Press.

27 Tomkins, G. S. (1986) *A Common Countenance: Stability and Change in the Canadian Curriculum*, Scarborough, Ont., Canada: Prentice Hall.

28 Rowell, P. M., and P. J. Gaskell (1988) "Tensions and Realignments: School Physics in British Columbia 1955-80." In I. F. Goodson (ed.) *International Perspectives in Curriculum History*, London and New York: Routledge.

29 Goodson, I. F. (ed.) (1988) *International Perspectives in Curriculum History*, 2d ed., London and New York: Routledge.

30. Ibid.

31 Cunningham, P. (1988) *Curriculum Change in the Primary School Since 1945*, London, New York, and Philadelphia: Falmer Press.

32 Musgrave, P. W. (1988) *Whose Knowledge?*, London, New York, and Philadelphia: Falmer Press.

33 Powers, J. B. (1992) *The Girl Question in Education: Vocational Education for Young Women in the Progressive Era*, London, New York, and Philadelphia: Falmer Press.

34. Meyer, J. W., D. H. Kamens, A. Benavot, with Y. K. Cha and S. Y. Wong (1992). *School Knowledge for the Masses*, London, New York, and Philadelphia: Falmer Press.

35. Goodson, I. F. (1990a) "Laronplansforskning: mot ett socialt konstruktivistiskt perspektiv," *Forskning om utbildning*, Vol. 1, pp. 4-

18; idem. (1990b) "A Social History of Subjects" *Scandinavian Journal of Educational Research*, Vol. 34, No. 2, pp. 111-121; idem. (1990c) "Zur Sozialgeschichte der Schulfacher," *Bildung und Erziehung*, pp. 379-389; idem. (1991a) "La Construccion del Curriculum: Posibilidades Y Ambitos de Investigacion de la Historia del Curriculum," *Revista de Educacion on Curriculum History I*, No. 295, pp. 7-37; idem. (1991b) "Tornando-se una materia academica: padroes de explicacao e evolucao," *Teoria and Educacao* (Brazil), No. 2, pp. 230-254; Goodson, I. F. and I. R. Dowbiggin, (1991) "Vocational Education and School Reform: The Case of the London (Canada) Technical School, 1990-1930," *History of Education Review*, Vol. 20, No.1, pp 39-60.

36   See Watson, F. (1909) *Teaching Modern Subjects*.

37   Goodson, I. F. (1990d) "Studying Curriculum: Towards a Social Constructionist Perspective," *Journal of Curriculum Studies*, Vol. 22, No. 4, pp. 299-312.

38.   Goodson, I. F. (1994) *Studying Curriculum: Cases and Methods*, Milton Keynes: Open University Press and Teachers College Press, New York.

39.   Goodson, I. F. (1990e) "'Nations at Risk' and 'National Curriculum': Ideology and Identity," *Politics of Education Association Yearbook 1990*, London, New York, and Philadelphia, Falmer Press, p. 231.

Chapter 5

Curriculum History, Professionalization, and the Social Organization of Knowledge: An Extended Paradigm for the History of Education

Ivor F. Goodson and
Ian Dowbiggin

One of the more striking trends within educational theory during the last twenty years is the growing interest in the history of the secondary-school curriculum.[1] This interest in curriculum history has perhaps been most visible in Great Britain and Australia, but there is evidence that it is gaining momentum in the United States, Canada, and other parts of the western world, thanks in part to the scholarly attention paid to recent historical studies of secondary school subjects.[2]

We maintain that this scholarly trend is a salutary one. It comes at a time when the possibilities for an extended paradigm of educational history are promising. This is not the first time that alternatives to mainstream history of education have been launched. In the 1960s and 1970s "revisionism" generated a range of interesting studies throughout the Anglo-American world. But to many historians the appeal of revisionist history of education is fading, largely as a result of dissatisfaction with the misuse of history to support broad sociopolitical interpretations or theories.[3] We too are critical of revisionist approaches, but rather more because like "mainstream" history of education they focus on the political and administrative contexts of schooling and remain "external" to the school. Instead, we are concerned with penetrating the "internal" patterns of schooling, but like the revisionists we hold to the view that historical studies have a valuable role to play in challenging and informing theory. We contend that a shift to an historical paradigm grounded in the study of curriculum constitutes in many ways a return to scholarly initiatives launched some sixty years ago by academic educators in Britain like S. S. Laurie and Foster Watson, initiatives that later Whiggish concerns with "Acts and Facts" overshadowed.[4]

A new yet complementary paradigm of curriculum history is particularly important because it enables us to penetrate a fundamental part of schooling that historians have tended to ignore: the internal processes or "black box" of the school. Curriculum history seeks to explain how school subjects, tracks, and courses of study have constituted a mechanism to designate and differentiate students. It also offers a way to analyze the complex relations between school and society because it shows how schools both reflect and refract society's definitions of culturally valuable knowledge in ways that defy simplistic models of reproduction theory.

Our contention is that curriculum history has a further significance. We maintain that it enables us to explain the role professions—like education—play in the social construction of knowledge.[5] Research into the social history of British secondary-school subjects has shown how teachers have been encouraged to define their curricular knowledge in abstract, formal, and scholarly terms in return for status, resources, territoriality, and accreditation. A subtle yet pervasive series of incentives has compelled those educators eager to improve their professional prerogatives and credentials to surrender solicitously to the definitions of valuable knowledge formulated by university scholars. We need to know more about this historical process because of its obvious implications for present-day decisions regarding curricular policies and practice.

From an historiographic perspective, this issue is also important because it agrees with recent studies in the history of other "liberal" professions: for instance, nineteenth-century asylum psychiatry. In both cases subordinate groups of institutional practitioners voluntarily legitimized high-status patterns of knowledge by deferring to academic definitions of their working lives. The conclusion to be drawn is that hegemonic forms of knowledge are reinforced less through the one-dimensional process of "socialization" than through the well-established connection between patterns of resource allocation and the associated work and career prospects these ensure.[6]

Our intention here is to review briefly what some recent research has revealed about the historical patterns followed by specific subjects in the British secondary-school curriculum. We shall then compare this research and its findings with equally recent work done in the history of French psychiatric knowledge in the nineteenth century. Without minimizing the patent differences between secondary school teaching and public-asylum psychiatry, we conclude that the history of both asylum mental medicine and secondary-school subjects enables us to understand how professions become part of the bureaucratic organizations that shape social, political, economic, and cultural life in the modern and postmodern eras. It shows that the more occupational groups and their representative associations have pursued the material incentives offered by the state, the more abstract and decontextualized professional knowledge has become. In the history of the British secondary curriculum, for example, the form of subject knowledge has grown increasingly irrelevant to the experience of learning, just as psychiatric knowledge in the nineteenth century grew increasingly irrelevant to effective therapy. The result is that formal knowledge has superseded practical and utilitarian knowledge as the central concern of professionals; and as a result, possibilities for the care, cure, enlightenment, and emancipation of client populations may have been postponed.[7]

We maintain that a history of education that accepts curriculum as a central factor of schooling will of necessity address itself to these concerns. Yet, its principal value lies in its capacity to probe the internal reality and relative autonomy of schooling. Curriculum history views the school as something more than the simple instrument of ruling-class culture. It uncovers the traditions and legacies of school bureaucratic systems, those factors that prevent men and women from creating their own history under circumstances of their own choosing. It analyzes the circumstances men and women experience as reality and explains how these have been negotiated, constructed, and reconstructed over time. The work of curriculum scholars such as David Layton, Mary Waring, and Harold Silver examines these internal processes of schooling and contributes to the eventual formulation of a dynamic model of how courses of study, pedagogy, finance, resources, selection, and the economy intersect.[8]

Studies in Curriculum History (I)

In making the case for curriculum history, we shall briefly examine the history of biology and science education in late nineteenth- and twentieth-century Britain. The history of these subjects leads to three general conclusions about the process of becoming a school subject, conclusions, we suggest, that have important implications for the historical study of other bodies of professional knowledge.

The first is that subjects are not monolithic entities but shifting amalgamations of subgroups and traditions that through contestation and compromise influence the direction of change. Second, the process of becoming a school subject features the evolution of the subject community from one promoting pedagogic and utilitarian purposes to one defining the subject as an academic "discipline" with ties to university scholars. Third, the debate over curriculum can be interpreted in terms of conflict between subjects over status, resources, and territory.

In addition, historical studies of secondary subjects in the British school curriculum disclose a steady shift from low-status marginality within the curriculum, through a utilitarian stage, and ultimately toward a definition of the subject as a discipline with a rigid and rigorous body of knowledge. This evolution from one stage stressing content to another stressing form has been sustained by the close connection between academic status and resource allocation that is a fundamental feature of the British educational system, a connection whose origins can be traced to the examination system created by universities in the nineteenth century and codified in the school certificate system in 1917. From this date the School Certificate and the university- controlled examination boards began to exert considerable influence over the secondary-school curriculum. The effect of this influence has been that subjects seek to be recognized as examinable bodies of knowledge because this status means that they will have abler students, higher salaries, better staffing ratios, higher capitation allowances, more graded posts, and generally better career prospects.

The history of biology as a school subject exemplifies this process of curricular change. In its pursuit of academic status it endorsed the control of university scholars over the subject. Initially, biology was overshadowed by botany and zoology during the nineteenth-century campaign to introduce scientific subjects into the secondary school curriculum. Yet with the discoveries in bacteriology, marine biology, physiological research, and agricultural science in the latter years of the century, agencies like the British Association for the Advancement of Science, the British Social Hygiene Council, and the Science Masters Association promoted the cause of biology as a school subject.

The twentieth century—period between the World Wars— witnessed a growth in the utilitarian aspects of the subject as promoters argued that "biology was capable of economic application and exploitation in industries such as fishing, agriculture, and forestry, and also in medicine."[9] This strategy proved to be successful because during the course of the 1930s biology gained an established place in the secondary-school curriculum. By 1931 all eight examination boards had adopted biology as a school certificate examination.

Yet these gains were offset by a growing disenchantment with the place occupied by advanced biological studies in schools. Complaints arose in the 1950s that biology was a subject for "vocational training rather than . . . an instrument of education."[10] Similarly, botany and zoology school teachers, reflecting the attitudes their university training tended to foster, resisted union. Consequently, biology was confined to the early years of the secondary school and to largely vocational training at O and A level.

This state of affairs by the 1960s sparked efforts to publicize a version of biology as a "hard science" emphasizing laboratory experimentation and mathematical techniques. Laboratories, thanks to the Nuffield Project, were status symbols that tended to attract money and resources. As biology grew as a laboratory-based science in the universities, a new generation of biology graduates was trained, and the subject's incorporation as a high-status O- and A-level school subject was assured. At the same time, concerns surfaced at the height of biology's successes in the 1970s. Even though there is a consensus today that biology must outgrow its pedagogic and utilitarian origins and pursue status and resources through the promotion of the subject as a hard, experimental, and rigorous science, there is an awareness that the subject's status as a scientific discipline is still vulnerable to calls from within and without the subject community for a more social and human teaching approach.

Therefore, biology followed an historical pattern that culminated in it becoming an academic discipline characterized by a body of knowledge whose content university specialist scholars selected. In return biology teachers received status, students, and resources that testified to their acceptance as purveyors of culturally valuable knowledge.

Historical studies of subjects like biology within the British secondary-school sector point to a phenomenon that warrants more attention from U.S. and Canadian historians of education. In Britain there was a discernible tendency in the history of school subjects to move away from an early stage when the content of the subject was oriented toward fulfilling practical and vocational aims. Because the material and professional conditions of school teaching were tied closely to its status as an examinable school subject ultimately defined by university specialist scholars, teachers were subtly encouraged to characterize their subject matter in ways that stressed academic and abstract features divorced from the interests and upbringing of most students. Indeed, the content of the school subject became increasingly irrelevant to classroom experience as the form and scholarly context of subject knowledge grew more and more germane to the interests of teachers. School-subject teachers gradually deserted their original clientele in the pursuit of professional objectives related to career and working conditions.

Perhaps no historical case study illustrates the conflict over the form of school subjects and exposes the hegemonic nature of academic knowledge as vividly as David Layton's account of "The Science of Common Things." Largely the creation of the Victorian Richard Dawes, "The Science of Common Things" was a type of science education taught in some English elementary schools in the 1840s. Its subject matter was secular and was drawn from

> things which interest [pupils] at present, as well as those likely to interest them in future—such as a description of their clothing, how it is manufactured, etc., the articles which they consume, from whence they come, the nature of the products of the parish which they themselves and those about them are helping to cultivate.[11]

Dawes's experiment in teaching "scientific knowledge as it applied to an understanding of familiar things," in Layton's words, quickly proved to be successful and by the next decade seemed poised to become the most important version of science education within the elementary-school curriculum.

However, this success was reversed during the 1850s, despite widespread official recognition of the effectiveness of "The Science of Common Things." Physical science changed form a compulsory to an optional subject. The supply of trained science teachers dried up. In 1859 grants for science teaching were slashed and in 1862, with the Revised Code and "payment by results," all specially targeted financial resources for science were withdrawn. The effect of these developments was to destroy systematically a successful early initiative in mass science education.

The conclusion to be drawn from the brief history of "The Science of Common Things" is that public schooling in Victorian Britain was being reconstructed and reorganized in a way that undermined real efforts to educate the lower orders. Support for this conclusion can be found in the parliamentary committee report of the British Association for the Advancement of Science, set up in 1860 to examine the form of science education that the upper classes required. For example, when confronted by the "lucid and intelligent . . . reply" of a child who had taken "The Science of Common Things," the chairman expressed his admiration of "the child's talents" but cautioned that "it would be an unwholesome and vicious state of society in which those who are comparatively unblessed with nature's gifts should be generally superior in intellectual attainments to those above them in station."[12] When science eventually reappeared in the elementary school curriculum some twenty years later it was in a very different form from "The Science of Common Things." A version of pure laboratory science had become accepted as the correct form of science, one that muted utilitarian purposes and stressed scholarship, research, and inquiry for its own sake, and the differences between abstract scientific concepts and the world of everyday experience. As Brian Woolnough has argued, this tradition of grammar school science with its rigid separation of scientific subjects has proven to be particularly resilient despite recent attempts to stop this symbolic academic drift by introducing "General Science Education."[13]

The case study of "The Science of Common Things" demonstrates that in the history of science as a school subject there is a firm link between status and the definition of the subject as a pure laboratory science divorced from "object teaching and nature study, with their pedagogical and utilitarian objectives."[14] But this link derives largely from the emergence of laboratory research in universities, a process that, beginning in Europe in the last quarter of the nineteenth century, found its way to North American shores. In Canada, for example:

> By the mid-1920s the institutional structures that produced the university professor as a research-oriented professional were securely in place in Canadian universities. Though on a modest scale, university physicists as well as chemists and biologists could now develop their research programmes in harmony with their institutional setting. Graduate programmes provided them with students and the NRC provided grants and fellowships, as did the better endowed universities also. In this way a system of production of scientific knowledge, the output of which was publication, was set in motion.[15]

As the university definition of science grew in power and prestige in the twentieth century, the pressure on school science teachers to conform to scholarly criteria rather than respond to the immediate problems of teaching the subject effectively has grown apace. In other words, the type of science education represented by "The Science of Common Things" is at a distinct disadvantage in an age dominated by postsecondary opinions of what constitutes high-status and culturally valuable knowledge.

The history of British school subjects is significant not only for what it reveals about the bureaucratizing and professionalizing tendencies within public education in the modern era. It is also important because it shares striking similarities with the social history of psychiatry. By comparing the histories of curricular knowledge and psychiatric knowledge, it is apparent that in both cases the context of professional practice is structured in ways that foster institutional ties with bureaucratic organizations whose hegemony in the definition of culturally valuable knowledge is difficult to counteract. Despite evidence of considerable professional resistance to this hegemonic pressure, the long-term outcome is the construction of bodies of knowledge that authorize a sharp dichotomy between professional prerogatives and the interests and needs of client groups. Of course, as William Reid has argued, following the insights of J. W. Meyer, professionals must be careful that this gap does not grow "to the point where credibility collapses." "Nonetheless," to quote Reid, "it remains true that what is important [for professional success] is not the delivery of 'goods' which can be publicly evaluated, but the development and maintenance of legitimating rhetorics which provide automatic support for correctly labelled activity." With educators as well as psychiatrists, "[t]he choice of appropriate labels and the association of these in the public mind with plausible rhetorics of justification can be seen as the core mission . . ."[16] Historians who explore how professionals take such action will shed valuable light on the series of constraints and rewards that engender occupational styles of discourse that have little practical usefulness for institutional populations.

Studies in Curriculum History (II)

Curriculum historians who address themselves to these issues can be heartened by the fact that scholars have identified similar gaps between knowledge and practice in the social history of science and medicine.[17] This conclusion is germane to the history of school subjects because it resembles what curriculum historians have discovered recently: that is, that the type of school knowledge found in curricula is chiefly important for its social value to teachers intent on pursuing professional rewards. The knowledge contained in medical theories, it appears, has fulfilled basically the same purpose.

The history of Western psychiatry in the nineteenth century confirms this hypothesis and also suggests that, like school-subject knowledge, psychiatric knowledge tends to grow more formal, abstract, and divorced from the context of their patients' lives. This insight is similar to that which curriculum scholars have recently reached regarding the social history of school subjects in the secondary curriculum and draws attention to the widening gap between the changing form and content of professional knowledge and the needs and interests of the clients/patients/pupils professionals were originally committed to serve.

While it is somewhat of an oversimplification, the evidence indicates that the early nineteenth-century origins of asylum psychiatry were characterized by a sincere commitment to the cure of mental patients. This era witnessed the introduction of the modern asylum, an institution self-consciously designed to provide a retreat through isolation from a disruptive, disorienting, and often dissatisfying world.[18] The nineteenth-century asylum was based on the notion that this cloistered environment would, in conjunction with the activist intervention of a sympathetic practitioner, enable the individual patient to return to his or her senses and rejoin the outside world. It was also based on the optimistic belief that insanity could be cured, not through the use of drugs and other physicalist measures, but through a psychological approach called the moral treatment, a form of therapy that was addressed to the distinctive emotional needs of the individual patient.[19]

While the chronology was not the same for every nation, it is generally true that during the middle third of the nineteenth century things had begun to change. Trained physicians began to oust the talented lay or clerical amateurs who had been involved initially in the institutional treatment of the insane. As licensed doctors gradually took over administrative control of asylums, professional considerations overshadowed the relationship between therapists and patients. Because the patient population was growing beyond the capacity of physicians to minister to individual patients, many doctors in mental hospitals found their time and energy increasingly devoted to administrative and managerial matters.

Thus, the difficulties in practicing "moral treatment" in asylums encouraged many physicians to concentrate on improving their dissatisfying professional circumstances. Psychiatrists in the middle third of the century looked increasingly to the state to build more asylums, hence providing better employment opportunities. In France, in particular, psychiatrists urged the government to centralize the national asylum system by establishing uniform standards for pay, promotion, pensions, and working conditions. They also encouraged the government to end the long-standing division of powers between doctors and laypeople or clerics by making physicians the lone authorities in the management and administration of mental hospitals.[20]

Nonetheless, there were still some psychiatrists who remained wedded to the original ethos of the modern asylum and refused to renounce the therapeutic optimism, psychological approach, and suspicion of theory that had characterized the early years of the century. Just as subject groups are not monolithic entities but actually shifting amalgamations of competing subgroups, so psychiatry in the middle third of the century embraced both this trend and a group who began to advocate a more biologically oriented approach to the interpretation of mental illness as a way of improving the profession's image of expertise and specialized knowledge.[21] This latter group felt that as long as mental disease was viewed as little more than a disorder of pure mind, there would be no way of plausibly justifying the sole intervention of physicians in the institutional treatment of insanity.

Symptomatic of this tension within mental medicine was the founding of psychiatric associations in France, Britain, and the United States in the 1840s and 1850s. The appearance of these organizations—like the formation of subject associations—indicated that asylum physicians wished to unify the profession's subgroups in order to better pursue professional interests.

By the final third of the nineteenth century, it was becoming clear that the faction within psychiatry in favor of a more biological or organicist orientation was gaining sway. The principal reason for the psychiatric swing away from a largely psychological approach to therapy and theory toward a more somatic and naturalist orientation was the psychiatric awareness that improved resources and career opportunities for asylum medicine hinged on its capacity to convince the state that it was a corps of expert practitioners privy to a scholarly and scientific body of medical knowledge; in other words, something more than "moral entrepreneurs," to use Eliot Friedson's term.[22]

Throughout the Western world—but especially in France—this psychiatric strategy often took the form of adherence to the hereditarian theory of degeneracy in the final third of the nineteenth century.[23] But psychiatrists also stressed the positivist qualities of psychiatric knowledge, maintaining that, by relating to most recent discoveries in the anatomy and physiology of the brain to the clinical observation of pathological mental symptoms, psychiatry had ceased to be a chiefly psychological endeavor. By following the "positivist method" of studying the anatomy and physiology of the brain and the factors that cause it to malfunction, French psychiatrists in particular hoped to improve their academic status and end the subservience to their patients that they felt they endured as long as they were viewed simply as "mad-doctors" and "alienists."[24]

The growing attraction to psychiatrists of degeneracy theory, positivism, and somaticism during the final decades of the nineteenth century indicated that doctors of psychological medicine were intent on creating the impression that as purveyors of esoteric and scientific knowledge they were entitled to the academic status that accompanied official recognition as a medical specialty by university faculties of medicine. This process was perhaps most vividly evident in France where psychiatrists were well aware that appeals to the cultural value of naturalist and scientific knowledge were congruent with the attitudes of leading Republican politicians. The early 1880s was a time when successive republican governments officially and explicitly defended the advantages of positivism in their campaign to eliminate clerical involvement in the state educational system. The effect of this promotion of positivism was to make it virtually the hegemonic form of knowledge in late nineteenth-century France, and encouraged substantial investment in and a great expansion of science faculties in the state university system.[25] The 1870-1890 period was also a time when concerted efforts were made to introduce in French medical faculties the German ideal of academic scientific activity based on laboratory research and scholarly publications. This led to reform of the medical-school curriculum through the addition of subjects like physiology, anatomy, histology, and microbiology. Reformers believed that this new model of academic scientific activity would substantially improve the prestige of academic medicine while "increas[ing] the effectiveness of reformers' demands for greater academic freedom and larger budget allocations."[26] In other words, when French psychiatrists exploited the rhetoric of positivism, they hoped to establish their specialty as a legitimate department within the university sector and as a bona fide part of the reformed curriculum at state faculties of medicine.

Behind this movement to shape psychiatric knowledge into a recognizably academic and scientific form was an aggressive psychiatric campaign to have chairs in the clinical study of mental and nervous diseases established at the state University Faculty of Medicine in Paris. A chair in mental pathology had been discontinued at the Faculty of Medicine in 1822 because of the left-wing political activism of students. From that date French psychiatrists had openly yearned for the reestablishment of this chair and the intellectual history of the profession had reflected this concern. When the new chairs were founded in 1877 and 1882, respectively, it meant that the Faculty of Medicine would conduct official clinical courses in psychiatry at the university level.[27] More to the point, asylum psychiatry was now linked firmly to the state university system and its faculties of medicine which, thanks to the considerable cultural and political status enjoyed by the natural and medical sciences during the Third Republic, had augmented autonomy and better students, salaries, buildings, and laboratory facilities and equipment in the 1880s and 1890s.

The capacity of late nineteenth-century French psychiatry to depict itself as a medical specialty with bioscientific credentials was crucial, then, to the effort of psychological medicine to establish a foothold in the state university system and cover the tracks leading back to mental asylums and their institutionalized inmates. Not that this trend has gone unchallenged: periodically psychiatrists have argued that mental medicine ought to return to a form of practice that stresses the emotional needs of the patient. But as the twentieth century has witnessed the growth of university psychiatry, so the fate of these sporadic movements to jettison the "biomedical model" of mental illness in favor of psychosocial explanations has been predetermined.

Summary

To summarize: like the subject-knowledge in biology and science, psychiatric knowledge in the nineteenth century revealed a tendency to move beyond utilitarian and practical aims toward an academic and scholarly form that reflected high-status and hegemonic definitions of knowledge. The historical pattern followed by psychiatric knowledge symbolized an abandonment of the therapeutic and palliative needs of asylum patients and the pursuit of professional objectives whose realization, from the psychiatric perspective, was contingent upon closer ties with the state and the material advantages it could offer. Psychiatric knowledge eventually lost any relevance to the therapeutic imperatives of asylum physicians, and thus became rigidified and virtually useless for psychiatrists intent on the delivery of effective health care to their institutionalized patients.

Yet its advantages in other respects were considerable. It enabled psychiatry to stake a place for itself in the centralized university system where psychiatrists could be taught and trained, and it authorized the process whereby the management and administration of public asylums would be placed solely in the hands of a trained and licensed physician. The academic and scholarly status that accompanied these achievements helped to convince the state that psychiatry warranted the resources that were fundamental to this professional survival and growth.

The resemblance between the history of psychiatric knowledge in the nineteenth century and the history of secondary-school subjects indicates that they have undergone roughly the same "morphology of reform," to borrow Carl Kaestle's terminology.[28] In both cases it is clear that knowledge increasingly became decontextualized and disembodied as the "disciplines" developed closer and closer ties with the state and with university scholars. As high-status knowledge has been increasingly identified with the characteristics of scholarly knowledge generated and reinforced by university academics, there has been a growing perception that the material self-interests of professionals lies in the cultivation of a scholarly and academic image. Thus, professional knowledge tends to become more abstract and formal as occupational groups seek to gain footholds within the bureaucratic departments of the modern university. The evidence suggests that the trend toward more academic qualities is animated by the professional desire to acquire the mystique of specialization that assures a monopoly of power, resources, and prerogatives in a specific sphere of occupational practice. The price professions pay for these advantages is that they must defer to the "kind of 'education' that produces a system of special examinations" and whose form is ultimately defined by university scholars, not practitioners themselves.[29]

Our belief is that an extended paradigm that takes curriculum as its focal point will, by drawing attention to the actual participants in this complex historical process, enable historians of education to explain why professionals comply with bureaucratic and corporate control of their occupational practice. In accounting for human process, it will shed light on the two levels of reality for historical actors: individual life-history and the experiences of specific groups or subgroups with interests in the organization of curricular knowledge. The ongoing negotiation of reality by both individuals and groups reveals the antecedent structures of power in education and suggests how the attitudes of dominant groups in society continue to influence schooling despite evidence of conflict and contestation. The political, social, economic, and cultural debates over both schools and asylums have traditionally been heated and divisive, yet professional practice has been remarkably resistant to change. Curriculum historians who devote themselves to examining the emergence and survival of what we define as "traditional" can do much to explain why schools have conformed to Kaestle's "morphology of reform." Perhaps their studies will also lead eventually to the formulation of theories and models that systematically investigate how existing curricula originate, are reproduced, and respond to new prescriptions.

The "traditional" link between academic status and patterns of resource allocation and career construction has been documented in the social history of British school subjects and the history of nineteenth-century French psychiatry. Whether or not the connection has been a reality in North American schooling remains to be seen. When U.S. and Canadian historians of education have explored this issue, we shall know more about the internal nature of schooling, the forces that push and pull both teachers and students to reproduce or challenge the social structure outside schools. In recommending an extended paradigm for the history of education, we are not implying that the possibilities of other paradigms have been exhausted. Instead, we contend that a move toward curriculum history assumes that we analyze the administration and organization of educational structures and systems through a broader analysis of the enduring legacies of status, resources, curriculum, and examination policy. We now need a history of education that encompasses the study of structures as well as the other piece in the puzzle of educational change: the curriculum. To date it has remained as secret to historians as to educational policymakers.

Notes

1. By "curriculum" we mean, in the words of the Canadian curriculum historian George S. Tomkins, the ostensible or official course of study, typically made up in our era of a series of documents covering various subject areas and grade levels together with statements of "aims and objectives" and sets of syllabi, the whole constituting, as it were, the rules, regulations, and principles to guide what should be taught. Tomkins, G. S. (1986) *A Common Countenance: Stability and Change in the Canadian Curriculum*, Scarborough, Ont., Canada: Prentice Hall, p. 1.

2. For example, see Goodson, I. F. (1983) *School Subjects and Curriculum Change*, London and Sydney: Croom Helm; Goodson, I. F. (ed.) (1985) *Social Histories of the Secondary Curriculum: Subjects for Study*, London, New York, and Philadelphia: Falmer Press; and idem. (1987), *International Perspectives in Curriculum History*, London and Sydney: Croom Helm. See also the series entitled *Studies in Curriculum History*, edited by Goodson and published by Falmer Press, and the *History of Education Review*, Vol. 17, 1988, particularly the articles by P. W. Musgrave, D. Layton, and G. McCulloch.

3. For an account of recent historiographic trends in education, see Gaffield, C. (1986) "Coherence and Chaos in Educational Historiography," *Interchange*, Vol. 17, pp. 112-121.

4. For a fuller version of this argument, see Goodson, I. F. (1988) *The Making of Curriculum: Collected Essays*, London, New York, and Philadelphia: Falmer Press, p. 41-58.

5. We use Bucher and Strauss's definition of professions "as loose amalgamations of segments pursuing different manners and more or less delicately held together under a common name at a particular period in history." Bucher, R., and A. Strauss (1961) "Professions in Process," *American Journal of Sociology*, Vol. 66, pp. 325-334.

6. For recent accounts of the theory of cultural hegemony and its relevance to the history and sociology of education, see Connell, R. W., et al. (1983) *Making the Difference*, Sydney: Allen & Unwin; Connell, R. W. (1988) "Curriculum Politics, Hegemony, and Strategies of Social Change," *Curriculum and Teaching*, Vol. 3, Nos. 1 & 2, pp. 63-71; Giroux, H. A. (1983) "Theories of Reproduction and Resistance in the New Sociology of Education: A Critical Analysis," *Harvard Educational Review*, Vol. 53, pp. 257-293; Labaree, D. F. (1986) "Curriculum, Credentials, and the Middle Class: A Case Study of a Nineteenth-Century High School," *Sociology of Education*, Vol. 59, pp. 42-57. See also Jack-

son Lears, T. J. (1986) "The Concept of Cultural Hegemony: Problems and Possibilities," *American Historical Review*, Vol. 90, pp. 567-593.

7.   One of the chief advantages of a different agenda grounded in curriculum history is that it links the history of education with equally innovative developments in the social history of knowledge, a field that, thanks to the insights of scholars such as Karl Mannheim, Michel Foucault, Pierre Bourdieu, Michael Young, Basil Bernstein, and Christopher Lasch, is making progress toward an understanding of the relationship between the historical construction of knowledge by professionals and the discipline, classification, and control of vulnerable social groups. For example, see Mannheim, K. (1972) *Ideology and Utopia: An Introduction to the Sociology of Knowledge*, London: Routledge & Kegan Paul; Foucault, M. (1979) *Discipline and Punish: The Birth of the Prison*, transl. Alan Sheridan, New York: Vintage; Bourdieu, P., and J. C. Passeron (1977) *Reproduction in Education, Society, and Culture*, Beverley Hills: Sage; Young, M. F. D. (1971) "An Approach to the Study of Curricula as Socially Organized Knowledge." In M. F. D. Young (ed.) *Knowledge and Control: New Directions for the Sociology of Education*, London: Collier-MacMillan; Bernstein, B. (1977) *Class, Codes, and Controls*, 3 Vols., London: Routledge & Kegan Paul; Lasch, C. (1978) *The Culture of Narcissism: American Life in an Age of Diminishing Expectations*, New York: Norton.

8.   Layton, D. (1973) *Science for the People*, London: Allen & Unwin; Waring, M. (1979) *Social Pressures and Curriculum Innovation: A Study of the Nuffield Foundation Science Teaching Project*, London: Methuen; Silver, H. (1983) *Education as History*, New York: Methuen.

9.   Tracey, C. W. (1962) "Biology: Its Struggle for Recognition in English Schools During the Period 1900-60," *School Science Review*, Vol. 93, p. 423.

10. Ministry of Education (1960) *Science in Secondary Schools*, Ministry of Education Pamphlet No. 38, London: His Majesty's Stationery Office.

11. Layton, D., *Science for the People*, p. 41.

12. Wrottesley, Lord J. (1860) Thoughts on Government and Legislation, London: John Murray. Cited in Hodson, D. (1987) "Science Curriculum Change in Victorian England: A Case Study of the Science of Common Things," in I. F. Goodson (ed.) *International Perspectives in Curriculum History*, London: Croom Helm, p. 36.

13. Woolnough, B. (1988) *Physics Teaching in Schools, 1960-1985*, London, New York, and Philadelphia: Falmer Press.

14. Tomkins, G., *A Common Countenance*, pp. 82-83.

15. Gingras, Y. (1986) "The Institutionalization of Scientific Research in Canadian Universities: The Case of Physics," *Canadian Historical Review*, Vol. 67, pp. 182-183.

16. Reid, W. A. (1984) "Curricular Topics as Institutional Categories: Implications for Theory and Research in the History and Sociology of School Subjects." In I. F. Goodson and S. J. Ball (eds.) *Defining the Curriculum: Histories and Ethnographies*, Lewes, England: Falmer Press, pp. 67-75. See also Meyer, J. W. (1978) "The Structure of Educational Organization." In J. W. Meyer, W. Marshall, et al. (eds.) *Environments and Organizations*, San Francisco: Jossey Bass; and *idem.* (1980) "Levels of the Educational System and Schooling Effects." In C. E. Bidwell and D. M. Windham (eds.) *The Analysis of Educational Productivity*, 2 Vols., Cambridge, Mass.: Ballinger.

17. Thackray, A. (1974) "Natural Knowledge in Cultural Context: The Manchester Model," *American Historical Review*, Vol. 79, esp. pp. 675, 678, 679, 682, 686, 693, 698. See also Berman, M. (1978) *Social Change and Scientific Organization: The Royal Institution, 1799-1844*, Ithaca, N.Y.: Cornell University Press; for a qualification of the Thackray thesis, see Inkster, I. (1982) "Variations on a Theme by Thackray: Comments on Provincial Science, Culture, ca. 1780-1850," *British Society for the History of Science Newsletter*, No. 8, pp. 15-18. A useful discussion of this general issue within the context of Anglo-American medicine in the nineteenth century is Shortt, S. E. D. (1983) "Physicians, Science, and Status: Issues in the Professionalization of Anglo-American Medicine in the Nineteenth Century," *Medical History*, Vol. 27, pp. 51-68. For the most extensive treatment of this issue in the history of medicine, see Ackerknecht, E. H. (1973) *Therapeutics: From the Primitives to the Twentieth Century*, New York: Hafner. For a more specific case study of this discrepancy between medical theory and therapeutics and the way scientific knowledge could be exploited by groups seeking professional objectives, see Brown, T. M. (1970) "The College of Physicians and the Acceptance of Iatromechanism in England, 1665-1695," *Bulletin of the History of Medicine*, Vol. 44, pp. 12-30. The pioneering study of discontinuity in the history of scientific ideas is Kuhn, T. S. (1962) *The Structure of Scientific Revolutions*, Chicago: University of Chicago Press.

18. In fact, one of the earliest modern asylums in Britain was named the York Retreat. See Digby, A. (1986) "Moral Treatment at the Retreat, 1796-1846." In W. F. Bynum, R. Porter, and M. Shepherd (eds.) *The Anatomy of Madness: Essays in the History of Psychiatry*, Vol. 2: *Institutions and Society*, London and New York: Tavistock, pp. 52-72.

19. There is now a considerable literature on the growth of public and private asylums in the nineteenth century in France and the Anglo-American world. The most important contributions are Rothman, D.

(1971) *The Discovery of the Asylum: Social Order and Disorder in the New Republic*, Boston and Toronto: Little, Brown; Scull, A. T. (1979) *Museums of Madness: The Social Organization of Insanity in Nineteenth-Century England*, Harmondsworth: Penguin; Grob, G. N. (1973) *Mental Institutions in America: Social Policy to 1875*, New York: Free Press; Castel, R. (1976) *L'ordre psychiatrique: L'age d'or de l'alienisme*, Paris: Editions de minuit; Tomes, N. (1985) *A Generous Confidence: Thomas Story Kirkbride and the Art of Asylum-Keeping, 1840-1883*, New York: Cambridge University Press; Shortt, S. E. D. (1986) *Victorian Lunacy: Richard M. Bucke and the Practice of Late Nineteenth-Century Psychiatry*, New York: Cambridge University Press; Goldstein, J. (1987) *Console and Classify: The French Psychiatric Profession in the Nineteenth Century*, New York: Cambridge University Press. The pioneering work in revisionist theory regarding the birth of the asylum is Foucault, M. (1973) *Madness and Civilization: A History of Insanity in the Age of Reason*, transl. Richard Howard, New York: Vintage. Some collections of essays in the history of psychiatry deal with the topic of the birth of the asylum. See, for example, Scull, A. T. (ed.) (1981) *Madhouses, Mad-doctors, and Madmen: The Social History of Psychiatry in the Victorian Era*, Philadelphia: University of Pennsylvania Press; Bynum, Porter, and Shepherd, *The Anatomy of Madness*.

20.   For the clearest expression of the professional objectives of late nineteenth-century French psychiatry, see Lunier, C., and D. Constans et Dumesnil (1878) *Rapport general a M. le Ministre de l'Interieur sur le service des alienes en 1874*, Paris: Imprimerie nationale.

21.   For an account of the eventual victory of the clinical, somatic, and pathological orientation in England, see Clark, M. J., "The Rejection of Psychological Approaches to Mental Disorder in Late Nineteenth-Century British Psychiatry." In Scull, *Madhouses*, pp. 271-312. The struggle between psychoanalysis and the biomedical model in American psychiatry and neurology in the early twentieth century is one of the topics dealt with by N. G. Hale (1971) *Freud and the Americans: The Beginnings of Psychoanalysis in the United States, 1876-1917*, New York: Oxford University Press.

22.   Friedson, E. (1970) *Professional Dominance*, New York: Atherton. Cited in Scull, *Museums of Madness*, p. 141.

23.   Historical interest in degeneracy theory has been growing recently. See, for example, Dowbiggin, I. R. "Degeneration and Hereditarianism in French Mental Medicine, 1840-1900." In Bynum, Porter, and Shepherd (eds.) *The Anatomy of Madness*, Vol. 1, pp. 188-232; Shortt, *Victorian Lunacy*, pp. 100-109.

24.   For examples of this attitude, see Ball, B. (1880) "La medecine a travers les siecles," *Annales medico-psychologiques*, Vol. 3, p. 28; and Camuset, L. (1882) Review of J. Luys's *Traite clinique et pratique des maladies mentales*, ibid., Vol. 7, p. 509.

25. For the influence of positivism on republican politicians, see Elwitt, S. (1975) *The Making of the Third Republic: Class and Politics in France, 1868-1884*, Baton Rouge: Louisiana State University Press, esp. pp. 170-229. See also Keylor, W. R. (1981) "Anticlericalism and Educational Reform in the French Third Republic: A Retrospective Evaluation," *History of Education Quarterly*, Vol. 21, pp. 95-103. For an account of the dramatic changes within science faculties in late nineteenth-century France, see Fox, R. (1984) "Science, the University, and the State in Nineteenth-Century France." In G. L. Geison (ed.) (1984) *Professions and the French State, 1700-1900*, Philadelphia: University of Pennsylvania Press, pp. 66-145.

26. Weisz, G. (1980) "Reform and Conflict in French Medical Education, 1870-1914." In R. Fox and G. Weisz (eds.) *The Organization of Science and Technology in France, 1808-1914*, Cambridge, England: Cambridge University Press, p. 65.

27. To use Eliot Friedson's words, prospective psychiatrists could now receive instruction in "a curriculum that includes some special theoretical content" that "may represent a declaration that there is a body of special knowledge and skill necessary for the occupation" of psychiatry. Friedson, *Professional Dominance*, pp. 134-135.

28. Kaestle, C. F. (1972) "Social Reform and the Urban School," *History of Education Quarterly*, Vol. 12, p. 218.

29. Weber, M. (1958) "Bureaucracy." In H. Gerth and C. W. Mills (eds.) *From Max Weber*, Oxford: Oxford University Press, pp. 240, 243. Cited in Redner, H. (1987) "The Institutionalization of Science: A Critical Synthesis," *Social Epistemology*, Vol. 1, pp. 37-59 and 52. We do not mean to suggest that the content of knowledge is inconsequential at any time in the social history of knowledge. We mean only that the explicitly instrumental application of bodies of knowledge diminishes in inverse relation to the seriousness and success of professional attempts to improve their material conditions.

Chapter 6

Docile Bodies: Commonalities in the History of Psychiatry and Schooling

Ivor F. Goodson and
Ian Dowbiggin

Preface

In this chapter, we extend our argument that there are important similarities between the ways in which French psychiatrists in the nineteenth century constructed their knowledge systems and the ways in which educators shape the form of their subjects within the secondary-school curriculum. In making the connection between psychiatric knowledge and school-subject knowledge we do not wish to obscure the many differences between the two. School teaching, is of course, unlike the activities of psychiatrists in several fundamental ways. But psychiatry and the teaching of school subjects might be viewed as sharing the same context of professionalization of knowledge within rigidly defined "disciplines."

As Young et al. have argued, those in positions of power are responsible for the assumptions that underlie the selection and organization of knowledge in society.[1] The task for the historian of curriculum, as for the historian of psychiatry, is to recover the complex patterns of structuration, and distributions of power that influence how a society selects, classifies, transmits and evaluates the knowledge it considers to be public.[2]

This involves reconstructing the relationship between profession and state and the struggle among constituencies and agencies with interests in the social consequences of professional practice. By so doing, the historian reveals what forms of knowledge are legitimized and sanctioned within an institutionalized structure; that is, what kinds of knowledge are authorized through patterns of resource allocation, status distribution, and career prospects. The historian also seeks to shed light on the way in which socially approved structures of knowledge legitimize the relations of power between professional and client at specific times in the past, for nineteenth-century asylums and public schools shared the institutional task of creating, transforming, and disciplining forms of behavior and character in order to produce mechanisms for what Foucault has called "constant policing." In other words, out of the power relations between state and profession emerge both a "discipline" and a mode of disciplining self, body, emotions, intellect, and behavior. "Power produces knowledge," as Foucault (1979) has written in *Discipline and Punish* and knowledge in the service of the modern nation state with its various interest groups and power brokers produces fields or "disciplines" whose authorities exercise an increasingly thorough and meticulous control over the body. To quote Foucault again, "the disciplines" become "general forms of domination" that create "subjected and practised bodies, 'docile' bodies."[3]

We maintain that this process is particularly visible through the historical study of subjects in the secondary curriculum and the construction of knowledge systems in organized psychiatry. We are left then with the full force of Foucault's warning in *Discipline and Punish*:

> Perhaps we should abandon a whole tradition that allows us to imagine that knowledge can exist only where the power relations are suspended and that knowledge can develop only outside its injunctions, its demands and its interests. Perhaps we should abandon the belief that power makes mad and that, by the same token, the renunciation of power is one of the conditions of knowledge. We should admit rather that power produces knowledge (and not simply by encouraging it because it serves power or by applying it because it is useful); that power and knowledge directly imply one another; that there is no power relation without the correlative constitution of a field of

knowledge, nor any knowledge that does not presuppose and constitute at the same time power relations. These 'power-knowledge relations' are to be analysed, therefore, not on the basis of a subject of knowledge who is or is not free in relation to the power system, but, on the contrary, the subject who knows, the objects to be known and the modalities of knowledge must be regarded as so many effects of these fundamental implications of power-knowledge and their historical transformations. In short, it is not the activity of the subject of knowledge that produces a corpus of knowledge, useful or resistant to power, but power-knowledge, the processes and struggles that traverse it and of which it is made up, that determines the forms and possible domains of knowledge.[4]

However, our analysis shows that Foucault's interpretation of the influence of professional knowledge is one-dimensional and fails to take into consideration the distinctive ways in which secondary schools and asylums practice domination and enforce docility. Indeed, we make a distinction between the docile bodies of professionals and the docile bodies of students and psychiatric patients. Docile bodies of knowledge discipline not only the subjectivities of the clientele whose interests and needs are presumed to be served; they also discipline the professions with which they are associated by encouraging their members to pursue agendas concerned chiefly with career structures, and in that sense they are highly effective in undermining the common interests of professional and client and postponing the emancipatory possibilities of this relationship. Similarly, while the disciplinary bodies of knowledge characteristic of professionalization are intended to enforce docility, their target groups or classes are never as pliant and docile as it might be hoped they will be. As recent accounts of psychiatry and schooling have shown, the human objects of domination demonstrate resistance and display oppositional behavior in the face of social reproductionist mechanisms. This is not to say, as Henry Giroux has astutely observed, that all oppositional behavior is emancipatory. However, it does point to the need for continued study of the way in which "domination," in Giroux's words, "reaches into the structure of personality itself" and engenders compliance as well as forms of resistance that both have radical significance and ultimately lead to the negation of dissent.[5]

Psychiatry in Nineteenth Century France

From roughly the beginning of the nineteenth century to the First World War, French psychiatry went from being a new medical specialty with an uncertain future to an accredited branch of organized medicine with academic and professional status. Yet this was not a painless or uncontested process. Throughout the nineteenth century French psychiatrists—or "alienists," as they called themselves—had to confront and surmount many obstacles. The most serious obstacle was the psychiatric failure to demonstrate in pathoanatomical terms what precise organic conditions corresponded to the varieties of psychological symptoms a typical asylum physician encountered. This failure made it extremely difficult for psychiatrists to maintain that they were legitimate physicians, for their medical credentials rested on the supposition that they cured the mind thanks to their understanding of the somatic conditions that caused madness. Without these medical credentials, they could not plausibly justify their efforts to oust the clerical orders of the Catholic Church from public asylums, arguably the most important professional task for nineteenth-century French psychiatrists. Nineteenth-century psychiatrists, then, longed to be recognized as bona fide physicians, and in pursuit of this goal they followed a strategy calculated to win the profession a foothold in the expanding university system of the 1870s and 1880s. Like school subject teachers, asylum doctors believed that the key to securing augmented resources and expanded career opportunities for their occupational practice lay in the establishment of their medical specialty as a distinctly academic discipline with university chairs, able students, examinations, and fully accredited clinical courses.

In the status passage from alienists to psychiatrists, the construction of particular kinds of knowledge played a vital role. As we argue, medical claims to expert knowledge of madness in the second half of the nineteenth century were valuable to psychiatrists interested in professionalization because they conveyed the impression that asylum alienists were something more than "moral entrepreneurs," to use Eliot Freidson's term, that they could lay claim, in Freidson's words, "to knowledge of an especially esoteric, scientific, or abstract character that is markedly superior" to the claims to knowledge of "amateurs" such as the clerical orders of the Catholic Church.[6] The evolution of psychiatric knowledge enabled alienists to forge "a political settlement" with the French state that guaranteed their status, material interests, and social authority in the face of persistent public criticism. As we shall see was the case with the teachers of school subjects and the associated bodies of school knowledge, so with psychiatrists and psychiatric knowledge a number of stages can be discerned in the evolutionary profile.

Psychiatry began by justifying its status as a medical specialty and as a socially useful profession with appeals to its utilitarian role in curing the disease of insanity. But, for a variety of reasons that we outline below, these appeals had become outmoded or irrelevant by midcentury. In order to enhance their prestige and power to command the material resources of the state Ministry of the Interior, psychiatrists in the second half of the nineteenth century gradually developed a body of abstract biomedical knowledge and empirical data regarding the pauper classes. When deployed by psychiatrists this body of knowledge enabled the struggling profession to gain the status and state support it coveted. As psychiatric knowledge became more academic and specialized, it assumed a positivist form that complied with the trend toward experimental medical science in the medical faculties of the state university system. This tendency in late nineteenth-century psychiatric knowledge symbolized a desertion of the medical responsibility to cure the mentally ill. Yet, the trade-off was not disadvantageous for the psychiatric profession. Thanks to the remarkable capacity of psychiatric knowledge to reproduce in abstract form the class relationships, division of labor, and cultural hegemony of late nineteenth-century France, psychiatry by 1914 had emerged as a bona fide profession with scholarly and institutional ties in the state university system and had played a pivotal role in the process of state formation begun in the 1840s.[7]

In order to understand the similarities between nineteenth-century French psychiatry and curriculum history, it is necessary to first discuss the main professional, social, and intellectual features of psychiatric life from 1800 to 1914. Psychiatry took root around the turn of the nineteenth century. The Revolution had swept away most of the royalist, clerical, and aristocratic corporations of the Old Regime, and in the process organized medicine had undergone its own revolution. No longer an elite corps of practitioners who wrote in Latin and served the upper classes, medicine after 1789 became a middle-class profession based on the hospital system created by the revolutionary leaders in the 1790s and consolidated under Napoleon in the early years of the century. Thus, from its revolutionary inception, psychiatry was a hospital specialty which, after the example of the renowned Philippe Pinel, committed itself to curing the patient population housed in institutions such as Salpêtrière and Bicêtre.

For the first third of the nineteenth century psychiatrists embraced an attitude of therapeutic optimism. They believed that they could cure a substantial number of institutionalized patients with "moral treatment." Moral treatment was the name given by Pinel and his follower Etienne Esquirol to a psychodynamic approach to therapy that featured reasoning, intimidation, persuasion, and education. Moral treatment was also consistent with a diagnostic classifications system organized according to mental symptoms rather than organic lesions. In other words, psychiatrists developed a discourse of professional knowledge that endorsed an optimistic approach to therapy based on the disposition, character, and emotional needs of the individual patient. It reflected the great hopes many early psychiatrists felt about the possibility of curing madness in asylums.

During the middle third of the nineteenth century, therapeutic optimism in psychiatry began to wane. In a development similar to that which took place in nineteenth-century America and described by David Rothman in his *Discovery of the Asylum,*[8] the mental hospitals of France, crowded even at the best of times, became seriously congested with patients suffering from incurable physical illnesses, mental retardation, or senile dementia. More and more psychiatrists confessed their doubts that the bulk of their patients could be cured with either individualized moral treatment or standard physicalist remedies. Instead they argued that the asylum psychiatrist's duty was to manage the hospitalized population by organizing the lives of the inmates down to the smallest detail. Psychiatrists began to advocate a collectively oriented moral treatment that stressed surveillance and conformity to moral norms rather than activist therapy. They did so not because it offered the best hope for curing patients, but principally because it enabled the psychiatrist to control them.[9]

This form of therapeutic pessimism, which satisfied itself with making patients docile and pliable, spread as the century progressed. But as the institutional possibilities for actively reducing the incidence of madness declined, other issues attracted psychiatric interests around midcentury. In 1838 the French government passed a law that established the guidelines governing admission to and release from asylums. It also authorized the departmental Prefects of France to build new public asylums, thereby improving the chances of employment for the growing number of physicians drawn to the study and treatment of mental illness. The problem was that the construction of new asylums was notoriously slow. Also, the relative decentralization of the French political structure led to conflict between psychiatrists and Prefects over the administration of mental hospitals. Psychiatrists reacted by making overtures to the Minister of the Interior, urging him to centralize the entire administration of the asylum system. They believed that the centralization of the asylum system would serve their material interests as a profession by establishing uniform standards for pay, promotion, pensions, and working conditions.[10] It was clear, then, that by the 1850s a host of issues had arisen to divert psychiatric attention from their original aims. As psychiatric commitment to the mental health of their patients became increasingly difficult to sustain, psychiatrists grew more aware of the need to enhance their professional status and their relations with the sources of political power and patronage in France in order to ensure that the allocation of material resources for the asylum system did not diminish with the fading of public enthusiasm for mental institutions.

An important part of the psychiatric campaign to improve the status and legitimacy of mental medicine in the middle third of the century was the successful attempt to form a psychiatric learned society that presumably would represent the profession's interests. Founded in 1852, and with its own journal, the *Annales médico-psychologiques*, the *Société médico-*

psychologique acted much in the same way as have subject associations in the history of curriculum: it increasingly served to unify the subgroups into a coalition promoting enhanced status and prerogatives. The timing of the *Société*'s founding is crucial: it came at a time when there was much psychiatric infighting and conflict. In the 1840s and 1850s tensions had developed between one group that essentially urged a return to the "moral treatment" of Pinel and a group that wanted psychiatry to become more "biological"—in other words, more closely associated with trends in academic medicine and science. The eventual triumph of the "organicists" is evident in the pages of the *Annales médico-psychologiques* and the history of the *Société médico-psychologique* in the second half of the nineteenth century. Thus, the centripetal tendency of the *Société* contributed to the transition in psychiatry from a loose amalgamation of subgroups or idiosyncratic individuals into a more or less unified profession dedicated to pursuing its own interests in terms of material resources and career opportunities.[11]

During the 1860s psychiatry pursued its professional interests by expressing its willingness to serve the French state in a variety of capacities. For example, psychiatrists eagerly performed "medical police" functions for the Imperial government of Louis Napoleon when an epidemic of hysteria broke out in the Alpine village of Morzine in 1862.[12] Yet, for the most part, psychiatrists remained wedded to their asylums as the prime locus of their professional activity. Their principal concern was to serve the state as salaried employees within the asylum system. To ensure that public disfavor did not tempt the state to revoke psychiatric powers or restrict funding of the asylum system, psychiatrists committed themselves to convincing the state of their political good faith.

Psychiatric efforts to ally themselves more closely with the French state and the dominant social classes began in the 1860s and continued until the First World War as psychiatrists increasingly cited and contributed to the formulation of degeneracy theory.[13] In the process, they constructed a biomedically and culturally resonant body of knowledge that enabled them to appear medical and scholarly. The emergence of degeneracy theory among psychiatrists in the final third of the nineteenth century supplied a rationale and a rhetoric for mental medicine that justified the psychiatric abandonment of its patients without, in any serious way, blaming asylum physicians for doing so. Degeneracy theory bolstered psychiatrists in their growing belief that their task lay less in ministering to the insane than in the institutional classification and subordination of patients. It also reinforced the image of psychiatrists as a corps of specialist and expert professionals who were dealing with a grave problem that threatened social peace and stability. Finally, it justified the place of psychiatrists in mental hospitals and the status of psychiatry as a genuine branch of medical science. In effect, psychiatry forged a kind of political settlement with the state on the basis of adherence to degeneracy theory, a settlement that benefited both parties, but particularly the material self-interests of mental medicine. Psychiatrists in the final third of the nineteenth century were crucial participants in the social organization of knowledge around the principle of degeneracy.

The history of degeneracy theory in French psychiatry is complex and warrants a fuller explanation than can be provided here, yet certain basic themes and developments can be identified. The first surge of interest in degeneracy theory occurred in the 1860s, following the publication of B. A. Morel's *Treatise on Degeneracy* in 1857. Morel, the founder of degeneracy theory, argued that there was a growing number of Frenchmen and women who were predisposed to a host of neurological and mental illnesses because of bad heredity. Most of those afflicted with hereditary degeneracy, Morel maintained, were members of the working or "pauper" classes. Their mental instability and poor health could be traced to the "immoral" lifestyle they pursued in the swelling urban and industrialized centers of France, a lifestyle characterized by alcoholism, indigence, crime, and sexual profligacy. Medically unsound conduct, Morel contended, weakened and destabilized the nervous system. It was then common for these pathophysiological conditions to be handed down to offspring through inheritance, according to Morel. Heredity, as Morel and his colleagues came to believe, assured that pathological characteristics would persist, change form, and actually proliferate from generation to generation.

Morel's formulation of degeneracy theory endorsed the continued existence of psychiatric asylums and institutional practice at a time when both were under heavy attack. According to his theory, the rising incidence of mental illness in French society—documented time and again by psychiatrists-was due to lower-class ignorance of proper morals, values, and hygienic principles. In other words, the insane poor were held to be responsible for their diseases. Degeneracy theory also neatly explained away the catastrophic overcrowding of insane asylums with chronically ill cases. These cases, Morel and his followers argued, were essentially due to heredity, the pathological extent of which limited the number of acute cases and hence the medical possibilities for achieving a cure. The asylum, according to Morel, became an important institutional site for the segregation, classification, and subordination of "degenerate," lower-class persons: its presence guaranteed the isolation from society of "tainted" and troublesome lunatics whose symptoms could only be identified consistently by an asylum-trained psychiatrist. Thus, Morel's theory vindicated asylum psychiatrists for their increasing failure to cure their hospitalized patients. At a time when the usefulness of both psychiatrists and asylums was being openly questioned in the press, in the Chamber of Deputies, and in medical learned societies, Morel was telling his colleagues that far from being responsible for the acknowledged, calamitous state of affairs regarding the public assistance to the insane, hospital psychiatry was in fact privy to expert knowledge of the national epidemic of madness.

Psychiatric interest in hereditarianism and degeneracy theory peaked in the 1880s. By this decade the new leader in mental medicine was Morel's follower Valentin Magnan. Thanks to Magnan's persuasive talents, more and more of the psychiatric community swung over to the theory of degeneracy. Naturally enough, there was not quite unanimity among France's psychiatrists, even by 1890. However, even Magnan's foes had to admit that in criticizing degeneracy theory they were in a distinct minority within psychiatry.

The growth of interest in degeneracy theory in the 1880s and 1890s was still tied to a significant degree to the professional ambitions of psychiatrists to vindicate their roles as medically qualified hospital physicians. Yet other considerations surfaced in the last two decades of the century to compel them to accept degeneracy theory. Psychiatrists were now more than ever eager to appear as biologically and medically erudite practitioners. They wished to be seen as possessors of a body of formal and scholarly knowledge, knowledge that was important for establishing the academic credentials of psychiatry as a medical science with a place for itself in the reformed curriculum of university medical faculties.

The acceptance of degeneracy theory turned out to be a felicitous choice for the French psychiatric community, for it wove together a variety of themes that reflected late nineteenth-century trends in French culture, biology, and medical science. As Robert A. Nye has shown, *fin de siècle* French scholarship and official culture was punctuated with concerns about the apparently declining biological and reproductive fitness of the nation.[14] Moreover, as biology developed into a prestigious science in the last half of the nineteenth century, mainstream medicine began to attribute more and more causal importance to heredity, especially in dealing with the chronic and constitutional diseases of the nervous system. It soon was conventional in late nineteenth-century French medicine to explain diseases of the nervous system as characteristics that the organism was forced to acquire and then transmit through heredity as it struggled to adapt to pathogenic environmental conditions, such as the domestic and occupational *milieus* of the working classes and the rural poor.

Therefore, in changing their professional discourse from the largely psychological terminology of the early nineteenth century to the rhetoric of degeneracy theory in the late nineteenth century, psychiatrists were able to appear biomedically and culturally up-to-date. The hereditarianism of degeneracy theory enabled psychiatrists to maintain that madness had an ineradicable biological component, that the otherwise bewildering plethora of psychological symptoms encountered in everyday asylum practice could be organized around and referred to a purely natural phenomenon like heredity. Doctors of psychological medicine could disguise their ignorance of the precise physiological and anatomical lesions responsible for the different categories of madness by basing their explanations of mental illness on the physical transmission of characteristics from one generation to the next. Finally, adherence to degeneracy theory as a seemingly coherent body of medical knowledge authorized psychiatrists to pose as trained specialists committed to the positivist ethos of order and progress through science. As institutional experts in the medical management of madness, psychiatrists could pose as prototypical Comtean scientists at a time—the early 1880s—when the French Republican state was attempting to reconstruct public subjectivity and consciousness through a flood of civil and educational legislation. In so far as their claims to academic and specialized knowledge were recognized as legitimate, psychiatrists could erase the stigma of social marginality and receive just remuneration as a professional group with unique contributions to the reconstitution of public morals and political order.

A sign that the psychiatric endeavor to make their knowledge claims appear more scientific was at least partially successful was the creation of a chair in mental pathology in 1877 at the Parisian Faculty of Medicine, one of the faculties of the centralized French university system. At one point early in the nineteenth century there had been a chair in mental pathology, yet during the Royalist purges of the university system in 1821-1822 it had been abolished and never reinstated. The appointment of Dr. Benjamin Ball as occupant of the chair in 1877 meant that there would be official courses in psychiatry delivered at the Faculty, addressing the long-standing complaint of asylum psychiatrists from the 1820s to the 1870s that there had been no formal university teaching in mental pathology. Before 1877 asylum psychiatrists themselves had to teach clinical courses in the subject if they wished to train young physicians for careers in mental medicine. After 1877 this would no longer be the case. The creation of the chair indicated that psychiatry was a genuine medical specialty with the prestige and resources that went along with this academic status. To cite Freidson again, prospective alienists could now receive instruction in "a curriculum that includes some *special* theoretical content (whether scientifically proven or not)," which "may represent a declaration that there is a body of special knowledge and skill necessary for the occupation" of psychiatry.[15] At the same time, the strengthened ties between asylum psychiatry and the state university system encouraged the trend in psychiatric theory toward more formalized and abstract bodies of knowledge.

This point constitutes a crucial link between the history of psychiatry and the history of school subjects in the secondary-school curriculum. While it is clear that university scholars have managed to impose a pattern of domination on the construction of knowledge, whether in the form of curricula or psychiatric theory, teachers and psychiatrists have been major participants in these patterns. In effect, psychiatrists, like their counterparts in teaching, were "socialized" or disciplined by patterns of resource allocation, and associated work and career prospects to legitimate high-status definitions of knowledge, definitions that largely derive from the pervasive influence exercised by scholars within the state university system. For late nineteenth-century French mental medicine, as for geography teachers in secondary schools, the hegemonic form of high-status knowledge stressed academic features that had less to do with the actual techniques employed by practitioners and the needs and wishes of clientele than with the material self-interest of professionals anxious to surrender solicitously to developing structures of power. By adopting the rhetoric of positivist science in their claims to scholarly, esoteric knowledge of insanity, French psychiatrists celebrated their liberation from what they perceived to be their original tutelage to their patients: as the occupant of the chair in the clinical study of mental illness argued in 1880, by shifting the "axis" of psychiatry away from psychology and toward the study of organic and biological conditions, mental medicine would no longer be limited to the role of "secretary" to patients, laboriously writing down everything their clients said.

To summarize: French psychiatric knowledge in the nineteenth century followed a distinct evolutionary pattern. The origins of psychiatric knowledge in nineteenth-century France were utilitarian and practical in nature. Psychiatrists devoted themselves to serving the "clientele" of the burgeoning public asylum system. They adopted an individual-oriented form of psychotherapy predicated on the curability of most mentally ill patients. When asylums quickly filled up with chronically ill and incurable patients, psychiatrists lost much of their therapeutic optimism. As a result, they began to devote the bulk of their attention to asylum administration and patient management rather than activist therapy. This process was reinforced by the fact that the new generation of psychiatrists who replaced the talented amateurs of the previous generation did not share the same sense of philanthropic commitment to their patients and were more concerned with the pursuit of professional status. The disengagement of psychiatry from its original objectives was reflected in the social history of knowledge by the emergence of a new form of psychiatric discourse called degeneracy theory. It represented the final break with the relatively humane and optimistic therapeutic approach to madness. It served the interests of psychiatry because it derived from a body of knowledge with great cultural, political, and medical resonance for a host of constituencies with their own interests in the management of deviance. Degeneracy theory symbolized the advent of university hegemony over the knowledge of occupational practice, the decontextualization and disembodiment of psychiatric knowledge fostered by its increasing definition according to standards set by scholars from the Faculty of Medicine. Psychiatric knowledge thus became rigidified and virtually useless for psychiatrists intent on the delivery of effective medical care to their institutionalized patients; in effect, it "disciplined" alienists by stifling innovation and directing their attention away from the therapeutic task endorsed by the original "moral treatment." Yet its advantages in other respects were considerable. It enabled psychiatry to win status and resources from the French state that were fundamental to its survival and growth as a profession. More ominously, it authorized the long-standing psychiatric treatment of the mental patient as an object to be classified and controlled rather than cured. In its desertion of its original clientele, psychiatry resembles the pattern of development we shall discern for school subjects.

School Geography in Twentieth Century England

In 1976 Foucault was interviewed for the Marxist Geographer's Journal *Hérodote*. The first question asked by the interviewers was about his work, which they argued

to a large extent intersects with, and provides material for, our reflections about geography and more generally about ideologies and strategies of space. Our questioning of geography brought us into contact with a certain number of concepts you have used—knowledge (**savoir**), power, science, discursive formation, gaze, **episteme**—and your archaeology has helped give a direction to our reflection. For instance the hypothesis you put forward in *The Archaeology of Knowledge*—that a discursive formation is defined neither in terms of a particular object, nor a style, nor a play of permanent concepts, nor by the persistence of a thematic, but must be grasped in the form of a system of regular dispersion of statements—enable us to form a clearer outline of geographical discourse. Consequently we were surprised by your silence about geography.[16]

As the interview progressed the imperial, military, and national aspects of geography were discussed, and Foucault talked of power/knowledge in relation to geography.

Once knowledge can be analysed in terms of region, domain, implantation, displacement, trans-position, one is able to capture the process by which knowledge functions as a form of power and disseminates the effects of power. There is an administration of knowledge, a politics of knowledge, relations of power which pass via knowledge and which, if one tries to transcribe them, lead one to consider forms of domination designated by such notions as field, region and territory. And the politico-strategic term is an indication of how the military and the administration actually come to inscribe themselves both on a material soil and with forms of discourse.[17]

By the end of the interview Foucault was clearer about some of the content of geography and its relationship to the "discourse of right":

The longer I continue, the more it seems to me that the formation of discourses and the genealogy of knowledge need to be analysed, not in terms of types of consciousness, modes of perception and forms of ideology, but in terms of tactics and strategies of power. Tactics and strategies deployed through implantations, distributions, demarcations, control of territories and organisations of domains which could well make up a sort of geopolitics where my preoccupations would link up with your methods. One theme I would like to study in the next few years is that of the army as a matrix of organisation and knowledge; one would need to study the history of the fortress, the 'campaign', the 'movement', the colony, the territory. Geography must indeed necessarily lie at the heart of my concerns.[18]

But in the history of a school subject there is an interesting relation and interrelation between the subject as *content* and the subject as *form*. In both cases the subject continues to func-

tion as a maker of *subjectivities*. Most of the focus of the interview with Foucault remained, no doubt, because of the *Journal
Geographers* preoccupation with their subject's content, on aspects of geographical content. But the power/knowledge relation crucially relates to the form that the school curriculum
espouses and embodies. This is because as well as serving to
carry content to pupils, the school subject also serves many
other constituencies—notably the state and the professional
groups involved in schooling. By focusing on the history of
school subjects in English schools in the twentieth century, it
is possible to explore analogies between the foregoing history
of psychiatry in France and aspects of schooling in England.
School subject teachers composed professional groups that,
as was the case with the French psychiatrists, were understandably concerned with the acquisition of status and resources.
Again, the state was an important sponsor and professional
groups of teachers sought the rhetorics that would maximize
state aid. In analyzing the rhetoric employed in the promotion
of school subjects we gain insight into the agendas of schooling. As we shall see there are a number of powerful analogies
with the manner by which state aid was secured for psychiatrists. Central in these analogies is the relationship between
the professionals and their clients/pupils/inmates; and alongside this the position of specialized knowledge as a central
indicator and ingredient of this relationship and of the relationship between the professional groups and the state.

The Establishment and Promotion of Geography as a School Subject

In the late nineteenth century geography was beginning to
establish a place in the curriculum of public, grammar, and
elementary schools of Britain. The subject was emerging from
the first stages when it appears to have been little more than a
dreary collection of geographical facts and figures which one
of the founding fathers of geography, H. T. MacKinder, contended "adds an ever-increasing amount to be borne by the
memory."[19] At this time this was a nongraduate subject, for
geography remained outside the universities. It was partly to
answer this problem that MacKinder, posed the question in

1887: "How can geography be rendered a discipline?" But MacKinder was aware that the demand for an academic geography to be taught in universities could only be engendered by the establishment of a more credible position in schools. Essentially it was in the high-status public and grammar schools that geography needed to establish its intellectual as well as pedagogical credibility. In these schools, without full-fledged academic status, the subject's position as an established part of the curriculum remained uncertain.

In the elementary schools geography was rapidly seen as affording utilitarian and pedagogic possibilities in the education of the children of working people. Hence the take-up of the subject grew considerably in the period following the 1870 Education Act. In 1875 "elementary geography" was added to the main list of "class subjects" examined in elementary schools.

Given the limited base in the elementary- and secondary-school sectors, the promoters of geography began to draw up plans for a subject association. In 1893 the Geographical Association was founded "to further the knowledge of geography and the teaching of geography in all categories of educational institutions from preparatory school to university in the United Kingdom and abroad."[20] The formation of the association in 1893 was well-timed, and it rapidly began to operate as a vocal "lobby" for the subject. Two years later the Bryce Commission reported, and its recommendations were built into the 1902 Education Act. Further, the 1904 Secondary Regulations effectively defined the traditional subjects to be offered in secondary schools; geography's inclusion in the regulations was a major staging post in its acceptance and recognition and in the broad-based take-up of external examinations in geography in secondary schools. The emergence of external examinations as a defining factor in secondary curricula around 1917 is clearly reflected in the sharp increase in the association's membership around this date. At this stage geography was included in many Examination Board regulations both at School Certificate and Higher School Certificate as a main subject. Certain Boards, however, included geography only as a "subsidiary subject."

The founding of a subject association was only a first stage in launching the subject; what was also required was an overall plan aimed at establishing the subject in the various educational sectors mentioned in the constitution. At a discussion on geographical education at the British Association in September 1903, MacKinder outlined a four-point strategy for establishing the subject:

> Firstly, we should encourage University Schools of geography, where geographers can be made . . .
>
> Secondly, we must persuade at any rate some secondary schools to place the geographical teaching of the whole school in the hands of one geographically trained master . . .
>
> Thirdly, we must thrash out by discussion and experiment what is the best progressive method for common acceptation and upon that method we must base our scheme of examination.
>
> Lastly, the examination papers must be set out by practical geography teachers.[21]

This strategy reads very much like trade union pleas for the closed shop. The geography teacher is to set the exams and is to choose exams that are best for the "common acceptation" of the subject—there is not even the facade that the pupils' interest should be the central criterion; the teaching of geography is to be exclusively in the hands of trained geographers and the universities are to be encouraged to establish schools of geography "where geographers can be made."

In the immediate period following this pronouncement the Geographical Association continued the earlier rhetoric about the subject's utility; the changeover was slowly implemented. Thus in 1927 we learn that: "Travel and correspondence have now become general; the British dominions are to be found in every clime and these facts alone are sufficient to ensure that the subject shall have an important place in the school time-table."[22] Alongside these utilitarian and pedagogic claims the Geographical Association began to mount more "academic" arguments. But the problems of the utilitarian and pedagogic emphases had by now surfaced. Thus in the 1930s the Norwood Committee was concerned with the way geography appeared to effortlessly change direction and definition, thereby intruding on the territory of other subjects and disciplines. Above all, they were concerned with the temptation afforded by what they called the "expansiveness of geography," for "environment is a term which is easily expanded to cover every condition and every phase of activity which makes up normal everyday experience."

The results of such "expansiveness" in school geography were later reported by Honeybone, who argued that by the 1930s, geography "came more and more to be a 'world citizenship' subject, with the citizens detached from their physical environment." He explained this partly by the spread "under American influence" of "a methodology, proclaiming that all education must be related to the everyday experience of children."[23] Thus through the work of those teachers untrained or badly trained in the subject, "by 1939 geography had become grievously out of balance; the geographical synthesis had been abandoned; and the unique educational value of the subject lost in a flurry of social and economic generalizations." The central problem remained the establishment of departments in universities where geographers could be made and the piecemeal changes in pursuit of pupil relevance and utility could be controlled and directed. To further this objective the Geographical Association began to promote more "academic" arguments for the subject. Hence in 1927 we learn that "the main objective in good geographical teaching is to develop, as in the case of history, an attitude of mind and a mode of thought characteristic of the subject."[24]

The increasingly academic presentation of the school subject applied more pressure on the universities to respond to the demand for the training of geography specialists. As a recent president of the Geographical Association has noted, "the recognition of our subject's status among university disciplines . . . could never have been achieved without (the) remarkable stimulus and demand injected from out of schools."[25] The contention, while correct, contains the origins of the status problems geography has encountered in universities. As David Walker recently noted, "some senior members of our ancient universities can still be found who dismiss it as a school subject."[26] As a result, until recently geographers remained a frustrated university profession because of what Wooldridge described as "the widespread belief among our colleagues and associates that we lack academic status and intellectual respectability. What has been conceded is that geography has a limited use in its lower ranges. What is implicitly denied by so many is that it has any valid claim as a higher subject."[27] Wooldridge, however, hints that acceptance at the lower level is the main threshold to cross. "It has been conceded that if geography is to be taught in schools it must be learned in the universities."[28]

The period following 1945 does seem to have been critical in geography's acceptance and consolidation within the university sector. Professor Alice Garnett explained in 1968 why this period was so important:

> Not until after the Second World War was it widely the case that departments were directed by geographers who had themselves received formal training in the discipline, by which time most of the initial marked differences and contrasts in subject personality and had been blurred or obliterated.[29]

By 1954, Honeybone could write a summary of the final acceptance and establishment of geography as a university discipline:

> In the universities, there has been unparalleled advance in the number of staff and scope of the work in the departments of geography. In the University of London alone, there are now six chairs, four of them of relatively recent creation. Students, both graduates and undergraduates, are greater in number than ever before. Many of the training colleges and university departments of education are taking a full part in this progress; employers are realizing the value of the breadth of a university training in geography; and the Civil Service has recently raised the status of geography in its higher examinations. In fact, on all sides, we can see signs that, at long last, geography is forcing its complete acceptance as a major discipline in the universities, and that geographers are welcomed into commerce, industry and the professions, because they are well educated men and women . . .[30]

So by the mid-1950s geography had progressed to the crucial stage in the acceptance of a subject. The selection of subject matter was "determined in large measure by the judgments and practices of the Specialist Scholars who lead inquiries in the field."[31] Of course the final takeover of geography by the universities meant that control of the definition of the subject was in the hands of Specialist Scholars. The context in which these scholars operated was substantially divorced from schools; their activities and personal motivations, their status and career concerns were situated within the university context. The concerns of school pupils, thereby unrepresented, were of less and less account in the definition of this well-established academic discipline. The implications within schools soon became clear. In 1967 the report on *Society and the Young School Leaver* noted that the student of geography felt "at best apathetic, at worst resentful and rebellious to geography . . . which seems to him to have nothing to do with the adult world he is soon to join." The report adds:

> A frequent cause of failure seems to be that the course is often based on the traditional belief that there is a body of content for each separate subject which every school leaver should know. In the least successful courses this body of knowledge is written into the curriculum without any real consideration of the needs of the boys and girls and without any question of its relevance.[32]

The threat to geography began to be appreciated at the highest level. A member of the Executive and Honorary Secretary of the Geographical Association recalls: "the subject began to lose touch with reality . . . geography got a bad name."[33] A college lecturer, David Gowing (1973), saw the same problem facing the subject and argued:

> One must recognize the need to take a fresh look at our objectives and to reexamine the role and nature of geography in school. It is not difficult to identify the causes of increasing dissatisfaction. Pupils feel that present curricula have little relevance to their needs and so their level of motivation and understanding is low. Teachers are concerned that the raising of the school leaving age and some forms of comprehensive reorganization may exacerbate the problems.[34]

The increasing control of geography by the university specialists plainly posed problems for the subject in schools. To recapture the sense of utility and relevance of earlier days the subject would have needed to focus more on the needs of the average and below-average school student. However, geography still faced problems of academic status within some universities and also among the high-status sections of the secondary sector.

The advances in university geography after the Second World War partly aided the acceptance of geography as a subject suitable for the most able children, but problems remained. In 1968 Marchant noted: "Geography is at least attaining to intellectual respectability in the academic streams of our secondary schools. But the battle is not quite over."[35] To finally seal its acceptance by the universities and high-status sixth forms, geography had to forever renounce its pedagogic and utilitarian intentions. The supreme paradox is that the crisis in school geography in the late 1960s led not to change, which might have involved more school pupils, but to changes in the opposite direction in pursuit of total academic acceptance. The final push for status centered around the "new geography," which moved away from regional geography to more quantitative data and model building. The battle for new geography was perhaps the final clash between those traditions in geography representing the pedagogic and utilitarian traditions (notably the fieldwork geographers and some regionalist) and those pushing for total academic acceptance.

Geography then achieved total academic acceptance both as a high-status, highly resourced school subject and, associated with this status passage, as a fully fledged academic university "discipline." Control of the subject passed toward the detached scholars in universities. The pupils/clients in the school are faced with school-subject knowledge defined by those divorced from their milieu and from the concern as to how learners learn. Not surprisingly most school pupils react to such alien knowledge "with passivity and resignation, a prelude to disenchantment."[36] In biography, as with all other "proper" subjects, the vast majority will leave school without the coveted A-level examination passes. In so doing they will be closing the door on the route to university for which, as we have seen, the whole subject had been avowedly restructured.

The processes and struggles that traverse the emergence of geography as a school subject in England point to salient features in the "professionalization" and modernization of the subject. In the early stages of the subject utilitarian arguments about the subject as a handmaiden to Empire prevail. The content of the subject reflects these national and imperial preoccupations. Children are being schooled into a particular version of national and economic identity. But geography still remains a marginal and low-status subject in the public and grammar schools where the upper- and middle-class children are located.

The content of the subject therefore clearly serviced certain interest groups, but the *form* of the subject remained problematic. The *Geography of Empire* was a dreary collection of facts and figures whether "capes and bays" or "homes in many lands." The professionalization of geography demanded that MacKinder's four-point strategy was painstakingly followed. There had to be "University schools of Geography, where geographers could be made." But once established such university departments began to "make Geographers" not in the image of secondary schools, not in the image of the Nation and Empire, but above all in the image of themselves. The patterns of status and prestige *within* the universities became the major factors in the subsequent definition of geography. The discursive formation of geography from here on was derived from the prevailing patterns and symbolic drift of university scholarship. The subject was presented as a "discipline," a coherent body of knowledge with status and rigor as a scientific discipline. The culminating discursive formation in geography's status passage resonated above all with the status and prestige concerns of contemporary university professionals. Ultimately geography, whether for secondary schools or for higher education, was driven by the needs and concerns of these professionals. In the process of academic establishment the Geography profession accepted the hegemony of university scholars, and the result was a particular content and form for the subject created in the image of those scholars.

The close connection between academic status and resources is a fundamental feature of our educational system. The origin of this connection is the examination system created by universities from the late 1850s and culminating in the school certificate system founded in 1917. As a result, the so-called "academic" subjects provide examinations that are suitable for "able" students, while other subjects are not.

Byrne's work has provided data on resource allocation within schools. She discerned that "two assumptions which might be questioned have been seen consistently to underlay educational planning and the consequent resource allocation for the more able children. First, that these necessarily need longer in school than non-grammar pupils, and secondly, that they necessarily need more staff, more highly paid staff and more money for equipment and books."[37] The implications of the preferential treatment of academic subjects for the material self-interest of teachers are clear: better staffing ratios, higher salaries, higher capitation allowances, more graded posts, better careers prospects. The link between academic status and resource allocation provides the major explanatory framework for understanding the aspirational imperative to become an academic subject. Basically, since more resources are given to the academic examination subject taught to able students, the conflict over the status of examinable knowledge is, above all, a battle over the material resources and career prospects of each subject teacher or subject community.

The allocation of resources from the state government and the "local authorities" thereby sponsored university influence over school geography. The professional groups involved in the promotion of the subject thereby had to accept the control of university scholars in the definition and academic establishment of their subject. The relationship between the professional body of knowledge and the clients in secondary schools has important analogies with the relationships discerned for psychiatric knowledge and its clients. The demands of professionals and of state sponsors would seem to have a great deal in common; certainly enough to warrant substantial further investigation.[38]

Conclusion

The comparison of French psychiatry and psychiatric knowledge with English schooling and school knowledge reveals some remarkable similarities. These similarities cross centuries as well as cultures, yet they appear to point toward certain continuities of social purpose.

French psychiatrists made a clear bargain with the state. In return for status and resources, psychiatrists reneged on their original therapeutic optimism and utilitarianism. The development of a body of knowledge—degeneracy theory—underpinned a practice and institutional power that in the asylum allowed for the surveillance of patients and their moralization through the regulatory internalization of ruling-class values and attitudes. This psychiatric style of disciplinary "treatment" was all the more effective because it seemed to be a humane and commonsensical alternative to letting the lunatics of the nation loose in the streets. It also constituted an important chapter in the French state's campaign to control and manage those social groups labeled as "dangerous," not through coercive policing, but through the construction of docile and socially approved mentalities during the second half of the nineteenth century.

In the development of schooling, school-subject knowledge evolved in a similar manner. The subject teachers, in the case of geography, reneged on their original social and pedagogic optimism in pursuit of status and resources. In the phase of successful academic establishment of the subject when geography was defined as a high-status school subject with major resources and finance, the students were, "at best apathetic, at worst resentful and rebellious to geography." At the high point of its political acceptance the clients of school geography were clearly "approaching passivity and resignation, a prelude to disenchantment." However, their alienation simply made them more deferential to the social hegemony and high-status definition of abstract subject knowledge, a process that reinforced the devaluation of practical/manual labor and the disqualification of the majority from the material rewards possible only through academic credentialism.

In a sense the history of psychiatry and geography may be seen as passing through three stages. At first there was a period of professional optimism and systematic close engagement with the concerns and interests of the clients/pupils. Second was a period where a body of professional/curricula knowledge is developed. In the case of psychiatry, it focused on degeneracy theory; in the case of geography, a body of knowledge focused on imperial and territorial concerns. These new bodies of knowledge began to substantially influence the nature of professional relationships with clients/pupils. Finally, in the third stage, a more systematically abstracted body of knowledge emerged in the universities where the subject became institutionalized. From this new detached site, future definitions of the professional body of knowledge are now produced and reproduced.

It seems then that psychiatry and education may have the same "morphology of reform," to use Carl Kaestle's words;[39] as public institutions, schools and asylums have more in common than meets the eye. In both cases, knowledge implied the power of trained and licensed professionals to displace talented amateurs in institutional practice and fulfill state agendas of classifying and subordinating disadvantaged groups. Yet, professionals, while gaining important advantages, underwent their own "policing" and disciplinary process. In many significant respects, the conditions of their practice ceased to be defined by practitioners themselves and were instead formulated by specialist "scholars" and administrators far removed from the sites of service. State tutelage replaced the relative flexibility and freedom to innovate that characterized the origins of public schools and asylum medicine. Teachers, for example, submitted to the increasing control exerted by examinations, syllabuses, textbooks, and teacher training. We contend that until insights into the complex relations between professional power and professional knowledge are recognized and scrutinized widely, this two-dimensional process of disciplining subjectivity into "docile bodies" will ensure that schooling never becomes true "education" and psychiatry never becomes synonymous with mental health.

Notes

1. Young, M. (1971) "An Approach to the Study of Curricula as Socially Organized Knowledge." In M. Young (ed.) *Knowledge and Control*, London: Collier Macmillan, pp. 19-46.

2. The field of curriculum history has expanded considerably of late. See Goodson, I. F. (ed.) (1985), *Studies in Curriculum History*, London, Philadelphia, and New York: Falmer Press series that began in 1985 that comprises Goodson, I. F. (ed.), *Social Histories of the Secondary Curriculum: Subjects for Study*; McCulloch, G., E. Jenkins, and D. Layton (1985), *Technological Revolution? The Politics of School Science and Technology in England and Wales Since 1945*; Cooper, B. (1985), *Renegotiating Secondary School Mathematics: A Study of Curriculum Change and Stability*; Franklin, B. (1986), *Building the American Community: Social Control and Curriculum*; Moon, B. (1986), *The 'New Maths' Curriculum Controversy: An International Story*; Goodson, I. F. (1983), *School Subjects and Curriculum Change*; Popkewitz, T. S. (ed.) (1987), *The Formation of School Subjects: The Struggle for Creating an American Institution*; Woolnough, B. E. (1988), *Physics Teaching in Schools 1960-85: Of People, Policy and Power*; Goodson, I. F. (1988), *The Making of Curriculum: Collected Essays*; Cunningham, P. (1988), *Curriculum Change in the Primary School Since 1945: Dissemination of the Progressive Ideal*; Musgrave, P. W. (1988), *Whose Knowledge? A Case Study of the Victorian Universities Schools Examinations Board 1964-1979*.

3. Foucault, M. (1979) *Discipline and Punish: The Birth of the Prison* (Transl. Alan Sheridan), New York: Vintage, pp. 27, 137-138.

4. Ibid., pp. 27-28.

5. Giroux, H. A. (1983) "Theories of Reproduction and Resistance in the New Sociology of Education: A Critical Analysis," *Harvard Educational Review*, Vol. 53, pp. 257-293.

6. Freidson, E. (1970) *Professional Dominance*, New York: Atherton, p. 106. Cited in Scull, A. T. (1979) *Museums of Madness: The Social Organization of Insanity in Nineteenth-Century England*, Harmondsworth: Penguin, p. 141.

7. For historical treatments of nineteenth-century French psychiatry, see Castel, R. (1976) *L'ordre psychiatrique: L'age d'or de l'alienisme*, Paris: Editions de minuit; Goldstein, J. (1987) *Console and Classify: The French Psychiatric Profession in the Nineteenth Century*, New York: Cambridge University Press; Semelaigne, R. (1930, 1932) *Les pionniers de la psychiatries francaise avant et apres Pinel*, Paris: J. B. Bailliere, 2 vols. For general accounts of the history of nineteenth-century psychiatry, see

Scull, A. T. (1981) *Madhouses, Mad Doctors, and Madmen: The Social History of Psychiatry in the Victorian Era*, Philadelphia: Universisty of Philadelphia Press; and W. F. Bynum, R. Porter and M. Shepherd (1985). Pinkney, D. H. (1986) *Decisive Years in France 1840-1847*, Princeton: Princeton University Press; Corrigan, P., and B. Curtis (1985) "Education, Inspection and State Formation: A Preliminary Statement, Canadian Historical Association," *Historical Papers*, pp. 156-171; Curtis, B. (1983) "Preconditions of the Canadian State: Educational Reforms and the Construction of a Public in Upper Canada 1837-1846." In *Studies in Political Economy: A Socialist Review*, Vol. 10, Winter, pp. 99-121. Dowbiggin, I., "Degeneration and Hereditarianism in French Mental Medicine 1840-90." In W. F. Bynum, R. Porter, and M. Shepherd (eds.) (1985) *The Anatomy of Madness: Essays in the History of Psychiatry*, Tavistock Publications, London, New York, Vol. 2.

8.   Rothman, D. J. (1971) *The Discovery of the Asylum: Social Order and Disorder in the New Republic*, Boston and Toronto: Little, Brown.

9.   There are several sources for the institutional history of the insane and French psychiatry in the first half of the nineteenth century. See, for example, Bleandonu, G. and G. Le Gaufey, "The Creation of the Insane Asylums of Auxerre and Paris." In R. Forster and O. Ranum (eds.) *Deviants and the Abandoned in French Society*; selections from the *Annales E.S.C.* (1978) (transl. E. Forster and P. M. Ranum) Vol. 4, Baltimore: The Johns Hopkins University Press, pp. 180-212; Jones, C. (1980) "The Treatment of the Insane in Eighteenth- and Early Nineteenth-Century Montpellier," *Medical History*, Vol. 24, pp. 372-390; and Petit, J. (1980) "Folie, language, pouvoirs en Maine-et-Loire 1800-1941," *Revue d'histoire moderne et contemporaine*, Vol. 27, pp. 529-564.

10. For an expression of these psychiatric demands, see Lunier, C. and D. (1876) *Rapport général a M. le Ministre de l'intérieure sur le service des aliénés*, Paris: Imprimerie nationale.

11. Ritti, A. (1913-1914) *Histoire des travaux de la Société médico-psychologique et éloges de ses membres*, 2 Vols., Paris: Mason; Dowbiggin, I. (1985) "French Psychiatry, Hereditarianism and Professional Legitimacy 1840-1900," *Research in Law, Deviance, and Social Control*, Vol. 7, pp. 135-165.

12. Goldstein, J. (1984) "'Moral Contagion': A Professional Ideology of Medicine and Psychiatry in Eighteenth- and Nineteenth-Century France." In G. L. Geison (ed.) *Professions and the French State 1700-1900*, Philadelphia: University of Pennsylvania Press, pp. 181-222.

13. For recent accounts of degeneracy theory, see Bing, F. "La Théorie de la dégénéréscence." (1983), *Nouvelle histoire de la psychiatrie*, Toulouse: Privat, pp. 251-356; see also Bynum, W. F., R. Porter, and M. Shepherd (eds.) (1985) *The Anatomy of Madness: Essays in the History of Psy-*

chiatry, 2 Vols., London and New York: Tavistock; Bynum, Porter, and Shepherd (eds.) *Degeneration and Hereditarianism*, Vol. 1, *People and Ideas*, pp. 188-232; and Shortt, S. E. D. (1986) *Victorian Lunacy: Richard M. Bucke and the Practice of Late Nineteenth-Century Psychiatry*, Cambridge: Cambridge University Press, pp. 100-109.

14. Nye, R. A. (1984) *Crime, Madness, and Politics in Modern France: The Medical Concept of National Decline*, Princeton: Princeton University Press.

15. Freidson, *Professional Dominance*, pp. 134-135.

16. Foucault, M. (1980) "Questions on Geography." In *Power/Knowledge: Selected Interviews and Other Writings 1972-1977*, Brighton: Harvester Press, p. 63.

17. Ibid., p. 69.

18. Ibid., p. 77.

19. MacKinder, H. J. (1887) "On the Scope and Methods of Geography," *Proceedings of the Royal Geographical Society*, Vol. IX.

20. Manifesto of Geographical Association printed on the inside cover of all copies of the journal, *Geography*.

21. MacKinder, H. J. (1903) *Report of the Discussion on Geographical Education*, London, England, pp. 95-101.

22. Board of Education (1927) "Report of the Consultative Committee: The Education of the Adolescent," *Hadow Report*, London: His Majesty's Stationery Office.

23. Honeybone, R. C. (1954) "Balance in Geography and Education," *Geography*, Vol. 34, p. 186.

24. Ibid.

25. Garnett, A. (1969) "Teaching Geography: Some Reflections," *Geography*, Vol. 54, p. 387.

26. Walker, D. (1975) "The Well-rounded Geographers." *The Times Educational Supplement*, November 28, p. 6.

27. Quoted in Wooldridge, D. T. (1973) "Against Geography." In Bale, D., N. Graves, and R. Wallford (eds.) *Perspectives in Geographical Education*, Edinburgh: Oliver and Boyd, pp. 12-13.

28. Ibid.

29. Garnett, "Teaching Geography," p. 368.

30. Honeybone, "Balance in Geography and Education."

31. Ibid.

32. Report (1967) *Society and the Young School Leaver,* Working Paper No. 11, London: Her Majesty's Stationery Office, p. 3.

33. Anonymous interview, Leicester University, June 30, 1976.

34. Gowing, D. (1973) "A Fresh Look at Objectives." In R. Walford (ed.) *New Directions in Geography Teaching,* London: Longmans, p. 153.

35. Marchant, E. C. (1968) "Some Responsibilities of the Teacher of Geography," *Geography,* Vol. 53, p. 133.

36. Ibid.

37. Byrne, E. M. (1974) *Planning and Educational Inequality,* Slough, England: National Foundation for Educational Research, p. 29.

38. Goodson, I. F. (1987) *School Subjects and Curriculum Change,* London, New York, and Philadelphia: Falmer Press; idem. (1988) *The Making of Curriculum: Collected Essays,* London, New York, and Philadelphia: Falmer Press.

39. Kaestle, C. F. (1972) "Social Reform and the Urban School," *History of Education Quarterly,* Vol. 12, p. 218.

Chapter 7

Curriculum Contests: Environmental Studies Versus Geography

Preface

Much of the literature promoting environmental education as "a just cause" assumes a rational discussion of curriculum options. In fact, the promotion of new curriculum areas threatens existing subject territories. Historically environmental education has threatened the boundaries of geography. Thus, by studying these "border wars" we learn more about the process of promoting new curriculum areas. This chapter seeks to build on previous work that has scrutinized the social history of school subjects. A conviction underlying this work has been that as well as studying the interactive nature of curriculum practice, also examining the conflict over the definitions of curriculum that precede classroom events (with the insights thereby provided into the vested interests involved) will further our understanding of "what counts as education." My earlier work has looked at the process of becoming an academic subject:[1] the stages that subjects pass through in pursuit of academic status, the "kind" of subject that has to be presented and promoted if academic status, and the associated flow of finance and resources, is to be conceded. In *School Subjects and Curriculum Change*[2] I trace the link between common factors discerned in the evolutionary profile of school subjects and the career imperatives of school teachers. The evolving "career" of the school subject presents a changing range of opportunities for its subject practitioners. In the case of geography the promotional process has moved from a position where initially schools-based utilitarian and pedagogic interdisciplinary versions of the subject were predominant toward a position with geography as an academic subject "discipline" occupying a well-established university base. Clearly, the link between the changing "rhetorics" of subject promotion and the curriculum practice of subject teachers is complex: the links are neither direct nor easily discernible, but they influence the parameters of curriculum practice, and in the study presented in this chapter it is intended that preliminary insights and questions will be generated from which to develop more detailed studies. The study focuses on the "defense" of geography in ways that build on the work on the "definition" of geography so as to set this historical legacy against claims on the curriculum that embody different intentions and pedagogic orientations. Central to this conflict is the historical relationship between geography, integrated studies, and environmental studies.

Geography and Integrated Studies: An Historical Background

Since the early beginnings in the nineteenth century, geographers in England have been preoccupied with finding an answer to MacKinder's question, "can Geography be rendered a discipline?"[3] The quest has been continuous, and more recently Honeybone has noted: "The question of internal balance in geography is . . . one which must, of necessity, be always with us. A discipline which recruits its students from the sciences and the humanities alike has continually to keep its synthesis under review."[4] This continuing identity crisis at the heart of geography is accentuated by the relationship between university geography and "school geography," and most of all by the relationship between geography and other subjects. As Williams has noted, these problems are interlinked for "If geographers divide over definitions of geography and school geography, it is not surprising that when geography is allied with other subjects the problem of definition of terms is almost insoluble."[5]

The relationship between geography and integrated studies has been historically difficult, notably because "complication arises from the nature of geography itself,"[6] but the fears relating to geography's identity that integrated studies evoke have been compounded by the complex historical relationship between geography and other subjects. Geography was in fact created by specialists from other disciplines whose studies were integrated by concentration on problems perceived as geographical. As Kirk has stated, "modern geography was created by scholars, trained in other disciplines, asking themselves, geographical questions."[7] At the level of scholarship, therefore, geography was one of the earlier "Integrated Studies," but this was also true in schools. To tentatively establish a position in schools, geography was initially presented as an ingredient of integrated courses, as Williams has noted: "The early attempts at introducing integrated courses stemmed from the struggle to introduce geography into secondary schools . . ."[8]

Integrated studies stands as a dual reminder to geographers of the prolonged and continuing quest for a stable subject identity and of the early days when the subject itself was a low-status ingredient of integrated courses. The changing philosophies, pedagogies, and content orientations of geography are symbiotically related to its presentation, acceptance, and status as a "subject."

The first opportunity to scrutinize this symbiotic relationship is in the period before the First World War, for "no sooner had geography taken its place as an accepted part of school curricula than it was subjected to pressure to relate more closely to other subjects."[9] The main pressure group at this time was concerned with "education for citizenship" and, as a result, attempts were made to link history and geography. One of the leading protagonists was MacKinder, who advocated "a combined subject" in 1913 in an address to the Geographical Association.[10] He was mindful of the vested interests of those who taught history, and recalled the fears of geologists twenty years before that geographers would "make inroads upon their classes" and that their careers would thus be limited as fewer posts became available. He added: "Well, even scientific folk are human, and such ideas must be taken into account." Thus he assured historians: "There need be no question of vested interests in connection with the two subjects . . . . There is no idea of attacking the teaching of history as such in training colleges and in similar institutions." He was concerned only with the "upper half of elementary education and the lower tiers of secondary education": "There what I suggest is the teaching of a single subject, geography and history. In those stages of education, let us have one subject, but let that subject be taught by a teacher who has learnt both geography and history, and learnt them separately."

MacKinder's arguments in favor of integration were clearly linked to a view about geography's aspirations as a school "subject":

> How are children going to use their curiosity? By taking up a 'subject'? That is an academic idea. A special subject will be taken up by a few scattered people as a hobby, but the vast majority will increase their knowledge not by the study of any definite subject, but by reading this and that cheap book, by reading the newspapers, by talking with friends and by seeing what they can when travelling.

This leads MacKinder to argue that for the vast majority

> what is important is not send them out with the rudiments of history as such and the rudiments of geography as such in their minds, but to send them out with some sort of orderly conception of the world around them. Whether a fact is historical or whether it is geographical matters not one straw to them.

Significantly, MacKinder added that: "It does, perhaps matter to those who are going to increase the knowledge of history or the knowledge of geography, or who are to be specialized teachers of those subjects, and who are going to prepare for examinations in those subjects."[11] In fact, the specialist teachers of geography reacted to MacKinder's suggestions in a manner that confirmed his last point. Thus, in the discussions that followed MacKinder's address Miss Spalding argued that the most effective way of achieving the better citizenship desired by MacKinder was to train pupils "to love one or two subjects so much that they really go on and study them by themselves."[12] Unstead agreed and offered an alternative view of geography as a school subject to that proposed by MacKinder:

> What is a subject? It is an organized body of knowledge, the different parts of which naturally hang together, and I think in practical teach-

ing it is well to develop it as a whole . . . in geography, the facts do hang together; children can see relations, they may get the sense of proportion if they have the thing treated as a whole. . . .[13]

A few years later the Council of the Geographical Association, alerted to the danger, issued a statement since "the question of the position of geography in the curricula of schools and universities is a fundamental one at the present time." They asserted that

It is first necessary to understand what is meant by geography and the reasons why it is studied. Among many of those who have not followed closely the recent development of geographical study, an impression prevails that there are important divergences of opinion on these points, that different authorities hold different and conflicting conceptions even of the subject. But a more careful scrutiny reveals the fact that a close agreement is being steadily reached.[14]

The statement then refers to the growing power of the Geographical Association and to a recent manifesto on the subject "which has met with practically universal acceptance." Geography, they argue, is a unique combination, "a balanced subject with a unity of its own," and may claim ". . . to contribute in a unique fashion to an education which aims at the appreciative interpretation of the modern world."[15]

Alongside the group pursuing a combined subject of history and geography was another group that felt that geography was "rapidly taking its place as a definite science." The danger of scientific aspiration was that taken to its logical conclusion it presented "a very strong argument in favour of geography being taught by the chemistry or physics master."[16]

In the interwar period, having escaped the embraces of history and science, geography was confronted with a new integrationist initiative in the form of the growing social studies movement. Thus, in 1935 Happold argued for a reconstructed curriculum to take account of the fact that "a boy comes to school not to learn geography or history or English, but to be trained how to live." He replaced these subject divisions by social studies, ". . . a unified course designed to give the boy a knowledge and understanding of his own age, considered not in isolation, but in relation to its origin-that is, a picture both of his environment and his heritage."[17]

After the war the moves toward social studies continued to be linked with the Association for Education in Citizenship and were seen primarily as courses in civic education. In 1949 the Ministry of Education, reporting on citizens growing up, saw geography and history as the most relevant of the traditional subjects:

> The question which teachers of these subjects have to ask themselves today is how far they will make this civic value their sole value and criterion in their syllabus and presentation. Many history and geography teachers have taken up advanced positions in this respect, and the older subject names have sometimes in such cases given place to 'social studies'—an indication of the change in point of view. But others are reluctant to allow the illumination of the contemporary scene to become the sole purpose in this range of work, and hold to the more traditional approach which proceeds historically through the centuries and geographically through the regions of the world.[18]

The position of these traditional geographers who were reluctant to embrace social studies was eloquently summarized in a memorandum prepared in 1950 by the Royal Geographical Society's Education Committee. The committee stated frankly that social studies would "destroy the value of geography as an important medium of education" and hence was "concerned at its spread in the schools."[19] The comments of the committee indicate considerable fear that geography might be replaced by social studies especially, it was noted, in secondary modern schools:

> It is difficult to estimate precisely how far this elimination of Geography as an ordered study has proceeded. There is, however, much evidence of a strong tendency to "break down the barriers between subjects" (an explanation given for the change) and to teach an amorphous hotch-potch of geography, history and civics under the heading of social studies.[20]

The report conceded that the nature of these amorphous hotchpotches varied considerably between schools and that most contained some geography, "but in a disjointed and attenuated form, insufficient to preserve the characteristic outlook and discipline of the subject."[21] Above all, the report sees any integration of subjects as likely to impair "standards of instruction" in geography.

> An attempt to study a group of subjects together introduces such com-
> plexity that children cannot see any general pattern or gain a clear
> and memorable educational experience. The geographer is well aware
> that knowledge is whole, but makes no apology for dividing it into
> separate subjects for the purpose of learning. History and geogra-
> phy, for example, are distinct branches of study, and each is recog-
> nized as having a unique contribution to make to the intellectual equip-
> ment of the educated citizen of today. But these contributions are
> different and cannot be made unless the recognized content and char-
> acteristic method of presentation of each subject are preserved.[22]

Thus the integrationist perspective of social studies is presented as wholly undesirable: "The result is exactly what happens when the lemon is squeezed: the juice is removed, and only the useless rind and fibres remain."[23]

The report of the Royal Geographical Society engendered considerable discussion at the time, and Ernest Fereday summarized some of the main objections to the views presented. He concentrated on the two most emotive phrases in the report: first, the dismissal of social studies as an "amorphous hotch-potch." Fereday argued that geography itself could easily be presented in this light:

> Any highly regarded textbook of geography affords ample evidence
> that school geography is a brilliant reconciliation of the carefully se-
> lected essentials of several specialized sciences. Most of us owe so
> much to those clear-thinking teachers of geography in the last gen-
> eration who patiently and purposefully expounded such well-ordered
> symposia to us that we should at once condemn as unkind any one
> who could characterise such work as an 'amorphous hotch-potch'.[24]

Secondly, Fereday argues that the "most ardent advocate of social studies could hardly better their image of the squeezed lemon." Thus in selecting the materials of study from a widely increased range of possibilities it would appear, he argues, sensible to "retain the nourishing and necessary while rejecting the noxious, the nebulous and the nugatory."[25]

In spite of the refutations of Fereday and other supporters of social studies, by the mid-1950s it was quite clear that the opposition to the new approach was succeeding. Channon reported that for social studies: "The period of post-war experiment had faded by the mid-1950s, by which time many schools appear to have returned to a traditional curriculum."[26] She adds that one of the main reasons was the criticism of geographers (and also historians) "who saw the new proposals as a threat to the integrity and status of their own subjects."[27]

From the geographers point of view the result of the opposition to social studies was presented differently. In 1954 Honeybone summarized the developments that followed:

> If the Social Studies controversy has no other effect than that of making us put our house in order, then it will have made a very important contribution to the development of geography teaching in school. It is a pity that by reason of its brevity, the Royal Geographical Society's pamphlet does not develop the case for geography at greater length. We have a very strong and positive case, and . . . the present time is particularly hopeful for a wide-spread advance in the teaching of geography in school.[28]

The Definition and Establishment of Geography

From its position as a low-status integrated school subject in the early twentieth century, geography has progressed to broad acceptance as a high-status university "discipline." The story behind this remarkable progress has been told elsewhere,[29] but the implications for curriculum practice need to be carefully explored. Basically, geography, particularly through the activities of the Geographical Association, has followed the four-point strategy recommended by one of the leading activists, H. J. MacKinder, in 1903:

> Firstly, we should encourage University Schools of Geography, where Geographers can be made . . . Secondly, we must persuade at any rate some secondary schools to place the geographical teaching of the whole school in the hands of one geographically trained teacher. . . . Thirdly, we must thrash out by discussion and experimentation what is the best progressive method for common acceptance and upon that method we must base our scheme of examination. Lastly, the examination papers must be set by practical geography teachers.[30]

Above all, then, in the galaxy of priorities, MacKinder was concerned with "how Geography could be rendered a discipline." Exams were to be chosen as part of the pursuit of "common acceptance" of the subject—in this internal subject debate there was not even the facade that pupil interest or motivation were important criteria.

The implications of such subject priorities for curriculum practice have been hinted at in a short 1972 article written by David Layton and no doubt partially derived from his studies of the history of science education. Layton suggests that there is a tentative model for the evolution of school subjects in the secondary curriculum. The model has three stages. In the first stage

> the callow intruder stakes a place in the timetable, justifying its presence on grounds such as pertinence and utility. During this stage learners are attracted to the subject because of its bearing on matters of concern to them. The teachers are rarely trained specialists, but bring the missionary enthusiasm of pioneers to their task. The dominant criterion is relevance to the needs and interests of the learners.

In the interim second stage

> a tradition of scholarly work in the subject is emerging along with a corps of trained specialists from which teachers may be recruited. Students are still attracted to the study, but as much by its reputation and growing academic status as by its relevance to their own problems and concerns. The internal logic and discipline of the subject is becoming increasingly influential on the selection and organization of subject matter.

In the final stage

> the teachers now constitute a professional body with established rules and values. The selection of subject matter is determined in large measure by the judgments and practices of the specialist scholars who lead inquiries in the field. Students are initiated into a tradition, their attitudes approaching passivity and resignation, a prelude to disenchantment.[31]

Layton's model has great relevance for geography, for progressively the subject came to be "made" in the universities, as MacKinder's strategy had intended. The existence of a base in schools as an integrated subject taught by nonspecialists was used to call for the setting up of university geography departments. The definition of geography through the universities instead of the schools confirmed the replacement of utilitarian or pedagogic rhetoric common in the early stages by arguments in favor of purer, more theoretical, academic "rigor." As early as 1927 for instance, Hadow had contended that "the main objective in good geographical teaching is to develop as in the case of history, an attitude of mind and mode of thought characteristic of the subject."[32] However, for several decades, even though university departments were being established, the subject was plagued by its image as essentially for school-children and by the idiosyncratic interpretations of the sub-ject emanating from the universities, particularly in respect to fieldwork. Thus, while establishment in the universities solved the status problems of the subject in the schools by confirm-ing the claims for academic rigor, within the universities them-selves the subject's status still remained low.

The launching in the 1960s of "new geography" as a rigor-ous quantitative subject has to be viewed in this context. Now the subject was promoted with full aspirations to the scientific or social scientific character that would finally establish its status at the highest level. In this respect the current position of the subject in universities bears elegant testimony to the success of "new geography" in establishing parity of esteem with other university disciplines.

In the final stage of establishment geography was being defined by university scholars as in Layton's stage three. The particular version of the school subject thereby embodied in school curricula is very much Unstead's "organised body of knowledge," described earlier. It is fascinating to reflect on how MacKinder, through his growing involvement with the promotion of the subject, was forced to discard his earlier honesty about the versions of school subjects we now tend to think of as the norm. To recapitulate he said, "How are chil-dren going to use their curiosity? (to learn). By taking up a subject? That is an academic idea . . . the study of any definite subject" would, he felt, not increase or help the education of the "vast majority."[33]

This tension between the definition of the subject as a ve-hicle for the status enhancement and advancement of subject specialists and as an educational vehicle for the majority of pupils can be clearly evidenced in the evolutionary profiles of a range of school subjects. The tension becomes especially vis-ible when examination syllabuses have to be defined in ways that reflect a subject's push for academic status. The contest for recognition as an A-level subject is a central point in such status establishment within secondary-school curricula. Before looking at the clash over this issue between geographers and advocates of environmental studies, I quote one teacher who was against the strategy of pursuing status through the definition of a new academic subject that could be taught at A level. Talking of the early days of the campaign to promote environmental studies, he said, "Once again we see the unwanted children of lower intelligence being made servants of the juggernaut of documented evidence, the inflated examination." He concluded:

> True education is not for every man the scrap of paper he leaves school with. Dare we as teachers, admit this? Dare we risk our existence by forcibly expressing our views on this? While we pause after the first phase of our acceptance, are we to rely on exams for all, to prove ourselves worthy of the kindly eye of the state?[34]

Geography versus Environmental Studies

The geographers, ever alert to the threat from integrated studies, first formally discussed the "problem" of environmental studies in 1969. The worry was of the pressures exerted by headteachers on specialist teachers of geography to teach environmental studies, often in the place of pure geography. As a result it was thought that "the Geographical Association should involve itself in a dialogue with practitioners of environmental studies, to discover the geographical content of such studies and to ensure that, if such studies continue to proliferate, geographers will be included in the appropriate teaching teams and will be able to contribute their distinctive concepts, skills and techniques." However, it was moved that "some members felt that to do so would be tantamount to admitting the validity of environmental studies or would indicate a measure of approval."[35]

In addition to the legacy of geographers' responses to the "threat" of integrated studies stretching back half a century, the reaction to environmental studies was complicated by internal dissent among geographers with reference to the growth of "new geography" in the 1960s. In large measure the opposition came from those with a "regional" or "fieldwork" orientation in their training and practice. The close relationship of regional geography and the fieldwork tradition was reflected in the work of Professor S. W. Wooldridge. He argued that the aim of geographical fieldwork is "regional synthesis,"[36] and in his obituary in *Geography* it was recorded by Wise, later an advocate of close links with environmental studies, that "Above all, geography was for him regional geography."[37]

In 1966 Professor Fisher read a paper to the Research Committee of the Royal Geographical Society, later published in extended form under the title "Whither Regional Geography?." Fisher argued that geographical research was in serious danger of "over-extending its periphery at the expense of neglecting its base."[38] For Fisher the "traditional core of geography" was regional study, as against the "new," systematic geography, but he noted, "While systematic geography now flourishes like the Biblical bay tree, regional geography (however defined) appears to be declining and even withering away." He added some details of this decline of regional geography:

> . . . not only has there been a noticeable decrease in the importance attached to it in the university syllabus, but this process is apparently also spreading to the schools, and it has been announced that the Southern Universities Joint Board 'O' level Geography examination for 1970 would include no paper in regional geography.[39]

The increasingly threatened supporters of regional geography were therefore faced with the pervasive challenge of new geography and the traditional challenge of integrated studies currently epitomized by environmental studies. For one the internal threat seems to have been deemed greater than the external dangers represented by the emergence of environmental studies. The obituary of Professor P. W. Bryan, an eminent regionalist, records that in 1967:

> Only twelve months before his death, and already a sick man, Pat Bryan attended a strenuous full-day conference at Leicester University on Environmental Studies. He probably felt that this term expressed more clearly his own life's work and ambitions as a geographer.[40]

Similarly, in 1970 P. R. Thomas asserted in *Geography* that

> the tendency towards an environmentalist approach to explanation in school geography is at least partly due to the survival of the re-

gional concept as the basis for syllabus construction, despite the progressive decline in the importance of regional geography at most universities and its virtual disappearance from some.[41]

But the alliance between regional geography and environmental studies was not to last. Partly this was because after 1970 the "new geography" tradition began to lose impetus and became increasingly assimilated into traditional patterns of geography: "The new geographers became less violent . . . they flushed regions out but then accepted regionalism back in not as facts . . . but as a spirit and concept." A college lecturer noted a further conclusive reason for ending the alliance:

> The crisis in Geography caused traditional regional geographers to flee into environmental studies . . . they wanted a refuge to go on teaching as they were teaching . . . but they were overtaken by the Environmental crisis and the rapid growth in Environmental Studies that followed it . . . The threat to all Geographers from this new subject became much greater than any internal disagreements.[42]

The increasing convergence of new, systematic geography and regional and field geography, together with the rapid growth of environmental studies, once again helped unite geographers in their opposition to the perceived external challenge.

The challenge came quite rapidly, as large numbers of newly reorganized comprehensives began drawing up teaching environmental studies courses; in addition several new universities set up courses with this title. Most notable were the initiatives from Hertfordshire, led by rural studies teachers, to promote environmental studies as a new school subject and "scholarly discipline," which culminated in the Offley Conference of 1971. This led to a working party being set up to submit an A-level syllabus in environmental studies. The advocates for geography at the conference reflected the growing concern. Douglas, for instance, sought to define environmental studies in a way that would not "overlap too much" with geography. Indeed, commenting on the claims the geographers made, Hartrop, in a manner reminiscent of the Norwood Reports' complaints at the "expansiveness of geography" nearly 30 years before, commented that "parts of geography could be expanded to consume almost everything." The reasons for the geographers' reaction can be partially deduced from the evidence of a sample survey of secondary schools carried out by Her Majesty's Inspectors in 1971/72. They found that while in grammar schools only one "combined studies" course had replaced geography (one out of 44 schools), in secondary modern schools 40 schools out of 104 had replaced geography by such courses and in comprehensive schools 20 out of 59 schools.[43]

That the geographers were intensely worried by the threat of Hertfordshire teachers defining an A level in environmental studies was illustrated when Carson, the leading advocate of the A level, went to speak to them at this time. In an interview (July 7, 1977), Sean Carson recalled the events:

> I was invited to go and speak on environmental studies . . . The Royal Institution was probably where it was held . . . (laughter). There was a really good start when the chairman said "I'm Chairman of this meeting but I can't adopt a neutral attitude on something I feel so strongly about . . ."
>
> Then I made my spiel about Geography not being God-given religion, but a range of knowledge we had assembled to our convenience, and there was not reason why we shouldn't reassemble it in any other form. This (i.e. Environmental Studies) was another form in which it might be reassembled and just because one had learnt things in a different tradition, there's no reason why you should go on repeating so other people repeat it after you . . .

After his speech:

> There broke out shouting and rude remarks and the Chairman was not willing . . . made very little effort to control it . . .
>
> IG: Were you nervous?
>
> SC: I wasn't nervous at all . . . I'm not nervous in that sense . . . On this occasion I was frankly amused and amazed! It was so irrational.
>
> IG: What kind of things did they say?
>
> SC: Well, I can remember one chap who stood up and said, "I'm a professor of geography and I turn out 60 honours graduates every year." So I said, "Well, what do they do? Do they produce more students for you to turn out honours graduates every year? What's the end of that?". . . There were things like that being said.
>
> IG: Did they take the line that they were doing it anyway?
>
> SC: Yes, and that I was out to destroy Geography . . . Rural studies was a hotch-potch of various subjects being put together for no particular purpose, it had no respectability . . . I remember thinking, "This is what it must be like, facing a Congressional meeting in America". It was quite an experience—a lot of people afterwards apologised to me . . . I think, pretty ashamed of it. I got a letter of

thanks from the Conference not mentioning it at all! I did think of writing a sarcastic reply, but I didn't.

The geographers' official reaction to environmental studies was summarized in a presidential address to the Geographical Association on January 1, 1973, by Mr. A. D. Nicholls. His speech began by asserting, somewhat wishfully: "It is not surprising that in the minds of most teachers environmental studies should be associated with geography rather than with the numerous subjects which, in greater or lesser degree, are considered to be constituent parts of this educational field." Having hinted at the thrust of his argument, he later stated: "The definitions given by well-known geographers to provide answers to the question 'What is geography' might equally well be used to answer the question 'What are environmental studies?'." And similarly: "In the first decade of this century the founding fathers of the then 'new' geography came from many and varied disciplines. Their original choice of discipline would make an admirable list of environmental studies."[44] Nicholls's views were undoubtedly shared by most geographers; one college of education lecturer remembers that at this time: "At an early Environmental Studies meeting we felt that geography had been doing it for years and we said so . . . "[45] Tony Fyson also claimed that:

> On a pragmatic level a new subject dealing with the environment is still going to leave a lot of geography teachers claiming that their traditional fare is the true way to approach the topic; on an academic level it is possible to argue that geography . . . can develop to include the aims of the environmental studies lobby.[46]

Nicholls's second argument turned on the need for "a subject"; again he drew on a long tradition. In 1913, Unstead had argued against MacKinder's advocation of a combined subject, saying that a subject is an organized body of knowledge and that "in geography, the facts do hang together."[47] Unstead's argument was again used in the 1960s when there were fears about school geography: "No subject can claim a place on the school curriculum unless it has a clear structure, a precise theme and a worthwhile purpose . . . if geography is to survive in school, it, too, must be a scholarly discipline with a clearly defined purpose and a carefully organised structure."[48]

Nicholls began by conceding that environmental studies were generally accepted as useful in teaching "young children" but then argued that:

> As the width and depth of knowledge acquired increase so does the need to specialise, subject divisions appear and the need for subject disciplines arises. These codes of study are the framework or basic principles which are necessary for specialised learning and under-standing. Indeed, without them we tend to accumulate only encyclopaedic, unrelated facts.[49]

The role of geography as a subject discipline ordering and unifying the "unrelated facts" of environmental studies was widely promoted by geographers at this time.

> Geography because it is an integrated discipline at the heart of Environmental Studies is better placed than any of the other constituents nuclei to co-ordinate and unify the larger body of studies of which it is the core. To adapt a well known analogy, it may well be the leaven which will make the loaf palatable.[50]

The implicit hierarchy contained in this statement is clarified by another geographer exploring the same relationship: "To put it in terms of a model, geography may be likened to a pyramid the base of which is environmental studies, but the apex is the sharp intellectual discipline fashioned in the university."[51] A university professor confirmed this view and explained the implications for school geography: "You need high level theoretical development first of all . . . then you break it down to digestible level in school."[52]

The third strand of Nicholls' argument, undoubtedly the most convincing aspect for the many teachers in the audience, dealt with the "practical realities" for "practicing teachers." Crucial to this argument was the recognition that

> It is likely, but by no means certain, that if environmental studies or environmental education is considered as a subject in its own right, some, but not all, of the time previously devoted to constituent subjects will be made available to the new omnibus subject. With constant pressure on teaching time, headmasters are ever searching for new space into which additional prestige subjects can be fitted, and the total loss of teaching time to environmental subjects may be considerable. Nor, in my experience, have I found departments very ea-

ger to surrender precious teaching time, particularly with the more able classes, to make good other departments' losses.

Nicholls stressed a further practicality:

> Next, as a practising teacher, I must refer to what is an all-important consideration in every type of school—the teaching staff available. Many among you will think I should have referred to the staff before considering the timetable. If undifferentiated environmental studies of an omnibus nature are to be introduced into a school curriculum, which of the academic disciplines is going to cater for suitably qualified men and women to take charge of them? Or instead of using one suitable member of the staff to cover all aspects of the studies, is team work by a mixed group drawn from the allied disciplines to share the work? Can you imagine the wrangling over the relative importance of their particular shares which might go on?[53]

A publication prepared by the Environmental Education Standing Committee of the Geographical Association, which included Mr. Nicholls, clarifies the nature of the fears over such "wrangling." They assert that "The concerns of Environmental Education render the presence of a person with geographical training in each team quite essential." And, similarly, ". . . a team with one would have a wider range of possible activities."[54]

Nicholls explored this theme in considerable detail in his address:

> Qualified men and women of academic stature have selected their subjects because of their interest in them and the importance they consider them to have. They also like to see the inspiration of their teaching reflected in their pupils 'advancement': indeed, this is one of the rewards for those who engage in a profession which has been described as richly rewarding but badly paid . . .

The relationship between subject expertise and pupil advancement is later elucidated:

> A shallow approach to any subject inevitably becomes less satisfying, and finally utterly boring both to teacher and class. Not every question from a class calls for an immediate answer in depth, but when the teacher's ignorance of the subject becomes evident to the class and pupils lose confidence in their teacher, and more pitifully, the teacher loses confidence in himself, and confusion becomes chaos. The teacher must know his subject . . .[55]

The relationship between the status of a "subject" and the pupils that traditional subjects attract is alluded to by Nicholls in discussing a Department of Education and Science (D.E.S.) survey's findings with regard to environmental studies. Four varieties were distinguished:

1. One comprehensive school used environmental studies for all first year pupils and thereafter separate subjects were taught;
2. Two schools gave environmental studies for slow learners in years 1, 2, and 3 only—the average and able pupils did ordinary subjects;
3. Two schools gave environmental studies in year 4 only for fourth-year leavers—these were nonexamination pupils—the rest did ordinary subjects;
4. One school gave environmental studies for able fifth year pupils for O level as an option against other subjects.

From these findings Nicholls concludes:

> First, average and above average pupils are considered to be able to cope with ordinary subjects, though it might be unsafe to assume they enjoy these subjects more or that they would rather not spread their abilities. Secondly, environmental studies are thought to be easier or can be made more attractive to less able scholars. Thirdly, separate subjects may be easier to teach successfully. Cynics might suggest that combined studies provide a more successful opiate to potentially rowdy classes. You as teachers, may reach other equally valid conclusions.[56]

The last sentence confirms that the message, despite its philosophical and logical shortcomings, aims to focus on the teachers' perception of the practical realities of their work.

The final strand of Nicholls's argument concentrates on the need to keep geography as a unified discipline. An earlier president had touched on the socializing role of the Universities.

> University departments have a duty to ensure that, at least at the first degree level, the core of our subject is neither forgotten nor neglected and that the synthesis of the specialist fields and their relevance to that core are clearly appreciated by our undergraduate students.[57]

The symbiotic relationship between the university geography and school geography is explored:

> There is now an intake from sixth forms, into our university depart-
> ments of at least one thousand students each year to read geography.
> The recognition of our subject's status among university disciplines
> which this gives, together with the now costly provision made avail-
> able for its study, could never have been achieved without this re-
> markable stimulus and demand injected from our schools. This is a
> matter that university teachers must not forget; we have a duty at all
> times and in every way possible to return help to our colleagues in
> schools and colleges and to forge closer links between school and
> university teachers.[58]

Nicholls argued from a similar position about what is required of geography as a subject:

> At sixth form level it must . . . provide a challenge to the young men
> and women who may have ambitions for the future and wish to carry
> their studies further and go to a university. They will become, in the
> best sense, students. Some of these will furnish the university schools
> of geography with young men and women who will expect to have
> some knowledge with sound and deep foundations so that understand-
> ing between them and their lecturers, readers and professors is mu-
> tual. We should be wise not to stray too far from the recognised routes—
> the frontiers of the subject are alluring, but not all are worth extending,
> at least not in school. If we provide the universities with undergradu-
> ates who have a wide but shallow acquaintance with many subjects,
> will they prefer these students before those with a sound foundation
> in fewer relevant subjects?[59]

Nicholls' conclusion stressed the need for staying within "the recognised routes":

> Ten years ago, almost to the day and from this platform, Professor
> Kirk said 'Modern geography was created by scholars, trained in other
> disciplines, asking themselves geographical questions and moving
> inwards in a community of problems; it could die by a reversal of the
> process whereby trained geographers moved outwards in a fragmen-
> tation of interests seeking solutions to non-geographical problems'.
> Might not this be prophetic for us today? Could it not all too soon
> prove disastrous if the trained teachers of geography moved outwards
> as teachers of environmental studies seeking solutions to non-geo-
> graphical problems?[60]

Nicholls's conclusion is as explicit a statement of the geographers' "party line" as it is possible to make: in effect he is saying we must not allow the process that created geography to be repeated.

This speech frankly elaborates a view of school subjects as vested interests, territories, and career bases for subject teachers. This view stands in stark contradiction to notions of subjects as essentially reflecting the changing distillations of dispassionate scholarship. That Nicholls's view was predominant among geographers was confirmed by events.

In the negotiations over the environmental studies A level in Schools Council the geography subcommittee was consistently unhelpful. As a result the A level was delayed for more than a year and when finally accepted it was only as an experimental syllabus. More important was the ruling noted with approval by the geography subcommittee chairman, that candidates could not take the examination with geography. The geographers filibustering tactics, together with the insistence on this qualification proved a sufficient barrier to ensure environmental studies was not taken up widely. Carson noted at the time "candidates may not take geography at the same examination . . . Some of our teachers particularly wanted to take the subject with geography but the decision was a 'political one' by a group of geographers (who gave me a rough reception at the G.A. annual conference)."[61] In 1975 a Schools Council working party on environmental studies confirmed this view, while phrasing the matter more diplomatically:

> At present students taking Environmental Studies at G.C.E. [General College Entrance] 'A' level are not allowed to combine this choice with geography. Subject compatibility is frequently a source of discord but it is important to prevent the perfectly legitimate misgivings of academics about subject demarcations being turned into obstacles unfairly placed in the path of students.[62]

Conclusion

Defining the Subject
The link between subject defense and "obstacles placed in the path of students" is at the heart of any study of school subjects in negotiation and evolution. This contradiction actually pre-

cedes the defense of academic status and is evident in the process of becoming an academic subject. Often this process is marked by a progressive movement away from the type of subject defined by teachers and involving considerations of pupil relevance to versions of the subject much influenced by the activities (and proclivities) of university academics. Layton's summary of this culminating phase and its implications for classroom practice are so important that it is perhaps worth repeating:

> The teachers now constitute a professional body with established rules and values. The selection of subject matter is determined in large measure by the judgements and practices of specialist scholars who lead enquiries in the field. Students are initiated into a tradition. Their attitudes approaching passivity and resignation, a prelude to disenchantment.

Defending the Subject

After much conflict and promotion geography had reached the culminating phase characterized by Layton, where it was viewed as an academic subject with an associated university base. At this point we have seen that the material interests of its teachers were tied up in defense of this academic status. Thereby they retained their departmental territories, graded posts, capitation allowances, together with their rights to the constituency of "able" pupils (for whom only "academic" subjects are suitable). On this point Nicholls was only too clear: "Average and above average pupils are considered to be able to cope with ordinary *academic* subjects," and these pupils at that time were taught geography. On the other hand, environmental studies were "thought to be easier or can be made more attractive to less able scholars".[63] If however, and here was the threat, environmental studies was somehow to be considered as an "academic subject in its own right," the "total loss of teaching time to environmental subjects may be considerable," Nicholls adds "Nor in my experience have I found departments very eager to surrender precious teaching time, particularly with the more able classes."

The threat of losing able students, departmental resources and, by implication, career prospects is thereby made real if academic parity were to be conceded to environmental studies. By placing this threat to material self-interest and conditions of classroom practice at the center of the debate over the definition and defense of geography the implicit exhortation was to subjugate the claims of pupil interest, subject context, pedagogic orientation and intellectual scholarship to those of individual and subject *self-interest.*

Above all, such a preliminary study as this raises a number of questions that need to be addressed in future research. Most importantly, further work is needed into how far the rhetoric of subject promotion actually impinges on school syllabuses and classroom practice. One suspects, for instance, that the concentration on academic and theoretical content might be strongest during the passage to subject establishment of the sort here followed by geography. Moreover, because of its continuing identity crisis, geography may well be an extreme case; hence, other subjects must be examined. In this wider-ranging examination the most generative focus might be on how socialization into the subject and the way the subject's "career" (and by association the teacher's career) is structured impinges on classroom practice and the development of classroom skills. If Layton is right, the definition and defense of school subjects is often diametric in its opposition to the development of successful classroom practice.

Notes

1. Goodson, I. F. (1981) "Becoming an Academic Subject: Patterns of Explanation and Evolution," *British Journal of Sociology of Education*, Vol. 2, pp. 163-180.

2. Goodson, I. F. (1993) *School Subjects and Curriculum Change*, 3rd ed., London, New York, and Philadelphia: Falmer Press.

3. MacKinder, H. J. (1887). "On the Scope and Methods of Geography," *Proceedings of the Royal Geographical Society*, Vol. 9.

4. Honeybone, R. C. (1954). "Balance in Geography and Education," *Geography*, Vol. 39, p. 70.

5. Williams, M. (ed.) (1976) *Geography and the Integrated Curriculum*, London: Heinemann, p. 8.

6. Ibid.

7. Kirk, W. (1963) "Problems of Geography," *Geography*, Vol. 48, p. 357.

8. Williams, *Geography*, p. 8.

9. Ibid.

10. MacKinder, H. J. (1913). "The Teaching of Geography and History as a Combined Subject," *The Geographical Teacher*, Vol. 7.

11. MacKinder, cited in Williams, *Geography*, pp. 5-6.

12. MacKinder, "Teaching of Geography and History," p. 10.

13. Unstead, J. (1913). "Discussion of MacKinder's Paper," *The Geographical Teacher*, Vol. 7, p. 10.

14. Council of the Geographical Association (1919) "The Position of Geography," *The Geographical Teacher*, Vol. 10; cited in Williams, *Geography*, pp. 15-16.

15. Ibid., p. 18.

16. Carey, W. MacLean (1913) "The Correlation of Instruction in Physics and Geography," *The Geographical Teacher*, Vol. 5.

17. Happold, F. C. (1935) *Citizens in the Making*, London: Christophers, p. 67.

18. Ministry of Education (1949) "Citizens Growing Up," Pamphlet No. 16, His Majesty Stationery Office; cited in Williams, *Geography*, pp. 62-63.

19. Royal Geographical Society (1950) "Geography and Social Studies in School," memo prepared by the Education Committee, as cited in Williams, *Geography,* p. 81.

20. Ibid., p. 110.

21. Ibid., p. 81.

22. Ibid., p. 82.

23. Ibid., p. 80-81.

24. Fereday, E. L. (1950) "Social Studies in the Secondary Modern School," *Journal of Education,* November; cited in Williams, *Geography,* p. 66.

25. Ibid., p. 67.

26. Channon, C. (1964). "Social Studies in Secondary School," *Educational Review,* Vol. 17, No. I, cited in Williams, *Geography,* p. 110.

27. Ibid., p. 112.

28. Honeybone, "Balance in Geography;" cited in Williams, *Geography,* p. 89-90.

29. Goodson, I. F. (1981). "Becoming a Subject: Patterns of Evolution and Explanation," *British Journal of Sociology of Education,* Vol. 2, p. 2; idem. (1983) *School Subjects and Curriculum Change: Case Studies in the Social History of Curriculum,* London: Croom Helm.

30. MacKinder, H. J. (1903) "Report of the Discussion on Geographical Education at the British Association Meeting, September. British Association, London, England.

31. Layton, D. (1972), "Science as General Education," *Trends in Education.*

32. Board of Education (1927) "Report of the Consultative Committee: The Education of the Adolescent," *Hadow Report,* His Majesty's Stationery Office.

33. MacKinder, "Teaching of Geography"; cited in Williams, M. *Geography,* pp. 5-6.

34. Ibid.

35. Geographical Association Executive Minutes.

36. Wooldridge, S. W., and G. E. Hutchings (1957) *London Countryside: Geographical Field Work for Students and Teachers of Geography,* London: Methuen, p. xi.

37. Wise, M. J. (1963) "Obituary: Prof. S. W. Wooldridge," *Geography,* Vol. 48, No. 3, p. 330.

38. Fisher, C. A. (1970) "Whither Regional Geography?" *Geography*, Vol. 55, No. 4, p. 374.

39. Ibid., pp. 315-316.

40. Ibid., p. 376.

41. Millward, R. (1969) "Obituary: Patrick Walter Bryan," *Geography*, Vol. 54, No. I, p. 93.

42. Thomas, P. R. (1970) "Education and the New Geography," *Geography*, Vol. 55, No. 4, pp. 274-275.

43. Department of Education and Science (1974) Education Survey 19, *School Geographical Teacher*, Vol. 10, p. 6.

44. Nicholls, A. D. (1973) "Environmental Studies in Schools," *Geography*, Vol. 58, No. 3, p. 197.

45. Interview, December 14, 1976.

46. Ward, C., and A. Fyson (1973). *Streetwork–The Exploding School*, London: Routledge & Kegan Paul, p. 106.

47. Unstead, "Discussions," p. 10.

48. Scarfe, N. V. (1965) "Depth and Breadth in School Geography," *Journal of Geography*, Vol. 24, No. 4, p. 24.

49. Nicholls, "Environmental Studies," p. 200.

50. Thomas, I. (1969) "Rural studies and environmental studies," *Society of Environmental Education Journal*, 2, I, Autumn, p. 12.

51. Wheeler, K. S. (1971) "Review of D. G. Watts' *Environmental Studies*," *Journal of Curriculum Studies*, Vol. 3, No. I, p. 87.

52. Interview, December 14, 1976.

53. Nicholls, "Environmental Studies," p. 200.

54. Geographical Association. Environmental Education Standing Committee (1972) "Environmental Studies," a discussion paper for teachers and lecturers, draft ed., January.

55. Nicholls, "Environmental Studies," pp. 200-201.

56. Ibid., p. 205.

57. Garnett, A. (1969) "Teaching Geography: Some Reflections," *Geography*, Vol. 54, No. 4, p. 389.

58. Ibid.

59. Nicholls, "Environmental Studies," p. 201.

60.   Ibid., p. 206.

61.   Sean Carson Interview, May 7, 1973.

62.   University of London (1975) "GCE A-level Environmental Studies," paper presented to schools Council Working Party on Environmental Education.

63.   Nicholls, "Environmental Studies," p. 206.

Chapter 8

Beyond the Subject Monolith: Traditions and Subcultures

A number of studies have confirmed the central role that subject subcultures and subject specialisms play in the preparation of teachers. In 1970 McLeish's research on college students and lecturers found that "The most remarkable differences in attitude of any in the total sample appear to be between subject specialists."[1] Developing a more differentiated model of "subject subcultures," Lacey noted in 1977 that "the subject sub-culture appears to be a pervasive phenomenon affecting a student-teacher's behaviour in school and university, as well as their choice of friends and their attitudes towards education." This leads on to arguing the case for "considering the process of becoming a teacher as a multi-stranded process in which subject sub-cultures insulate the various strands from another."[2]

While studies of teacher preparation have thereby pointed up the part played by subject specialisms and subcultures, these have often been presented as "undifferentiated epistemological communities sharing knowledge and methodology."[3] This chapter contends that a variety of "traditions" exists within subject subcultures. These traditions initiate the teacher into widely differing visions of knowledge hierarchies and content, teacher role, and overall pedagogic orientation.

To understand subject subcultures as a "pervasive phenomenon" in teacher preparation the major "traditions" within these subcultures need to be identified and studied. We shall see that just as "there are important differences within subject boundaries of the same order as the differences between subjects,"[4] so also are there certain major traditions, which exist with varying degrees of articulation and allegiance, *within* most school subjects. It is these subject traditions that act as the main agency of teacher initiation into subject communities, so that they are the sharp end of the pervasive phenomenon of the subject subculture.

The study of school subject traditions should focus on the intentions and forces that underpin such traditions. Hopefully it will be possible to discern certain patterns underlying subject traditions, and this chapter argues that by studying school subjects and subject cultures in evolution certain historical imperatives can be identified. The forces that lead school subjects to follow broadly similar patterns of evolution are inevitably related to the forces that intrude on each individual teacher's judgment of how his or her career and material interests are pursued during his or her working life. However, the focus of this chapter is on academic subject cultures, so teachers involved in mainly pastoral careers are not considered. Above all, the chapter follows the aspiration voiced in a 1980 paper from Mardle and Walker that viewed the location of classroom processes "as part of a patterned historical framework" as a way of developing links between current micro and macro levels of analysis.[5]

Subject Tradition and Subcultures

School subjects are made up of groups of individual elements with varying identities, values, and interests. One is often reminded of Bucher and Strauss's characterization of professions as "loose amalgamations of segments pursuing different objectives in different manners and more or less delicately held together under a common name at particular periods in history."[6] The study of school subjects in evolution discerns a close relationship between the promotion of certain "traditions" and subcultures and the pursuit of status and resources. Layton's study, *Science for the People*, traces a number of traditions in nineteenth-century science that sought to relate science to people's lives.[7] The book generates a number of hypotheses as to why this version of science was ultimately replaced by a more thoroughly academic version pursued in laboratories and defined in new textbooks and syllabuses. The focal role played by subject associations in this pursuit of more academic status is documented by Hanson with reference to the Society of Art Masters.[8] The society showed great concern for the academic dress and that bestow, or appeared to bestow, high status on other knowledge categories.

Dodd has recently reviewed the history of design and technology in the school curriculum, following earlier work on design education by Eggleston. A major theme in the work is the desire among teachers of the subject for higher status:

> Heavy craft activities have been referred to by a number of different titles as their nature and contribution has changed. Concealed in this ongoing discussion is the matter of 'status' and 'respectability', and although the most recent change from Handicraft to Design and Technology reflects a change of emphasis, there is something of the former argument. 'Practical' describes quite adequately an essential part of the subject, but it is an adjective which is little used because in the terms of the Crowther Report, it is an 'emotionally charged word'. As the subject has developed there have been efforts made to encourage its acceptability by participation in certain kinds of external examinations (which have not always been the best instruments of assessment), the use of syllabuses (often malformed to make them acceptable by other institutions), and by euphemisms like the 'alternative road', but these have failed to hide the underlying low status which practical subjects have by tradition.[9]

Among more general studies of the history of curriculum, Raymond Williams' brief work relating educational philosophies to the social groups holding them is deeply suggestive. He writes:

> an educational curriculum, as we have seen again and again in the past periods, expresses a compromise between an inherited selection of interests and the emphasis of new interests. At varying points in history, even this compromise may be long delayed, and it will often be muddled.[10]

This view of the history of curriculum has been recently extended by Eggleston, who contends that "the fundamental conflicts are over the identity and legitimacy of the rival bute knowledge and the power these confer."[11]

Banks's study, *Parity and Prestige in English Secondary Education*, written in 1955, though even more out of date than Williams' work, is a valuable complement. The same theme relating curriculum to social class emerges. Williams has noted that the academic curriculum was related to the vocations of the upper and professional classes. The curriculum related to the vocations of the majority was slowly introduced, and Banks notes that "as the proportion of children from artisan and lower middle class homes increased, it was necessary to pay more attention to the vocational needs of the pupils, and even to amend the hitherto academic curriculum to admit subjects of vocational nature."[12] But the subjects related to majority vocations were persistently viewed as of low status. Banks quotes a Trades Union Congress (TUC) pamphlet that in 1937 maintained:

> School time used for vocational training not only gives a bias to study but takes up valuable time and effort better employed in a wider and more useful field. Moreover, it stamps at an early and impressionable age the idea of class and inferior status on the scholar, which it is the aim of a noble education to avoid.[13]

Viewed in this way, vocational training is seen not to refer to the pervasive underlying objective of all education as preparation for vocations but to the low-status concern of preparing the majority for their work. The academic curriculum is, and has historically been, in purpose vocational, but the preparation is for the high-status professions. Indeed, Banks's study concludes that "the persistence of the academic tradition is seen as something more fundamental than the influence, sinister or otherwise, of teachers and administrators. It is the vocational qualification of the academic curriculum which enables it to exert such a pressure on all forms of secondary education."[14]

Layton has analyzed the evolution of science in England from the nineteenth century, and we saw on pages 102-103, suggests a tentative model for the evolution of a school subject in the secondary school curriculum. While the conflict between vocational and academic traditions is studied in Williams, Banks, Dodd, and Eggleston, Layton's work points toward a more complex and differentiated model of subject traditions. Layton's first stage clearly shows the "pedagogic" as well as vocational origins of school subjects: not just "utility" but also "relevance to the needs and interests of the learners." The concern with pupil relevance constitutes another tradition, and a continuing one, in the definition of the subject's content. In short, Layton's model warns against any monolithic explanations of school subjects and leads us toward identifying the motivations behind certain traditions and to studying the fate of these traditions as school subjects evolve over time.

Defining Subject Traditions: Academic, Utilitarian, and Pedagogic

The historical study of school subjects defines certain "traditions" that can often be related to the social-class origins and occupational destinations of their pupil clienteles. Hence the curricula of public and grammar schools aimed mainly at the middle and upper classes preparing for professional life were primarily academic; while the elementary schools educating the majority stressed vocational training.

Writing of the traditions in English primary education, Blyth discerned three different trends: the preparatory, the elementary, and the developmental. The preparatory tradition was "almost exclusively related to what we now call grammar school education, which developed in its turn mainly as an upper middle class phenomenon," the elementary tradition "with its characteristic emphasis on the basic skills" was aimed at the lower classes. "For those who were unfortunate, indolent or culpable enough to be poor, the minimum of education was proper and sufficient." The third tradition, the developmental, bases its principles on concern with each child along the lines recommended by Rousseau or Pestalozzi. Broadly speaking, Blyth's three primary traditions can be equated with the three traditions discerned within secondary education: the academic, utilitarian, and pedagogic traditions.[15]

The definition of public- and grammar-school subjects in the nineteenth century, established in the 1904 Regulations and confirmed in the School Certificate Examinations, clearly followed the aims of education as a preparation for professional and academic life. Eggleston, commenting on the early nineteenth century, states:

A new and important feature of the time that was to prevail, was the redefinition of high-status knowledge as that which was not immediately useful in a vocation or occupation. The study of the classics now came to be seen as essentially a training of the mind and the fact that a boy could be spared from work long enough to experience this in full measure was in itself seen as a demonstration not only on the high status of the knowledge itself but also of the recipient—the mark of a 'gentleman' rather than a worker.[16]

Eggleston's last sentence points up the contradiction: it was not so much that classic liberal education was nonvocational but that the vocations were only those fit for upper-class gentlemen. "As educational history shows," Williams reminds us, "the classical linguistic disciplines were primarily vocational but these particular vocations had acquired a separate traditional dignity, which was refused to vocations now of equal human relevance."[17]

For this reason we have avoided the use of the terms "vocational education" or "vocational knowledge." Instead, we refer to the subject-based curriculum confirmed by the examination system as the *academic* tradition, and to low-status practical knowledge as the *utilitarian* tradition. Utilitarian knowledge thus becomes that which is related to those nonprofessional vocations in which most people work for most of their adult life. In addition to the basic skills of numeracy and literacy, this includes commercial and technical education.

Neither commercial nor technical education was ever seriously considered as a new dimension that could be added to the existing classical curriculum. It was specialized training for a particular class of man, and its confinement to low-status areas of the curriculum has remained a constant feature of English curriculum conflict. For example, Layton's research on the development of science education in the nineteenth century has shown how the emphasis was increasingly placed on abstract knowledge with a consequent separation from the practical world of work. Nevertheless, the alternative view of a narrowly utilitarian curriculum is still powerful, as is shown by the constant pressure for utilitarian subjects in spite of their recurrent failure to earn high status. The manpower needs of a changing industrial economy demand that utilitarian training will be consistently advocated by many industrialists. When widespread industrial failure is endemic the continuing ambivalence of educational status systems causes serious concern and pressure for change. The Great Debate was one symptom of this concern, and as was recently argued in *The London Times*:

> Strategies for furthering the inter-relationship between industry and the educational system need to address the complex question of status systems. The established patterns of status represent an enormously powerful historical legacy, a kind of indirect pressure group. Only if high status areas in the educational system such as the public schools and Oxbridge are willing to remodel their value systems do current strategies stand any chance of success.[18]

The low status of utilitarian knowledge is shared by the personal, social, and common sense knowledge stressed by those pursuing a child-centered approach to education. This approach, with its emphasis on the learning process can be characterized as the *pedagogic* tradition within the English curriculum. Child-centered or progressive education does not view the task of education as preparation for the "ladder" to the professions and academia or as an apprenticeship to vocational work but as a way of aiding the child's own "inquiries" or "discoveries," and considers that this is best facilitated by "activity" methods.

The pedagogic tradition normally challenges the existing professional identity of teachers at two levels: (1) as a "specialist" in a school subject, for which the teacher had normally been specifically trained; and (2) as an all-pervading authority figure within the classroom. The Interdisciplinary Enquiry (IDE) workshops run by Goldsmiths College in the 1960s clarify and exemplify the dual nature of the challenge. The workshops were specifically instituted as pilot courses for experienced teachers involved with those school leavers staying on as a result of Raising of the School Leaving Age (ROSLA).

The IDE booklets contained a series of stark messages for teachers of traditional subjects:

> We suggest that the subject based curriculum has fundamental educational disadvantages. The school day is fragmented into subject periods and time allocated to each subject is always regarded as insufficient by the subject specialist, as indeed it is.

Apart from the disadvantages in terms of time

> The arbitrary division of knowledge into subject-syllabuses encourages a didactic form of teaching with the pupil's role reduced to passive assimilation. Any enquiry resulting from a keen interest shown by children in a section of work they are doing in a subject inevitably takes them over the boundaries of the subject into another, perhaps several others. Good teachers would like to encourage this evidence of interest, but they simply cannot afford the time, especially if their syllabus is geared to external examinations.[19]

As a solution to the problems engendered by the didactic teaching of traditional subjects Goldsmiths' team advocated organizing schemes of work around interdisciplinary enquiries.

Another curriculum project aimed at young school leavers underlined both the need to reappraise "subjects" and to clearly define new pedagogic relationships. The Humanities Curriculum Project (HCP) began in 1967 with Lawrence Stenhouse as its director. HCP pursued the pedagogic implications of curriculum reform through the notion of "neutral chairmanship." This meant "that the teacher accepts the need to submit his teaching in controversial areas to the criterion of neutrality . . . i.e. that he regards it as part of his responsibility not to promote his own view," and further that "the mode of enquiry in controversial areas should have discussion, rather than instruction as its core."[20]

The pedagogic tradition has been closely allied to the so-called "progressive" movement in education. As Shipman noted in 1969, the more progressive curricula have come to be concentrated on those sections of the pupil clientele not considered suitable for O- and A-level examinations. In this way the pedagogic tradition has often suffered from the comparatively low status also accorded to the utilitarian tradition.

Examinations and Academic Subjects

The connection between certain subjects taught in school and external examinations was established on the present footing with the birth of the School Certificate in 1917. From this point on the conflict over the curriculum began to resemble the contemporary situation in focussing on the definition and evaluation of examinable knowledge. The School Certificate rapidly became the major concern of grammar schools and because of the subjects thereby examined confirmed that academic subjects would dominate the school timetable.

By 1943 the Norwood Report assessed the importance of examinations in the following manner:

> A certain sameness in the curricula of schools seems to have resulted from the double necessity of finding a place for the many subjects competing for time in the curriculum and the need to teach these subjects in such a way and to such a standard as will ensure success in the School Certificate examination. Under the necessities the curriculum has settled down into an uneasy equilibrium, the demands of specialists and subjects and examinations being nicely adjusted and compensated.[21]

Despite the warnings, the academic subject-centered curriculum was strengthened in the period following the 1944 Education Act. The introduction of the General College Entrance (G.C.E.) in 1951 allowed subjects to be taken separately at O-level (whereas the School Certificate was a 'block' exam in which the main subjects all had to be passed), and the introduction of A level increased subject specialization in a manner guaranteed to preserve if not enhance the largely "academic" nature of the O-level examination. There was little chance that a lower-status examination, such as the Certificate of Secondary Education (CSE), which was introduced in 1965, would endanger the academic subject-centeredness of the higher-status O and A levels.

Indeed, it has proved remarkably adaptive to maintaining the status differentiation noted by Shipman and has even extended it. A recent study by Ball shows four bands within a comprehensive school allocating pupils as follows: Band 1 to subject-based O levels; Band 2 to subject-based CSE Mode 2; Band 3 to integrated or watered-down subjects (e.g., Maths for Living) for CSE Mode 3; and Band 4 to nonexamined "remedial" classes.

The hegemony of the academic subject-based curriculum for O-level candidates was confirmed by the organizational structure of the Schools Council. An early role for the council in the examinations field was advising the Beloe Committee set up to consider the proliferation of examinations in secondary modern schools. Beloe employed the subject-based framework of the Secondary Schools Examination Council, set up in the interwar years to ensure uniformity of examinations, mainly at O and A levels. As Robert Morris, one of the two founding Joint Secretaries, explained: "You can now see why the Schools Council developed a committee structure based on subjects. It was simply logical . . . we just inherited the structure of the Secondary Schools Examination Council who had already developed a pattern for examinations in academic subjects." (Personal communication). The attempts of interest groups to promote new subjects have focused since 1917 on the pursuit of high-status examinations and qualifications. Subjects like art, woodwork and metalwork, technical studies, bookkeeping, typewriting and needlework, domestic science, and physical education have consistently pursued status improvement by arguing for enhanced examinations and qualifications. But as we have seen, few subjects have been able to challenge the hegemony of the academic subjects incorporated in the 1904 Regulations and 1917 School Certificate. This academic tradition has successfully withstood waves of comprehensive reorganization and associated curriculum reform. The upheaval of the Great Debate is a reminder that this survival appears to have been at the expense of certain "dominant interests" in the economy.

Academic Subjects, Status, and Resources

The historical connection between academic subjects and external examinations is only partly explained because of "the need to teach these subjects in such a way and to such a standard as will ensure success in the School Certificate examination."

The years after 1917 saw a range of significant developments in the professionalization of teachers. Increasingly with the establishment of specialized-subject training courses teachers came to see themselves as part of a "subject community." The associated growth of subject associations both derived from and confirmed this trend. This increasing identification of secondary teachers with subject communities tended to separate them from each other, and as schools became larger, departmental forms of organization arose that reinforced the separation. Thus the subject-centered curriculum developed to the point where the Norwood Report in 1943 expressed considerable concern:

> Subjects have tended to become preserves belonging to specialist teachers; barriers have been erected between them, and teachers have felt unqualified or not free to trespass upon the dominions of other teachers. The specific values of each subject have been pressed to the neglect of the values common to several or all. The school course has come to resemble the 'hundred yards' course, each subject following a track marked off from the others by a tape. In the meantime, we feel, the child is apt to be forgotten.[22]

Norwood summarizes the position by saying that "subjects seem to have built themselves vested interests and rights of their own." In explaining the continuing connection between external examinations and academic subjects the part played by the vested interests of the subject groups needs to be analyzed. The dominance of academic subjects within high-status examination credentials would need to be in close harmony with the vested interests of subject groups to explain the strength of this alliance over so long a period.

The "subject" label is important at a number of levels: obviously as a school "examination" category, but also as title for a "degree" or "training course." Perhaps most important of all the subject defines the territory of a "department" within each school. The subject is the major reference point in the work of the contemporary secondary school: the information and knowledge transmitted in schools is formally selected and organized through subjects. The teacher is identified by the pupils and related to them mainly through his or her subject specialism. Given the size of most comprehensive schools a number of teachers are required for each subject and these are normally grouped into subject "departments." The departments have a range of "graded posts" for special responsibilities and for the "head of department." In this way the teacher's subject provides the means whereby his or her salary is decided and career structure defined.

Within school subjects there is a clear hierarchy of status. This is based upon assumptions that certain subjects, the so-called "academic" subjects, are suitable for the "able" students, while other subjects are not. In her study of resource allocation in schools, Eileen Byrne has shown how more resources are given to these able students and hence to the academic subjects:

> Two assumptions which might be questioned have been seen consistently to underlie educational planning and the consequent resource allocation for the more able children. First, that these necessarily need longer in school than non-grammar pupils, and secondly, that they necessarily need more staff, more highly paid staff and more money for equipment and books.[23]

Byrne's research ended in 1965 before widespread comprehensivization, and therefore refers to the tripartite system. However, referring to the now-comprehensive system, she wrote in 1974:

> There is . . . little indication that a majority of councils or chief officers accept in principle the need for review and reassessment of the entire process of the allocation of resources in relation to the planned application, over a period of years, of an approved and progressive policy, or coherent educational development.[24]

Hence it is likely, if Byrne's judgment is correct, that the discrimination in favor of academic subjects for the able pupils continues within the comprehensive school.

That comprehensive schools do place overwhelming emphasis on academic examinations, in spite of the growth of "pastoral systems," has been recently confirmed by Ball's study of Beachside Comprehensive. He notes that "once reorganised as a comprehensive, academic excellence was quickly established as a central tenet of the value system of the school."[25] He provides a range of qualitative and statistical indicators to confirm this contention and concludes that "while the division is less clear-cut and stark than in the grammar school" nonetheless it is evident that "the teacher-resources within the comprehensive school are allocated differently according to the pupil's ability." Thus the most experienced teachers spend most of their time teaching the most able pupils. This is a reflection of the fact that the social and psychological rewards offered by the school to its pupils accrue to those who are academically successful and that academic achievement tended to be the single criterion of "success in the school."[26]

Through the study of Beachside Comprehensive consider-able evidence is assembled to prove Marsden's prediction that "if we give the new comprehensive the task of competing with selective schools for academic qualifications, the result will be remarkably little change in the selective nature of education. Selection will take place within the school and the working-class child's education will still suffer."[27]

The importance of different curriculum traditions for each ability band of pupils is central in confirming these selective patterns. After the first term we learn "the increasing differ-ences of syllabus and curriculum which develop between the bands mean that band 2 or band 3 pupils would have to per-form exceptionally well if not brilliantly to overcome the limi-tations placed upon them by the organisation of the syllabus."[28] Ball notes that the pattern of curriculum differentiation is "not unlike that made in the Norwood Report for fourth and fifth year pupils."[29] At the top of the hierarchy of subjects are the traditional O-level subjects like maths, English, the languages, sciences, history, and geography. These high-status subjects have

> an academic orientation in common; they are concerned with theo-retical knowledge. They are subjects for the brighter, the academic, the band 1 pupil. Below these in status come O-levels in practical subjects like technical studies and metalwork. For band 2 and 3 pu-pils there are traditional CSEs and lowest of all in status new Mode III CSEs.[30]

In a detailed and illuminating study of how the option sys-tem works it is possible to discern how curriculum categories and pupil clienteles (and futures) are "matched" by the teach-ers. Ball shows how this works for two classes—the band 1 class 3CU and the band 2 class 3TA. After the option system has worked the "3TA pupils have been directed away from the 'aca-demic' to the practical, while the reverse has happened for the 3CU pupil."[31] The study shows clearly that working-class pupils concentrate in bands 2 and 3, and further that the "dif-ferentiation of access to high-status knowledge with high ne-gotiable value is crucially related to socio-economic status." He concludes:

Option-allocation is a point at which school careers become firmly differentiated and at which the informal differences between pupils in terms of social reputation and their experiences of the curriculum lower down the school are formalised into separate curricular routes and examination destinations. It is here that the stratified nature of the occupation structure is directly reflected in the ability stratification within the school.

Both the differential status of the knowledge areas in the curriculum and the access to the sixth form that certain courses provide are aspects of the selection of pupils for further and higher education and the occupation market. The selection process and negotiation of meanings that go to make up the option-allocation procedure are part of the structural relationships within the school which label pupils with different statures and educational identities.[32]

But the study of internal process in an individual school can only take us so far. Reflecting the reality of the teacher's view inside the school, such a study takes the differentiated curriculum traditions that play such a central part in pupil differentiation as given. Truly "men make their own history but not in circumstances of their own choosing." The comprehensive school has had to accept the "circumstances" of curriculum traditions derived from the tripartite system and earlier.

A number of studies confirm the status hierarchy of subjects. Warwick reports that a 1968 survey showed that over 7 percent of male teachers who had studied within the languages and literature group (forming just over 19 percent of the total sample) had become headteachers, compared with less than 1 percent of those who had studied in the field of technology and handicraft (who formed just over 11 percent of the total sample). Similarly, among male teachers "former students of languages and literature had apparently four times as many chances as former students of music and drama, and one and a half times the chances of former students of science and mathematics of becoming headmasters."[33]

The hierarchy of subjects is clearly derived from traditional grammar-school preferences. Stevens reports that here

English, Science, Languages and Mathematics are in general the subjects in which success or lack of it is significant for the children. The fact that practical subjects come low on the scale does not in itself support an assumption that more intelligent children are weak, even comparatively, at practical subjects. . . .The figures are rather as indicating the degree of importance with which several people, but chiefly the staff, invest subjects for the children.[34]

School Subjects and Teachers' Interests

Three major subject traditions have been identified: the academic, utilitarian, and pedagogic. The link between external subject examinations for the able student and the flow of status and resources has been clearly demonstrated. Conflicts between separate subject traditions have to be viewed within this context of status and resource allocation.

The aspirational imperative to become an academic subject is fundamental and very powerful and can be summarized as follows: school subjects comprise groups of people with differing interests and intentions. Certain common factors unite these subgroups, most notably that the material self-interest of each subject teacher is closely connected with the status of the subject in terms of its examinable knowledge. Academic subjects provide the teacher with a career structure characterized by better promotion prospects and pay than less academic subjects. Most resources are given to academic subjects that are taught to able students. The conflict over the status of examinable knowledge is above all a battle over the material resources and career prospects available to each subject community or subject teacher.

The definition of a subject as an O- and even more as an A-level examination postulates acceptance of the academic tradition. Even subjects with clear pedagogic or utilitarian origins and intentions such as art, craft (in aspiration design and technology) and rural studies (in aspiration environmental studies/science) have had to present themselves as theoretical academic subjects if A-level status is to be seriously pursued. Of course, once granted, A-level status, alongside acceptance as a university discipline, ensures "establishment." Layton's profile brings out the often contradictory directions in which pupil relevance and teacher and pupil motivation move as against the pursuit of academic status and the consequent definition of subject content by scholarly academics. The fate of subject traditions is clearly exhibited in close linkage with knowledge patterns and classroom pedagogy: the historical imperative in the case of science is clear, but so also are the implications in terms of teacher preparation.

A more recent historical study (Layton's model was devised in 1972) has allowed some of the tentative assertions Layton made from the case of science to be tested for geography, biology, and rural studies.[35] In the case of geography, the subject was initially dominated by utilitarian and pedagogic arguments: "we seek to train future citizens" and the citizen "must have a topographical background if he is to keep order in the mass of information which accumulates in the course of his life."[36] At this point the subject was largely taught by teachers untrained in geography. In 1903 MacKinder outlined a strategy for the improvement of geography: the first demand was that "University Schools of Geography" be established "where geographers can be made."[37] By this time the Geographical Association, which had been formed in 1893, was actively promoting the subject's academic potential, so much so that when the Hadlow Report came out in 1927 it contended that: "The main objective in good geographical teaching is to develop . . . an attitude of mind and mode of thought characteristic of the subject."[38]

By that time the university schools of geography demanded by MacKinder were being established for, as Wooldridge noted, "It has been conceded that if Geography is to be taught in schools it must be learned in the universities."[39] However, not until after 1945, Garnett tells us, were most school departments of geography directed by specialist-trained geographers. As a result of this training, she noted, "most of the initial marked differences and contrasts in subject personality had been blurred or obliterated."[40]

In fact, for several decades university geographers were plagued both by the image of the subject as essentially for school children and by the idiosyncratic interpretations of the various university departments, especially in respect to fieldwork, which encapsulated many pedagogic and utilitarian objectives. Thus, while establishment in universities solved the status of problems of the subject within schools, within the universities themselves the subject's status still remained low. The launching, in the 1960s, of "new geography" with aspirations to full scientific or social scientific rigor is therefore to be largely understood as a strategy for finally establishing geography's status at the highest academic level. New geography stressed the "scientific" and theoretical side of the subject at the expense of "fieldwork" and "regional studies."

The history of biology, from low-status origins in elementary and secondary schools to establishment in universities, is similar to that of geography. The utilitarian and pedagogic elements in biology that so retarded its progress were mainly confirmed by the fieldwork aspects of the subject. Hence, the development of field biology ran counter to the pressures for status escalation. Status through a vision of biology as "hard science" was increasingly pursued in the 1960s through an emphasis on laboratory investigations and mathematical techniques. In 1962 Dowdeswell had conceded the crucial importance of laboratories as status symbols and had directed much of the Nuffield Foundation's money and resources toward their development.[41] The rise of molecular biology with the work of Crick and Watson finally confirmed biology as a laboratory-based hard science. As a result, the subject was rapidly expanded in the universities (themselves expanded apace). With the training of a new generation of biology graduates the subject's incorporation as a high-status O- and A-level school subject was finally assured.

The case of rural studies provides a different pattern of evolution. The origins of the subject were clearly and avowedly utilitarian, and pedagogic arguments for the subject were continuous, but academic arguments were never seriously entertained or deployed. After 1944 the subject was almost exclusively confined to the secondary moderns, and with the growth of comprehensives in the 1960s it was faced with extinction, as schools were reluctant to teach an ex-secondary modern subject with no examination status. As a result the newly formed rural studies subject association began to promote the subject as an "academic discipline." The name was changed to environmental studies, and a protracted battle ensued to have the subject accepted at A level. Unfortunately, although one board did accept the subject at A level, there was never any possibility of a university base, and hence no specialist scholars to define the discipline for broad-based A-level acceptance. Lacking this university base, status passage to academic acceptance has been denied to environmental studies.

While aspiration to academic status has been discerned by Layton for science and confirmed in the case of biology and geography and (unsuccessfully) in the case of rural studies, utilitarian and pedagogic traditions and subgroups owe their existence to radically different visions about the assumptions and intentions that underpin school subjects. Despite the continuing support for these traditions, the flow of resources and attributions of status plainly operate against them and in favor of the academic tradition. The implications of this imperative for the individual teacher's specialization and career pattern are fundamental and wide-ranging, affecting his or her view of the role and associated pedagogic predictions. In the study of the history of geography the author concluded:

> To further their own material self-interests school subject teachers must hand over control of their subject to those who are given the power to define 'disciplines'. Inevitably the subject is now defined by university scholars for their peers and students in line with the pervasive theoretical and scientific vision which characterises our academic institutions . . . whatever the original intentions or content areas of that subject may have been.[42]

In the evolution of the subject and through the promotion of different traditions over time the teacher's role therefore moves (following Layton) from an initial stage as "an untrained specialist" to a final stage where as "a professional" he is trained to teach pupils an examination subject defined by university scholars and examination boards. The stark differences in the teacher's role and associated pedagogy reflect the different visions embodied in the various subject "traditions."

Conclusion

Subcultures, as well as initiating teachers into particular subject traditions, also offer arenas wherein those teachers can redefine and redirect educational patterns. But the direction in which school subjects move toward the culminating academic tradition is a reflection of the patterns of material interest and career aggrandizement that receive support inside the educational system and that crucially influence an individual teacher's assessment of the subcultural tradition that gains his or her allegiance.

The material interest of subject teachers is closely connected with the status of the subject in terms of examinable knowledge. "Academic" subjects provide the teacher with a career structure characterized by better promotion prospects than less academic subjects. More resources are given to those academic subjects that are taught to "able" children.

Hence the historical imperative is toward socialization into and acceptance of the academic tradition within subject subcultures. This tradition predicates fundamental assumptions about teacher role, pedagogic orientation, hierarchies of knowledge, and the fabric of relationships that underpin these. We have noted that Layton sees the academic tradition as the prelude to disenchantment for pupils; likewise Witkin has shown how working-class pupils actively prefer and choose lessons they can relate to the everyday world; and Halsey's recent research shows the radical difference between working-class recruitment to technical schools (utilitarian tradition) and the far lower take-up of grammar schools (academic tradition). Plainly, the historical imperatives that lead teachers into acceptance of the academic tradition will be at the expense of other aspirations encapsulated within pedagogic and utilitarian traditions.

We have noted the recurrence of challenges to the dominance of the academic tradition and to the emergence of "pastoral" careers within schools. At the present time, under the threat of falling rolls, some education authorities are reviewing their fundamental assumptions about curriculum planning. In some areas this has led to a concern for "whole curriculum needs," which leads to planning according to the range of subjects required by all pupils. Were this questioning of assumptions to become more general, it would clearly question the mechanisms that currently maintain the academic/able pupil alliance.

Detailed consideration of subject traditions, together with an appraisal of the benefits and costs of each for the individual teacher, might seem a useful perspective from which to begin teacher preparation. By focusing on these themes teacher trainers could ensure a discussion about teacher roles, pedagogies, and relationships that are closely related to actual choices with which the teacher will be confronted in his or her working life.

Notes

1. McLeish, J. (1970) *Students' Attitudes and College Environments*, Cambridge; quoted in Lacey, C. (1977), *The Socialisation of Teachers*, London: Methuen, p. 64.

2. Lacey, C. (1977) *The Socialisation of Teachers*, London: Methuen, pp. 63-64.

3. Ball, S. J., and C. Lacey (1978) "Subject Disciplines as the Opportunity for Group Action: A Measured Critique of Subject Sub-cultures," paper presented at the SSRC Conference, Teacher and Pupil Strategies, St Hilda's College, University of Oxford, Oxford.

4. Ibid.

5. Mardle, G., and M. Walker, (1980) Introduction to book on Teacher Preparation, mimeo.

6. Bucher, R., and A. Strauss (1976) "Professions in Process." In M. Hammersley and P. Woods (eds.) *The Process of Schooling: A Sociological Reader*, London: Routledge & Kegan Paul, p. 19.

7. Layton, D. (1973) *Science for the People*, London: Allen & Unwin.

8. Hanson, D. (1971) "The Development of a Professional Association of Art Teachers," *Studies in Design Education*, Vol. 3

9. Dodd, T. (1978) *Design and Technology in the School Curriculum*, London: Hodder and Stoughton.

10. Williams, R. (1961) *The Long Revolution*, London: Penguin, p. 172.

11. Eggleston, J. (1977) *The Sociology of the School Curriculum*, London: Routledge & Kegan Paul.

12. Banks, O. (1955) *Parity and Prestige in English Secondary Education*, London: Routledge & Kegan Paul, p. 5.

13. (1937) *Education and Democracy*, London: Trade Union Congress.

14. Banks, *Parity and Prestige*, p. 248.

15 Blyth, W. A. L. (1965) *English Primary Education: A Sociological Description*, Vol. 2, London: Routledge & Kegan Paul, pp. 21, 30, 124-125.

16 Eggleston, *School Curriculum*, p. 25.

17 Williams, *The Long Revolution*, p. 163.

18. Goodson, I. F. (1978) "Why Britain Needs to Change Its Image of the Educated Man," *The London Times*, February 14.

19. University of London, Goldsmiths College (1965) "The Raising of the School Leaving Age: Second Pilot Course for Experienced Teachers," Autumn Term.

20. The Humanities Project: An Introduction (1972) London: Heinemann, p. 1.

21. *Curriculum and Examinations in Secondary Schools* (The Norwood Report) (1943) London: His Majesty's Stationery Office, p. 61.

22. Ibid.

23. Byrne, E. M. (1974) *Planning and Educational Inequality*, Slough, England: National Foundation for Educational Research, pp. 29.

24. Ibid.

25. Ball, S. J. (1981) *Beachside Comprehensive*, Cambridge, England: Cambridge University Press, p. 18.

26. Ibid.

27. Ibid., p. 21.

28. Ibid., pp. 35-36.

29. Ibid., p. 138.

30. Ibid., p. 140.

31. Ibid., p. 143.

32. Ibid., pp. 152-153.

33. Warwick, D. (1976) "Ideologies, Integration and Conflicts of Meaning." In M. Flude and J. Ahier (eds.) *Educability, Schools and Ideology*, London: Croom Helm, p. 101.

34. Stevens, F. (1972) *The Living Tradition: The Social and Educational Assumptions of the Grammar School*, 3d ed., London: Hutchinson, pp. 117-118.

35. Goodson, I. F. (1982) *School Subjects and Curriculum Change: Case Studies in Curriculum History*, London: Croom Helm.

36. Council of the Geographical Association (1919) "The Position of Geography," *The Geographical Teacher*, Vol. 10.

37. MacKinder, H. J. (1903) "Report of the British Association Meeting, September 1903," *The Geographical Teacher*, Vol. 2, pp. 95-101.

38. Board of Education (1927) "Report of the Cpmsultative Committee: The Edication of the Adolescents,"*Hadlow Report*, London, His Majesty's Stationery Office.

39. Quoted in Wooldridge, D. T. (1973) "Against Geography." In J. Bale et al., *Perspectives in Geographical Education*, Edinburgh: Oluf and Boyd, pp. 12-13.

40. Garnett, A. (1969) "Teaching Geography: Some Reflections," *Geography*, Vol. 54, p. 368.

41. Dowdeswell, W. H., as Director of the Nuffield Biology Project.

42. Goodson, I. F. (1981) "Defining and Defending the Subject," paper presented at St Hilda's College, University of Oxford, Oxford.

Chapter 9

Distinction and Destiny: The Importance of Curriculum Form in Elite American Private Schools

Ivor F. Goodson,
Peter W. Cookson, Jr. and
Caroline H. Persell

In 1971 Basil Bernstein pointed to the *principles* for the classification and framing of curriculum. Significantly, however, he
emphasized the relationships between subject *content*. It is instructive that this concern with subject content is continued in
Shulman's recent work on the knowledge base required for
teaching. In Shulman's leading section on scholarship in the
"disciplines" one learns that "the first source of the knowledge base is content."[1] The issue of relationships *within* subject matter has remained unexplored and untheorized.

Goodson has previously developed and elaborated the concept of curriculum form as it applies to the evolution of curriculum in Great Britain. Goodson found that the "higher order" mentalities were judged to be intellectual, abstract, and
active. The "lower order" mentalities were found to be sensual, concrete, and passive.[2] In time, these polarized mentalities were built into the deep structures of curriculum—they
were, so to speak, internalized. In this way the process of mentality "production" was extended because school subjects became the makers of subjectivities. A self-confirming circle was
drawn around different social groupings. Given the resonance

with patterns of cultural capital, this was to prove a resilient settlement. At the time that these constellations of mentalities were emerging, a system of state schooling began to develop. The patterns of mentalities became institutionalized into a system of separate schools for students from the dominant classes and for students from the subordinate classes. The mental/manual division of labor was institutionalized in a division of curriculum. State schools favored and promoted an academic curriculum that elevated the head over the hands and, in effect, institutionalized curricula that favored students whose education was intellectual, abstract, and classical. Thus, a pattern of prioritizing certain social groups was replaced by an ostensively neutral process of prioritizing certain curriculum forms.

Though the name was changed the game was much the same. Not surprisingly, similar social groups continued to benefit and, likewise, other social groups as before, were disadvantaged. The internalization of differentiation, however, effectively masks the social process of preferment and privilege. The focus on conflicts within curriculum responds to this internalization of social differentiation. In short, to fully understand the process that is schooling, we must look *inside* the curriculum. It is critical to look inside curricula if we are to identify the relationship between the social division of labor and the social division of knowledge. To our way of thinking, curriculum knowledge is not a "given," but is a result of the social struggle embedded in the unequal distribution of wealth and power. Curricula can be usefully seen as an ideological justification of class relations. Moreover, curricula can be conceptualized in a narrow sense (i.e., classroom knowledge) or in a broad sense (i.e., the sum total of a student's exposure to a school's ideology).

In this study we adopt a definition of curriculum that is inclusive. The founders of the elite schools never believed that they should define curriculum merely in general terms of academic subjects; they were quite similar to Catholic educators who believed that an effective curriculum included character training, ideological indoctrination, and strict discipline. In this sense, curriculum is a universal experience rather than a discreet knowledge base. This definition of curriculum includes ends and means and is "total" in the sense that it aims at a definable outcome: a graduate who embodies the values of the organization. What is outside the curriculum is essentially the student culture which, in some ways, mirrors the popular culture with its glorification of pleasure, instant gratification, and celebrity. The total elite school curriculum is consciously thought of by teachers and administrators as an intervention to protect young people from their inclinations to participate in the larger popular culture. Naturally, this is a struggle that must be fought and refought on a daily basis, hence, the need for deep structural regulation of the students' inner and outer lives.

In this chapter we employ some of the initial insights first developed through analyzing British data to the curriculum form of academically and socially elite American private schools. We analyze the curricula of elite American private schools in the broad sense because we are convinced that the curricula of these schools shape the social consciousness of their graduates and reinforce the belief that the classical curriculum represents "the very best in Western Civilization" and by ideological extension, therefore, the very best civilization. The curricula of elite private schools express the social division of labor and mask class dominance by promoting classical knowledge as above social conflict and historically inevitable. Moreover, we maintain that the classical curriculum of academically and socially elite private schools serves as an intellectual model to some public school educators and, as a consequence, the social relations embedded in the curriculum of private schools suffuse the curricula of public-sector schools. As a consequence public school students come to accept the social division of knowledge as a matter of course rather than as a matter of social contest. Apple has written, "one does not take for granted that curricular knowledge is neutral. Instead, one looks for social interests embodied in the knowledge form itself."[3]

We are convinced that curriculum forms are related to institutional charters and, thus, have a significant impact on the social distribution of life opportunities. This is because the social influence of elite private schools is far greater than the number of these schools would indicate. While less than one percent of American high school students attend these schools, the graduates of these schools can be found in positions of cultural, political, and economic authority. Possession of an elite private school diploma credentializes class position and opens status doors. Useem found that thirteen elite boarding schools educated 10 percent of the members of the board of directors of large American business organizations.[4] Several U.S. presidents and scores of federal cabinet officers have been graduates of elite private schools. Private school graduates are also among the most active creators and consumers of culture, especially "high" culture.[5] A former Director of Development at one elite school indicated, "There is no door in this entire country that cannot be opened by a Choate graduate. I can go anywhere in this country and anywhere there is a man I want to see . . . I can find a Choate man to open that door for me."[6]

Not all American private schools are equally socially or academically elite. There is a high degree of stratification among the elite schools; in this chapter we define the world of elite schools in much the same way Baltzell did.[7] He indicated that there is a core group of eastern Protestant schools that "set the pace and bore the brunt of criticism received by private schools for their so-called 'snobbish,' 'un-democratic,' and even 'un-American values'."[8] The sixteen schools that Baltzell identifies as socially elite are Phillips (Andover) Academy, Phillips Exeter Academy, St. Paul's School, St. Mark's School, Groton School, St. George's School, Kent School, The Taft School, The Hotchkiss School, Choate Rosemary Hall, Middlesex School, Deerfield Academy, The Lawrenceville School, The Hill School, The Episcopal High School, and Woodberry Forest School. These schools represent the most elite of the 289 leading secondary boarding schools.[9] The key difference between the schools mentioned by Baltzell and other schools is that the former are more socially elite than the latter. Some of the most socially selective schools have student bodies where 40 percent of the students' parents are social registerites.[10]

Of course, it is not that these schools alone "produce" these results, but rather the complex interplay of family and school together that reinforce the powerful role of certain families and social classes. Most research about these schools has focused on the social status of the schools' student bodies and the linkages that these schools make with selective colleges and through these colleges to high status employers and high status social networks.[11] While some scholars have examined the curricula of these schools,[12] there has been relatively little study about how the curricula of these schools have internalized the division of labor. The classical curriculum signals to the larger society that its possessors are qualified for positions of leadership within society. In effect, the social interests internalized within the classical curriculum justify the social division of knowledge and legitimize the social division of labor in dominant and subordinate classes. The implication of this argument is that curricula are always political and that to the reform American education in a deep sense will require a curriculum form that legitimizes those very mentalities that are held in contempt by those who have been intellectually socialized by the classical curriculum.

We argue in this chapter that the socialization effects sought by the schools' teachers and administrative staff are achieved by immersing students in a curriculum that is subtle, but persuasively ideological, and by an institutional structure that requires students to live the schools' ideological imperative. There is considerable evidence that the elite-school experience shapes the individual's perceptions and connects them to similarly minded others throughout the life cycle.[13] An elite-school education provides its graduates with more than an educational credential, it provides a way of life, friendships throughout the adult life cycle, and a world view that is deeply internalized.

The data for this chapter are drawn primarily from research conducted in American boarding schools in the 1980s.[14] Fifty-five schools were visited. Researchers observed classes, assemblies, chapel services, sports contests, cultural events, discipline committee meetings, and student and faculty parties. Schools heads, teachers, directors of admission, college advisors, deans of students, deans of faculty, dorm supervisors, school psychologists, doctors, and students were interviewed. Schools gave the researchers a full complement of their printed materials, including catalogues, curricular listings, school newspapers, alumni magazines, application forms, and brochures. At twenty of the schools anonymous questionnaires were administered to 2475 freshman and senior students, exploring their family backgrounds, views about the academic climates of their schools, what they liked best and least about boarding school, why they came, whether they thought it had changed them and how, and what their educational, occupational, and life goals were.

The Super Elaborated Code

Borrowing from the British, early American headmasters and teachers advocated an elite private school curriculum that was classical, conservative, and disciplined. In Bernstein's vernacular, we might speak of the classical curriculum as a super elaborated code.[15] In Bernstein's words, a code is a "regulative principle, tacitly acquired which selects and integrates: (a) relevant meanings, (b) forms of their realization, and (c) evoking context."[16] In his work Bernstein distinguished between elaborated and restricted codes. He hypothesized that there are four aspects to consider when distinguishing these two codes: orientations, location, distribution, and performance. It should be clear, from even a cursory reading of Bernstein's work, that the classical curriculum is the apotheosis of the elaborated code. He writes: "The more complex the social division of labour, the less specific and local the relation between an agent and its material base, the more indirect the relation between meanings and a specific material base, and the greater the probability of an elaborated coding orientation."[17] In short, in societies with a complex class system, elites are likely to develop linguistic and cultural modalities that are abstract, defuse, and seemingly detached from the material base. High culture is not only ideological, it is also something of a mystification. Thus, the social consequence of the classical curriculum is to symbolically invest those who have access to it with a social status that transcends the material base upon which domination rests.

For a long time, a classical education was the only path to admission to universities such as Harvard that required candidates to demonstrate proficiency in Latin and Greek.[18] The disciplined and trained mind is still the major objective of the boarding school curriculum.

The Groton curriculum is predicated on the belief that certain qualities of mind are of major importance: precise and articulate communication; the ability to compute accurately and to reason quantita-
tively; a grasp of scientific approaches to problem solving; an
understanding of the cultural, social, scientific, and political background of western civilization; and the ability to reason carefully and
logically and to think imaginatively and sensitively.[19]

The preceding sentence provides ample demonstration of
what is meant by the super elaborated code. It is complex, sophisticated, self-assured, and imperial in its suppositions about
the nature of knowledge and who possesses it. The not so subtle
message of this code is that knowledge is power.

But one might ask if the super elaborated code is the exclusive possession of elite-school pedagogues and students. Are
not the elite schools simply good high schools, as their headmasters sometimes claim? How different are the curriculum
forms of the elite schools and college-preparatory public
schools? While it is clear that there is some overlap between
public and private schools that serve the same or very similar
class constituencies, we are convinced that the mentalities internalized within the super elaborated code differ significantly
from those found in the elaborated code (à la Bernstein) that
is internalized within the public school college- preparatory
curriculum. There are differences in degree between the elaborated and the super elaborated code, but there are also differences in kind. Briefly, the super elaborated code internalizes
and legitimates key assumptions about culture (an upper-class
possession), property (the basis of social power), and distinction (the key signaling device). The super elaborated code does
not emphasize meritorious achievement, but rather an historical record of the triumph of the dominant classes. Public school
students may read many of the same books as private school
students, but the context of their understanding concerning
the cultural significance of these books in quite different.

The elite-school student is treated as a recipient of class culture, but also the legitimate heir and possible creator of further expressions of class culture. Instructional techniques uti-
lized in the transmission of the super elaborated code do not
focus on the retention of facts, but on initiating the novitiate
into a cultural canon that is the social property of the upper

class. Attending an elite school does not certify students' knowledge, but their class position. The nominal egalitarianism required of American educational rhetoric can disguise the hierarchical and class-based division of educational labor that is expressed in the differentiated educational tracks between schools and within schools.

Diploma requirements at boarding schools usually include four years of English, three years of math, three years in one foreign language, two years of history or social science, two years of laboratory science, and one year of art. Many schools require a year of philosophy or religion and may also have such diploma requirements as four years of physical education, a library skills course, introduction to computers, and a seminar on human sexuality. Compared to public school curricula, elite private school curricula are extremely enriched. A course on the presidency at one school includes the following readings: Rossiter, *The American Presidency;* Hofstadter, *The American Political Tradition*; Hargrove, *Presidential Leadership*; Schlesinger, *A Thousand Days*; Kearns, *Lyndon Johnson and the American Dream*; and White, *Breach of Faith.* Social science courses require a great deal of reading. In a course called, "An Introduction to Human Behavior," students are assigned eleven texts, including works from B. F. Skinner, Sigmund Freud, Erich Fromm, Jean Piaget, and Rollo May.

Students are given many homework assignments and their work is graded regularly. Teachers know each student individually and are held accountable for student progress. There are few frills in a private school classroom. On the assumption that one learns through hard work and repetition, private school teachers employ a form of autonomous visual pedagogy that is seldom seen in the public sector. Private school teachers expect that their students will achieve at a high level. Unlike the soft pedagogy or the market-dependent visible pedagogy found at many public schools, the pedagogy at most private schools is "hard." That is, students are routinely expected to stand and deliver. It is the student's responsibility to study and to learn significant elements of the classical curriculum. Very often, students are expected to recite in class and there is the expectation that students will participate in class discussions on a regular basis. It is not uncommon for private school teachers or masters to refer to students by their last names only. There is little grade inflation within the elite schools, especially when compared to the public sector.

Private school students are expected to do an hour of homework per subject per night. Seventy-three percent of public high school students report doing five hours or less of homework per week, compared to 82 percent of elite private school students, who report doing ten or more hours of homework per week. Twenty-six percent of the students at private schools claim to spend more than twenty hours a week on their homework. Many of these students enroll in advanced placement courses and few, if any, watch television while they are in school. Students report that their academic experience helps them to have their "mind stretched." Other comments include: "It taught me to think," "It taught me to think critically and independently," "It has convinced me of the importance of broad knowledge and a clear mind," and "I have become a more effective speaker." It is not surprising, then, that the academic climates of the elite schools are extremely high compared to most public schools.[20] Not only are the curricula of elite private schools demanding, they are supplemented by a wide range of extracurricular activities, which include public service experiences, illustrious outside speakers, and the opportunity to engage in independent studies.

The catalogue of clubs at private schools is nearly endless. There are clubs for chess, cooking, sailing, woodworking, debate, music, drama, travel, and horseback riding. One elite boys' school has a "war games" club. Private school students are more apt than public school students to be involved in extracurricular activities; one in three private school students is involved in student government, compared to one in five public school students, and two in five are involved in the school newspaper or the yearbook, compared to one in five in public school. Sports are the most important private school extracurricular activity. Virtually every private school student must do athletics. A typical coed or boys' school will offer football, soccer, cross-country, water polo, ice hockey, swimming, squash, basketball, wrestling, winter track, gymnastics, tennis, golf, baseball, track, and lacrosse. Learning to compete is an important part of the elite rite of passage. Pep rallies are common, as are assemblies when athletics awards are given. Private schools make an effort to bring public personalities to their campuses; often these speakers are private school alumni. In the Groton School's main hallway hangs a letter from a president of the United States to the headmaster, reminding the students that Groton "boasts a former President of the United States and some of America's finest statesmen."

Elite private school educators place a great deal of importance on moral education.[21] Character development is an important aspect of acquiring the super elaborated code. It may be difficult to think of character development as class based or ideologically grounded, but the ethics that are taught within a private school environment play a major role in shaping a world view where power and righteousness are intertwined and inseparable:

> You are important to Lawrenceville, for you help to set the tone of the school, help to establish its character, help to make it a good place to be—or its opposite. Therefore, it is important that you meet your responsibilities, be considerate of others, face up to challenges, discipline yourself, and grow intellectually and socially.[22]

As this quote makes clear, the purpose of the classical curriculum is not only to create a literate mind, but to transform the student through a moral career. Elite private school students, in effect, undergo a rite of passage in which they become assimilated into attitudes and behaviors that prepare them for their future statuses. Of course, moral development is a complicated process, and because many elite private schools are total institutions, students are subjected to a great deal of authority. Students and teachers describe their lives as like "living in a fishbowl," where everything they do is visible to others.

Processes of Internalization

As mentioned earlier, curriculum can be viewed in a narrow or a broad sense. Generally speaking, the curriculum at elite private schools is meant to be transformative; that is, it is the hope of the school's staff that the curriculum will mold students into "ladies and gentlemen." It is for this reason that many private schools are residential. Lambert, who spent years studying the effect of British public school life on students, wrote this about life in the elite total institutions:

> The key to the public school ethos is that its end and means are one. Its values are embodied in a total social system; divesting its pupils of many of the roles and attributes they possess in the larger society, school provides them with its own structure, role patterns, relationships, style and norms. It is in living out its subtle, complete and all-inclusive way of life that the values are so effectively and permanently imbibed.[23]

Behavior modification in the elite private school generally takes three forms: through discipline schools try to enforce certain types of outward behavior; through the manipulation of ritual and symbol schools try to instill certain collective loyalties; and by what might be called "deep structure" regulation they try to control students' emotional and somatic needs. Discipline at an elite private school is thought of as a consistent form of socialization. The pendulum of justice at these schools balances between the rights of individuals and the larger community. Justice is also defined in terms of its primary objectives—retribution and redemption. Most schools have developed an elaborate legal system that includes faculty and student discipline committees, elaborate rules about behavior, and a system of appeals. Elite schools, however, are not content to socialize their students through discipline alone. They rely instead on an elaborate system of symbols and rituals that is meant to convince students that upper-class life and hegemity are rooted in timeless values. Thus, the chapel plays a large role in the curriculum of elite private schools because the chapel is the locus where the power relations that structure the curriculum are sanctified. According to Wakeford the religious rituals in private schools, "though based on moral egalitarianism, serve to emphasize, or to identify, hierarchical levels in the school."[24] One way they do this is by specifying who sits where, according to their social rank.

Hierarchy is the underlining concept that gives cohesiveness to the classical curriculum. Students at elite schools are exposed to multiple hierarchies, which are only graspable through total immersion. These multiple hierarchies include economic, social, cultural, academic, aesthetic, moral, dress, and sports hierarchies. Each of these hierarchies has underlying codes that novitiates need to understand. What students wear, the language that they use, and their sense of being special all contribute to a belief in their personal distinctiveness and their class destiny. Concern with cultural identity and distinction is evident in borrowings from the English public schools. These legacies include terminology such as "forms" instead of "grades," headmaster instead of principal, and in such English sports as fives (similar to handball for two or four players) and crew (rowing). The Anglophilia that is pervasive at the most elite private schools is an attempt to increase the value of the cultural capital students acquire. Curriculum is a medium for the self in a hierarchy of power. One of the tasks of young members of the upper class is to socially construct a self that is equal to, or superior to, anyone, including the president of the United States. The primary modality for internalizing hierarchical social relations is through deep structure regulation. To control an individual's body is to have great power over him and her. Schools attempt to reach inside students' psyches by regulating their eating habits and sex lives. Social domination starts with the repression of self, and where better to learn the tactics of self-denial than in a total ideological environment. Elite schools pay close attention not only to what students eat but how they eat. So-called "private food" smuggled into the schools by the students is often confiscated. Moreover, the schools with varying degrees of success, attempt to regulate students' sex lives. The prevailing norm seems to be that sex is an off hours activity done in privacy, with little or no "public display of affection" or PDA. Compared to most public high school campuses most elite school campuses seem almost asexual. As in so much of private school life it is not so much what you do, but with whom you do it.

The nonformal curriculum of elite private schools often reflects a continual tension between the official culture and value of the schools and the unofficial peer culture of the students. Many students feel they need a clique to help them deal with the efforts of the school to control their behavior. They learn to cover for their friends and to keep silent with the authorities. Students and alumni tell of helping their best friends through an unwanted pregnancy, family breakup, or attempted suicide. In some ways, they become each other's parents in their homes away from home. This crucible can either break or make a young person's character. Some private school students become depressed, withdrawn, or suicidal. Many turn to alcohol and drugs. One student wrote that their education "has created a deep cynical streak which will carry me into the darker side of life." Students who survive the pressure of this crucible often come out feeling they are entitled to privilege because they are, indeed, superior. As one student phrased it, "Boarding school has made me quite arrogant. I cannot reasonably believe that I am not better than most people."

Managing Modernity

When and where do changes enter into the classical curriculum? How adaptive is the super elaborated code? Private schools operate in a market environment. They compete with each other for the children of the "right" families. The organizational field of the elite school is complex; the schools must enroll the right students, maintain alumni loyalty, and gain favorable treatment by prestigious colleges. Observable changes in curriculum (and structure such as coeducation) tend to come from one or more of these relevant constituencies. Three examples of curricular change include computers, the arts, and internationalism. In the early 1980s private schools began to invest in computers on the assumption that for students to compete educationally and economically, they would have to be computer literate. Early acquisition of new knowledge can be described as "primitive accumulation of cultural capital."[25] One of the key intellectual resources of the present and future is the computer, a tool that allows users to create new knowledge and control existing knowledge. As Scheck notes, "Those individuals who obtain a greater understanding and an ability to use computers will have . . . the power to control information and through such control, the power to control the lives of others."[26] Goodson and Mangan found that the drive to include computers in schools in Ontario was dominated by an ideological belief in technical innovation that had little to do with broad-based pedagogic change. In short, the continuity of class position implies a willingness of class members and their agents to adapt to innovation as part of their strategy of social reproduction.[27] The classical curriculum is not ossified in its content but in its adherence to a particular patterning of curriculum form.

In the last twenty years many elite schools have instituted arts programs that are extensive and professional. Many schools have built large music and art studios and theaters. The rise of the arts in private schools is not incidental to the belief that the upper class are the guardians and promoters of high culture. Knowledge of the arts has become a necessary form of symbolic signaling, as it indicates an awareness of what constitutes high culture. Corporations have also become supporters of and investors in the arts; the contemporary manager must appreciate the social value of art. Finally, many elite schools have become more conscious of internationalism, in part because more and more of their students are coming from foreign countries and in part because most large corporations are now multinational. Private school graduates must develop a cosmopolitan view of economics and politics, if they are to compete with their peers from other countries.

Bourdieu has argued that continuity of class position implies the willingness of class members and their agents to adapt to innovation as part of their strategy of reproduction. Curriculum innovations in elite schools are best seen in this light.[28] Viewed from the outside the introduction of computers, the arts, and internationalism into the classical curriculum might appear to indicate that the schools are embracing alternate forms of knowledge and modes of understanding the world. Previously, Persell and Cookson discussed how the introduction of computers into the boarding school curriculum did little to alter the internal social assumptions of the curriculum.[29] Innovation is essentially a gloss for the sake of modernity without altering the fundamental curricular allegiance to abstract and traditional knowledge.

Goodson and Mangan concluded that in Canada ". . . . this innovation was as much a fundamental symbolic and ideological action, geared to mold the image of schools as functional components of the 'Information Age,' as it was an attempt to improve pedagogy."[30] In effect, computers are not instruments that transcend curriculum forms, but are symbolic instruments that are introduced in a disembodied and somewhat decontextualized manner into the curriculum. This type of innovation in no way challenges the stratification of mentalities as represented in the hierarchy of curriculum forms. In effect, one can introduce innovations into the classical curriculum that appear technical, or even egalitarian, without in any way diffusing the super elaborated code in its abstractness and imperial suppositions. The apparent blurring of the classical curriculum by the introduction of innovation only serves to emphasize that the class relations inherent in differentiated curriculum forms may take a variety of disguises, but the reality is as unalterable as class relations.

Conclusions and Implications

We have seen that the classical curriculum of American private schools is an apt example of a socially constructed set of beliefs that internalize and legitimize power relations within society. By this example, it seems reasonable to argue that the social division of labor and the social division of knowledge fall along the same social class lines; thus reinforcing each other and thereby creating a consistent and cohesive world view. Students who are exposed to this curriculum feel themselves socially distinctive and share with their social-class peers a sense of social destiny. Of course, adolescents learn these lessons imperfectly and many of their beliefs about the social world come from cultural experiences outside the classical curriculum. Undoubtedly, one of the justifications for creating total institutions for the young of the upper class was the knowledge that without strong reinforcement any curriculum will have little impact on young minds. Boarding school graduates, in particular, are saturated with an ideology of social hierarchy.

In one sense, this study represents only the beginning of what ought to be a larger study of the American elementary- and secondary-school systems. There are those who would argue that the elite private school is so isolated from the currents of public education that the classical curriculum has little impact on American education in general. We have argued that the classical curriculum sets the tone for the academic curricula for nearly all American public schools, and thus influences the perceptions of students who may not even know about the existence of the elite private schools. There are also those who have argued that schools are socially powerful, not because of their internal relations but because of their external connections.[31] This dichotomy may significantly oversimplify how education acts as a signifier of status. A school's external relations are shaped in part by its curriculum. Whether students master or are simply acquainted with the classical curriculum is less important than the fact that they have been "baptized" as true believers in Western civilization. In short, the internal relations embedded in curriculum play a significant role in shaping a school's external relations.

Further research might profitably explore the curriculum of public-sector schools to identify whether or not these schools' curricula internalize the social division of labor as has been hypothesized in this research. Curriculum form provides us with an analytic tool for examining the social interests that are internalized within the knowledge form itself. The examination of curriculum forms across the social spectrum of schooling may well reveal a consistent pattern whereby the social division of labor and the social division of knowledge correspond.

Notes

1. Shulman, L. (1987) "Knowledge and Teaching Foundations of the New Reform," *Harvard Educational Review*, Vol. 57, No. 1, p. 8.

2. Goodson, I.F. (1992) "On Curriculum Form: Notes Toward a Theory of Curriculum," *Sociology of Education*, Vol. 65, No. 1, pp. 66-75.

3. Apple, M. (1979) *Ideology and Curriculum*. Boston: Routledge & Kegan Paul, p. 17.

4. Useem, M. (1984) *The Inner Circle: Large Corporations and the Rise of Political Activity in the U.S. and U.K.*, New York: Oxford University Press, pp. 67-68.

5. Baltzell, E. D. (1958). *Philadelphia Gentlemen-The Making of a National Upper Class*, Chicago: Quadrangle Books; idem. (1964) *The Protestant Establishment*, New York: Random House; Domhoff, G.W. (1967) *Who Rules America?*, Englewood Cliffs, N.J.: Prentice Hall; idem. (1967) *The Higher Circles*, New York: Sage; Cookson, P. W., Jr., and C. H. Persell (1985) *Preparing for Power: America's Elite Boarding Schools*. New York: Basic Books.

6. Prescott, P. S. (1970) *A World of Our Own: Notes on Life and Learning in a Boys' Preparatory School*, New York: Coward-McCann, p. 67.

7. Baltzell, *Philadelphia Gentlemen*.

8. Baltzell, *Philadelphia Gentlemen*, pp. 307-308.

9. Persell, C. H., and P. W. Cookson, Jr. (1985) "Chartering and Bartering: Elite Education and Social Reproduction," *Social Problems*, Vol. 33, No. 2, pp. 114-129.

10. Ibid.

11. Cookson and Persell, *Preparing for Power*; Zweigenhaft, R. L., and G. W. Domhoff (1991) *Blacks in the White Establishment? A Study of Race and Class in America*, New Haven, Conn.: Yale University Press.

12. Levine, S. B. (1980) "The Rise of American Boarding Schools and the Development of a National Upper Class," *Social Problems*, Vol. 28, pp. 63-94; Cookson and Persell, *Preparing for Power*.

13. Cookson and Persell, *Preparing for Power*; Domhoff, *Who Rules America?*; Domhoff, *The Higher Circles*; Baltzell, *The Protestant Establishment*; Useem, *The Inner Circle*.

14. Cookson and Persell, *Preparing for Power*.

15. Cookson, P. W., Jr., and C. H. Persell (1995) "Knowledge for Power's Sake: Bernstein's Theoretical Contributions to the Study of Elite Education." In A. R. Sadovnik (ed.) *Knowledge and Pedagogy-The Sociology of Basil Bernstein*, Norwood, N.J.: Ablex, pp. 283-293.

16. Bernstein, B. (1990) *Class, Codes and Control*; Vol. 4: *The Structuring of Pedagogic Discourse*, London: Routledge & Kegan Paul, p. 14.

17. Ibid. p. 20.

18. Levine, S. B. (1980) "The Rise of American Boarding Schools and the Development of a National Upper Class," *Social Problems*, Vol. 28, pp. 63-94.

19. Groton School (1981-1982) *Groton School Bulletin*, Groton, Mass., p. 15.

20. Cookson, P. W., Jr. (1981) "Private Secondary Boarding School and Public Suburban High School Graduation: An Analysis of College Attendance Plans," Ph.D. Dissertation, New York University, New York.

21. Cookson, P. W., Jr. (1982) "Boarding Schools and the Moral Community," *Journal of Educational Thought*, Vol. 16, pp. 89-97; Cookson and Persell, *Preparing for Power*.

22. *The Lawrenceville Experience* (1982-1983) *Lawrenceville School Bulletin*, Lawrenceville, N.J., p. 8.

23. Lambert, R. (1977) "The Public School Ethos." In M. MacDonald (ed.) *The Education of Elites*, Milton Keynes, England: Open University Press, p. 67.

24. Wakeford, J. (1969) *The Cloistered Elite*, New York: Praeger, p. 124.

25. Bourdieu, P., and J. C. Passeron (1977) *Reproduction: In Education, Society and Culture*. Beverly Hills, Calif.: Sage, p. 187.

26. Scheck, D. C. (1985) "Promoting Computing Literacy in the Schools: Some Humanistic Implications," *Humanity and Society*, Vol. 9, p. 284.

27. Goodson, I. F. and M. Mangan (1992) "Computers in Schools as Symbolic and Ideological Action: The Genealogy of the ICON," *The Curriculum Journal*, Vol. 3, No. 3, pp. 261-276.

28. Bourdieu and Passeron, *Reproduction*.

29. Persell, C. H., and P. W. Cookson, Jr. (1987) "Microcomputers and Elite Boarding Schools: Educational Innovation and Social Reproduction," *Sociology of Education*. Vol. 60, No. 2, pp. 123-134.

30. Goodson and Mangan, "Computers in Schools," p. 12.

31. Meyer, J. (1977) "The Charter: Conditions of Diffuse Socialization in School." In W. R. Scott (ed.) *Social Processes and Social Structure*, New York: Holt, Rinehart & Winston.

Chapter 10

On Curriculum Form:
Notes Toward a Theory of Curriculum

Sociologists of education who are interested in the school curriculum have long faced a paradox. The curriculum is avowedly and manifestly a social construction. Why, then, is this central social construct treated as a timeless given in so many studies of schooling? In particular, why have social scientists, who traditionally have been more attuned than most to the ideological and political struggles that underpin social life, largely accepted the "givenness" of the school curriculum? As the curriculum wars rage in American higher education over the choice of "canon," it seems to be a good time to begin again to theorize the school curriculum.

In many Western countries, the school "curriculum" is back on the political agenda. In the United States, following the Holmes Group and the Carnegie Task Force and such publications as the author's article "Nations at Risk," it is clearly in evidence; in Britain, the givenness of curriculum is being literally enshrined by parliamentary legislation in the form of a "national curriculum"; in Australia, the provinces are "mapping" their curricula to discern commonalities, some scholars would argue, as a precursor to defining more "national" curricular guidelines.

In these circumstances, it is important to review the state of sociological knowledge with regard to the curriculum, for our knowledge of the school curriculum remains severely undertheorized. Much of the work in this domain has been carried out by sociologists of knowledge, but pioneering work in this area remains partial and flawed if we are concerned with developing our theoretical understanding of curriculum. As Apple conceded, a good deal of the significant work in this field has been conducted in Europe: Emile Durkheim's and Karl Mannheim's early work remains important, as does that of the late Raymond Williams and, in the 1960s and 1970s, the work of Pierre Bourdieu and of Basil Bernstein. In the work of Williams, most of the theoretical focus was on the *content* of the curriculum.[1] Meanwhile, Bernstein pointed to underlying principles for the classification and framing of curriculum, but emphasized the relationship *between* subject content.[2] It is interesting that the obsession with subject content is continued in Shulman's work on the knowledge base required for teaching. In Shulman's leading section on "scholarship in content disciplines," one learns that "the first source of the knowledge base is *content.*"[3]

The issue of relationships *within* subject matter has remained unexplored and untheorized. In this chapter, the question of the internal relations of curriculum—the *form* of curriculum— is analyzed: As Apple said, "for methodological reasons one does not take for granted that curricular knowledge is neutral. Instead, one looks for social interests embodied in the knowledge form itself."[4] The social conflict within the subject is central to understanding the subject itself (and hence relations among subjects). Because subject is not a monolithic entity, analyses that view subjects and relations among subjects in this manner mystify a central and ongoing social conflict. On this analysis an understanding of the internal relations of curriculum would be an important precursor to the kind of work that Bernstein has exemplified on the external relations and modalities of curriculum.

A less theoretical justification for analyses of curriculum form is the pervasiveness of what Connell called the "competitive academic curriculum." This form of curriculum sets the agenda and the discourse for schooling in many countries. The results are fairly generalizable:

> To say it is hegemonic is not to say it is the only curriculum in those schools. It is to say that this pattern has pride of place in those schools; it dominates most people's ideas of what real learning is about. Its logic has the most powerful influence on the organisation of the school and of the education system generally; and it is also to marginal or subordinate the other curricula that are present: Above all 'the com-

petitive academic curriculum makes the sorting and the hardening of hearts a central reality of contemporary school life'.[5]

Yet the continuing dominance of the competitive academic curriculum is the result of a continuing contest within school subjects.

Conceptions of "Mentalities"

By way of exemplifying a broader conception for studying school subjects, I will examine the emergence of certain conceptions of "mentalities," since they provide antecedent assumptions for our contemporary social construction of school knowledge. In doing so, I am building on the work of others and am not following a consistent line of development. Therefore, I may be justifiably accused of raiding history, of dipping into periods without full knowledge or portrayal of the complexity of context. But my objective is not so much to provide a sustained historical explanation as to show how antecedent factors could be a factor in contemporary construction and consciousness. The aim is to show how we may pursue a longer time perspective on current events and how in doing so we may provide a reconceptualization of the mode of curriculum study that will allow us to connect specific acts of social construction to wider social impulses.

The notion of "mentality" owes a good deal to the work of the Annales school of historians. Following them, I take the view that in studying historical periods, it is important to generate insights into the worldviews held by distinct cultural and subcultural groups. In this sense, mentality is related to the microconcept of "habitus," as developed by Bourdieu and Passeron[6] or "resistance" as a distinctive view held by British working-class "lads" in the work of Willis.[7]

In his work on Australian school reform, which derives from the Annales school, Pitman argued that "with a given civilization, there are multiple cultures related to location, class, occupation, gender and any other relevant criterion":

> The dialectic relationships of the various groups with their material worlds and with each other permit the development of world views, or mentalities (mentalities) within these groups which are distinct from each other. For example, in the division of labor and the class ex-

change of labor to organizers of labor and owners of the means of production, then the participants in the asymmetrical exchanges interact differently with their material worlds, at least in relation to the nature of work.[8]

Shapin and Barnes examined a selection of educational writings on pedagogy in Britain in the period 1770-1850. In examining the "rhetoric" of pedagogy, they found "remarkable agreement upon the mentality of the subjects of those programmes." Different mentalities were ascribed, depending on whether the persons in question came from "the higher orders" or "the lower ranks."[9]

Three Dichotomies

Three central dichotomies were discerned. The first places the *sensual* and *concrete* character of the thought of the lower orders against the *intellectual, verbal,* and *abstract* qualities of upper-class thoughts. The second places the *simplicity* of the lower-orders' thought against the *complexity* and *sophistication* of their betters'.

In *Wealth of Nations*, Adam Smith provided the crucial link between the division of labor and the division of mentalities (and, of course, curriculum). In patterns of exploitation and domination, this is the crucial rationalization to enshrine. Thus, Smith stated:

> In the progress of the division of labour the employment of the far greater part of those who live by labour, comes to be confined to a few very simple operations; frequently to one or two. But the understandings of the greater part of men are necessarily formed by their ordinary employments. The man whose whole life is spent in performing a few simple operations, of which the effects too are, perhaps, always the same or very nearly the same, has no occasion to exert his understanding or to exercise his invention . . . He naturally . . . becomes as stupid and ignorant as it is possible for a human creature to become.[10]

For the elite, Smith was similarly strident: "The employments, too, in which people of some rank or fortune spend their lives, are not, like those of the common people, simple or uniform. They are almost all of them extremely complicated, and such as exercise the head more than the hands."[11]

The third central dichotomy concerns the *passive* response of the lower orders to experience and knowledge compared with the *active* response of the upper ranks. This spectrum of passivity to activity is perhaps the most crucial part of the conundrum of mentalities when related to the evolution of school knowledge. Hence

> the sensually-based, superficial and simple thoughts of the lower orders did not allow them to produce mediated responses to experience, or to make deep connections between different pieces of information, such as would permit them to be generalised for use as resources in a wide range of contexts.[12]

From these early stages, the link between the lower orders and specific, contextualized knowledge was forged. This need for immediate contextualized knowledge provided the diagnosis "which justified the characterization of their learning process as passive and mechanical".[13] Knowledge was presented and accepted in such a way that connections were not made between specific and contextualized facts; the lower orders did not act upon knowledge or generalize from data. A devil's bargain emerged: The lower orders were taught specific, contextualized "facts" mechanically, but the capacity to generalize across contexts was not provided or encouraged. Decontextualized knowledge was for others, then; for the lower orders, it became an alien and untouchable form of knowledge. In due course, it, too, ensured passivity.

In contrast, the upper orders could incorporate their perceptions, intuitions, information, and knowledge into coherent systems of thought and inference.

> By so doing, they could, on the one hand, extend their range of applicability, and, on the other, bring a range of abstract principles and symbolic operations to bear upon them. Thus, they could, unlike the lower orders, make *active use* of knowledge and experience. Whatever it was, it served to extend the possibilities of their thought. [Hence] in society, as in the body, the head was reflective, manipulative and controlling; the hand, unreflective, mechanical, determined by instructions.[14]

Therefore, Shapin and Barnes judged that "as one moved up into the higher ranks of society, one increasingly encountered more abstract, refined and complex modes of thought, and more extensive, finely structured and profound bodies of 'knowledge'." But alongside this definition of knowledge was the requirement that knowledge should be "properly distributed," not "improperly graded" or taught "out of place." Thus

> properly distributed, it could operate as a symbolic display of social standing, enabling the various orders better to recognise the hierarchy and sectors to which deference was due. And it might also serve as a medium enabling communication between the top and the base of society, a vehicle through which head could control hand. Incorrectly distributed, knowledge could stimulate the masses to aspire upwards and give them the resources to use in doing so. Although, perhaps, their natural inferiority would doom these aspirations to ultimate failure, the temporary turbulence would be troublesome and inconvenient.[15]

The two distinct mentalities defined for the upper and lower orders were essentially cultural resources employed in a whole range of debates and discourses:

> They are a tribute to man's skill and endless creativity in the construction of rationalizations and adaption of cultural resources to the exigencies of concrete situations. And it is as situated responses to particular polemical requirements and not necessarily as the coherent philosophies of individuals that we must treat these individuals.[16]

In the process of favoring the "head more than the hands," new patterns of differentiation and examination were emerging in English secondary schooling in the mid-nineteenth century. By the 1850s, schooling was developing links with universities through the founding of the first examination boards. Here was a structural response to the privileges of the higher orders and their allied abstract knowledge of the head. The universities, of course, were for "fine minds" and developed curricula to "train the mind." They were unequivocally for the "head more than the hands"; indeed, "training the mind" was their exclusive preserve.

The links with the social order were then clear and were often explicitly stated as the university examination boards were constructed. For instance, the University of Cambridge Local Examination Syndicate was founded in 1858: "The establishment of these examinations was the universities' response to petitions that they should help in the development of 'schools for the middle classes'."[17] Also at this time, the feature of curriculum mentioned earlier, the power to differentiate, was being institutionalized. The birth of secondary *examinations* and the institutionalization of curricular *differentiation* were then almost exactly contemporaneous. For instance, the Taunton Report in 1868 classified secondary schooling into three grades, depending on the time spent at school. The report stated:

> The difference in time assigned makes some difference in the very nature of education itself; if a boy cannot remain at school beyond the age of 14 it is useless to begin teaching him such subjects as required a longer time for their proper study; if he can continue till 18 or 19, it may be expedient to postpone some studies that would otherwise be commenced earlier.[18]

The report noted that "these instructions correspond roughly but by no means exactly to the gradations of society." (This statement could, as will be shown, be equally well applied to the Norwood Report nearly a century later.) In 1868 schooling until age 18 or 19 was for the sons of men with considerable incomes independent of their own exertions, or professional men, and men in business whose profits put them on the same level. These students were taught a mainly classical curriculum. The second grade (up to age 16) was for the sons of the "mercantile classes." The curriculum for these students was less classical in orientation and had a certain practical orientation. The third grade (until age 14) was for the sons of "the smaller tenant farmer, the small tradesmen [and] the superior artisans." The curriculum of these students was based on the three Rs, but taught up to a fairly high level. These gradations cover secondary schooling. Meanwhile, most working-class students received only an elementary-school education and were taught rudimentary skills in the three Rs.

In the post-Taunton period, as the university examination boards came into being, a hierarchy of social orders and associated curricula were, in effect, being established and linked to a system and structure of schooling. At the top, schools were for "training the mind" and they developed links at the level of examinations, and at times future destinations, with the universities and with their classical curriculum. As one descended the levels of schooling, one found that the curriculum became progressively more rudimentary, was taught mechanically, and had a practical "orientation."

The Contest over Science

In the decades that followed, there were, of course, challenges to this "political settlement" on levels of curriculum that corresponded so well to the gradations of society. Most notable was the battle over the inclusion of science. The perceived social danger of science, particularly applied science, was partly that education could be related to the cultural experience of the lower orders. There was knowledge that could be contextualized—not abstract, not classical, not quintessentially decontextualized but the opposite—knowledge whose relevance and interest might be secured for the lower orders. For the masses, a possible educational medium was at hand. Here, then, was a litmus test of the interestedness or disinterestness of school knowledge. In the early nineteenth century, opinions on science had been clear. Thus, a "country gentleman" judged in 1825 that "if the working classes are to be taught the sciences, what are the middle and higher classes to learn, to preserve the due proportion? The answer is obvious enough. There is nothing they can be taught by which they can maintain their superiority."[19] In his early work, Mannheim thought science to be "disinterested knowledge," but science as school knowledge was plainly another matter, much more a case of "interested knowledge."

The problems raised by the "country gentleman" grew in the period following 1825, for some successful experiments were under way to teach science to the working classes in the elementary schools. For instance, the Reverend Richard Dawes opened a National Society School in King's Somborne in England in 1842. Here he proceeded to teach science as applied to "the understanding of common things." In short, he taught contextualized science, but with a view toward developing the academic understanding of his pupils from the lower orders. Scientific knowledge, then, was contextualized within the culture and experience of the common people's children, but taught in a way that could open the door to understanding and the exercise of thought. This was schooling as education—and, what is more, for the laboring poor. But the curriculum was limited to elementary schools with predominantly working-class students. There is a clear evidence in contemporary governmental reports that the science of common things allowed considerable practical success in classrooms. One would be wrong, however, to assume therefore that the problem was solved and that the science of common things provided the basis for the definition of school science. Far from it. Other definitions of school science were being advocated by powerful interests. Lord Wrottesley chaired a parliamentary committee of the British Association for the Advancement of Science on the most appropriate type of science education for the upper classes. Hodson argued that the report

> reflected a growing awareness of a serious problem: that science education at the elementary level was proving highly successful, particularly as far as the development of thinking skills was concerned, and the social hierarchy was under threat because there was not corresponding development for the higher orders.[20]

Wrottesley gave an example that confirmed his worst fears:

> a poor boy hobbled forth to give a reply; he was lame and humpbacked, and his wan emaciated face told only too clearly the tale of poverty and its consequences . . . but he gave forthwith so lucid and intelligent a reply to the question put to him that there arose a feeling of admiration for the child's talents combined with a sense of shame that more information should be found in some of the lowest of our lower classes on matters of general interest than in those far above them in the world by station.
>
> It would be an unwholesome and vicious state of society in which those who are comparatively unblessed with nature's gifts should be generally superior in intellectual attainments to those above them in station. [21]

Soon after Wrottesley's comments in 1860, science was removed from the elementary curriculum. When it eventually reappeared in the curriculum of the elementary schools some 20 years later, it was in a different form from the science of common things. A watered-down version of pure laboratory science had become accepted as the *correct* view of science, a view that has persisted, largely unchallenged, to the present day. Science, as a school subject, was powerfully redefined to become similar in form to so much else in the secondary curriculum—pure, abstract, a body of knowledge enshrined in syllabuses and textbooks.[22]

The fundamental insight is that even with a subject that is conceived of as a challenge to the traditional academic curriculum, incorporation can take place. Hence, science, which was thought of as practical and pedagogical, ended up as "pure laboratory science."

Continuities and Complexities

The early nineteenth-century pattern of differing "mentalities" and differing curricula that Shapin and Barnes noted has had considerable durability. Of course, the continuities that can be discerned must be fully related to the complexity of each historical period. In this sense, I am only pointing to an agenda for future historical work.

The apparent continuities are sufficiently clear, however, as to warrant substantial further historical study. For instance, almost a century later, the Norwood Report advocated the notion of different mentalities and of different curricula and, indeed, of different schools to serve these mentalities. This report led, in Britain, to the 1944 Education Act, which may be seen as institutionalizing a social and political order for schooling, built on a hierarchy of mentalities.

The Norwood Report argued that throughout Europe, "the evolution of education" had "thrown up certain groups, each of which can and must be treated in a way appropriate to itself." In England three clear groups could be discerned. First,

> the pupil who is interested in learning for its own sake, who can grasp an argument or follow a piece of connected reasoning, who is interested in causes, whether on the level of human volition or in the material world, who cares to know how things came to be as well as how they are, who is sensitive to language as expression of thought, to a proof as a precise demonstration, to a series of experiments justifying a principle; he is interested in the relatedness of related things, in development, in structure, in a coherent body of knowledge.[23]

These pupils form the continuing clientele of the traditional subject-based curriculum, for as the Norwood Report stated, "such pupils, educated by the curriculum commonly associated with the Grammar School, have entered the learned professions or have taken up higher administrative or business posts."[24] Second, the needs of the intermediate category, the pupil whose interests and abilities lay markedly in the field of applied science or applied art, were to be fulfilled by the technical schools. Third, the report stated, with a partial view of educational history: "There has of late years been recognition, expressed in the framing of curricula and otherwise of still another grouping of occupations." This third group was to provide the clientele for the new secondary modern schools.

> The pupil in this group deals more easily with concrete things than with ideas. He may have much ability, but it will be in the realm of facts. He is interested in things as they are; he finds little attraction in the past or in the slow disentanglement of causes or movements. His mind must turn its knowledge or its curiosity to immediate test; and his test is essentially practical.[25]

This curriculum, although ruling out certain occupational futures, certainly facilitated those who were destined for manual work. It "would not be to prepare for a particular job or profession and its treatment would make a direct appeal to interests, which it would awaken by practical touch with affairs."[26]

The Norwood Report summarizes the patterns of curricular differentiation that had emerged through "the evolution of education" over the past century or so. The close alliance between patterns of curricular differentiation and social structure was often conceded (as in the Taunton Report in 1868): Different curricula are explicitly linked to different occupational categories. The academic tradition was for the grammar school pupil, who was destined for the learned professions and higher administrative or business posts. The more utilitarian curriculum in the technical schools was for the pupil who was destined to work in "applied science or applied art." For the future manual worker in the secondary modern school, the emphasis was on utilitarian and pedagogical curricula; these studies were to "make a direct appeal to interests which it would awaken by practical touch with affairs."[27] The close identity between different curricular traditions, occupational destinations (and social classes), and educational sectors was confirmed in the 1944 Education Act, which organized schools into grammar schools for the academic pupils, technical schools for the "applied" pupils, and secondary modern schools for the "practical" pupils.

The 1944 act therefore produced an organizational pattern that was in close resonance with social configurations that were in the tradition established by the Taunton Report. However, in 1945 the election of a socialist Labour government initiated a period in which the entrenched and explicit class-based educational organization came under substantial attack. In Britain the battle for the common school was fought late—a symptom of the entrenched class structure of the country. The comprehensive school was thus "won" only in 1965. The 1965 circular had sought to "eliminate separatism in secondary education."[28] But a close reading of the circular implies that the major concern, perhaps understandably at the time, was with eliminating separatism in the form of different types of schools and buildings.

Indeed, there were clear indications that far from expecting a new synthesis of curricula, the main concern in 1965 was to defend and extend the grammar school education that had been confined mainly to the professional and middle classes. The House of Commons motion that led to Circular 10/65 was fairly specific:

> This House, conscious of the need to raise educational standards at all levels, and regretting that the realization of this objective is impeded by the separation of children into different types of secondary schools, notes with approval the efforts of local authorities to reorganize secondary education on comprehensive lines which will preserve all that is valuable in grammar school education for those children who now receive it and make it available to more children.[29]

What was unclear and unspoken was whether the logic of providing a comprehensive education for all in the common school would also extend to providing a common curriculum.

Yet if it seems that the comprehensive school had thereby been achieved, a more systematic historical analysis of internal curricular patterns tells another story. In a sense, the move to the common school represents a change only in the geometrical axis of differentiation. Thus, in Table 1 differentiation from 1944 is vertical, being based on separate school sectors.

Table 1. Tripartite Schooling:
Educational System after 1944 Act

Grammar School	Technical School	Secondary Modern
Academic: route to universities	Technical knowledge	Practical/manual

Comprehensive schooling limited all these separate types of schooling "under one roof." The class-based recruitment to the three types of school was thereby challenged by the fact that every child had the same "equal" opportunity to attend the same, comprehensive school (notwithstanding those "children of rich" parents who continued to go to private schools). But the results of this reform were less substantial when internal patterns were established, for *inside* the comprehensive school the old tripartite system was reestablished with a pattern of horizontal differentiation: that is, academic subjects, technical subjects, manual/practical subjects.

In many cases the last two categories effectively merged: the crucial distinction was between academic and nonacademic subjects. Pupils were clearly categorized along these lines as "academic" and "nonacademic." Close studies of the reform of schooling from tripartite to comprehensive affords an opportunity for scholars of curricular history to reconceptualize curricular reform. Reform therefore provides a "matrix of possibility" when the conflict over whether to redefine or simply renegotiate differentiation takes place (see Figure 1 p. 194).

In this matrix a range of possible combinations of curricula can be discerned. For instance, Option A in Figure 1 represents a situation that prevailed for a long time in Britain, in which the elite alone received schooling of an academic nature. Combining A with B provides recontextualized academic schooling for the higher orders and contextualized practical training for the lower orders—in effect, a hierarchical and stratified "caste curriculum."

Attempts to reform curricula can be top-down (A to C) or bottom-up (B to D). In the top-down model, academic decontextualized knowledge is distilled and made available to a wider audience (many of the curricular reforms in the 1960s

Figure 1. Curriculum Form

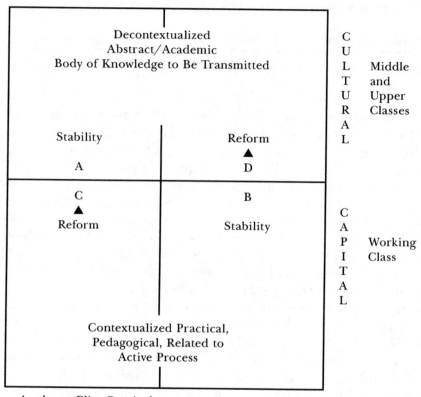

A—alone	Elite Curriculum.
A + B	Caste Curriculum. Hierarchical, Stratified
A → C	Top-down Reform. Exversion
B → D	Bottom-up Reform. Inversion

The material interests of teachers—their pay, promotion, and conditions—are intimately interlinked with the fate of their specialist subjects. In schools, school subjects are organized in departments. The subject teacher's career is pursued within such a department and the department's status depends on the subject's status. The "academic" subject is placed at the top of the hierarchy of subjects because the resources are allocated on the basis of assumptions that such subjects are best suited for the "able" students (and vice versa, of course), who, it is further assumed, should receive favorable treatment.

Thus, in secondary schools, the material and self-interest of subject teachers is interlinked with the status of the subjects, judged in terms of their examination status. Academic subjects provide the teacher with a career structure that is characterized by better prospects for promotion and pay than are less academic subjects.

The pattern of finances and resources that emerged in the period 1904-1917 proved durable and has only recently been subject to substantial challenge. As a result, a common process of promoting and developing school subjects began to emerge in response to the "rules of the game," defined in this manner for those who pursue financing, resources, and status.[32]

Conclusion

This chapter has noted that a polarized pattern of mentalities emerged in Britain in the period 1770-1850. For the "higher order," mentalities were judged to be intellectual, abstract, and active, whereas for the "lower orders," they were considered sensual, concrete, and passive. In time, these polarized mentalities were built into the deep structures of curriculum—they were, so to speak, internalized. In this way, the process of mentality "production" was extended, for school subjects themselves became, in turn, the makers of subjectivities. A self-confirming circle was drawn around different social groupings. Given the resonance with patterns of cultural capital, this structuring of curriculum form was to prove a resilient settlement.

At the time that these constellations of mentalities, curriculum, and cultural capital began to form, a state schooling system was emerging. In time, therefore, these patterns were institutionalized—initially into a system of separate schools for distinct mentalities and curricula. Later, as common schooling was "developed" (or "conceded," depending on your location), the pattern of distinct mentalities and curricula remained a mechanism of differentiation *within* what was ostensibly unified and common. It is as if the mental/manual "division of labor" is institutionalized in a "division of curriculum." Certainly with regard to the current policy associated with the new British "national curriculum," the emerging patterns of traditionalism, demarcated from new vocationalism, seem set to continue and strengthen this division.[33]

In the historical period considered here, the deliberate structuration of a state schooling in which the head rather than the hands was preferred can be clearly discerned. The academic form of curriculum was systematically favored by the structure of resources and finances. Hence, a pattern of prioritizing certain social groups was replaced by an ostensibly neutral process of prioritizing certain forms of curricula. But though the name changed, the game was much the same. It is not surprising, therefore, that similar social groups continued to benefit and, likewise, that other social groups, as before, were disadvantaged. But the internalization of differentiation effectively masked this social process of preferment and privilege.

Thus, the focus on conflicts *within* the curriculum responds to this internalization of social differentiation. In short, to understand fully the process that is schooling, one must look *inside* the curriculum. Part of the complex conundrum of schooling is to be understood by capturing the internal process of stability and change in the curriculum.

Notes

1. Apple, M. (1979) *Ideology and Curriculum*, Boston: Routledge & Kegan Paul.

2. Bernstein, B. (1971) "On the Classification and Framing of Educational Knowledge." In M. F. D. Young (ed.) *Knowledge and Control: New Directions for the Sociology of Education*, London: Collier-Macmillan, pp. 47-69.

3. Shulman, L. (1987) "Knowledge and Teaching Foundations of the New Reform," *Harvard Educational Review*, Vol. 57, No. 1, pp. 1-22.

4. Apple, *Ideology and Curriculum*, p. 17.

5. Connell, R.W. (1985) *Teachers Work*. London: Allen & Unwin, p. 87.

6. Bourdieu, P., and J. C. Passeron (1977) *Reproduction in Education, Society and Culture*, Beverly Hills, Calif.: Sage.

7. Willis, P. (1977) *Learning to Labour*, Westmead, England: Saxon House.

8. Pitman, A. J. (1986) *A Study of School Reform from the Perspective of the Annales School of French Historiography: Restructuring Victorian Schooling*, unpublished doctoral dissertation, University of Wisconsin-Madison, p. 60.

9. Shapin, S., and S. Barnes (1976) "Head and Hand: Rhetorical Resources in British Pedagogical Writing, 1770-1850," *Oxford Review of Education*, p. 231.

10. Quoted in Shapin and Barnes, "Head and Hand," p. 231.

11. Quoted in Shapin and Barnes, "Head and Hand," p. 234.

12. Smith, quoted in Shapin and Barnes, "Head and Hand," p. 234.

13. Ibid.

14. Quoted in Shapin and Barnes, "Head and Hand," p. 235.

15. Shapin and Barnes, "Head and Hand," p. 236.

16. Ibid., p. 237.

17. University of Cambridge Local Examinations Syndicate. (1958) *One Hundredth Annual Report to University*, Cambridge, England: Cambridge University Press.

18. *Report of the Royal Commission on School Inquiry* (The Taunton Report) (1868), London, p. 587.

19. Shapin and Barnes, "Head and Hand," p. 239.

20. Hodson, D. (1987) "Science Curriculum Change in Victorian England: A Case Study of the Science of Common Things." In I. F. Goodson (ed.) *International Perspectives in Curriculum History*, London: Croom Helm, p. 166.

21. Quoted in Hodson, "Science Curriculum," p. 167.

22. See Goodson, I.F. (1988) *The Making of Curriculum: Collected Essays*, London, New York, and Philadelphia: Falmer Press.

23. *Curriculum and Examinations in Secondary Schools* (The Norwood Report) (1943) London: His Majesty's Stationery Office.

24. Ibid.

25. Ibid., p. 4.

26. Ibid.

27. Ibid.

28. Department of Education and Science [D.E.S.] (1965) *Organisation of Secondary Education* (Circular 10/65), London: Her Majesty's Stationery Office, p. 1.

29. Ibid.

30. University of Cambridge Local Examinations Syndicate, *One Hundredth Annual Report*, p. 1.

31. Byrne, E. M. (1974) *Planning and Educational Inequality*, Slough, England: National Foundation for Educational Research, p. 29.

32. For a detailed analysis, see Goodson, I. F. (1987) *School Subjects and Curriculum Change*, London, New York, and Philadelphia: Falmer Press; idem. (1988) *The Making of Curriculum: Collected Essays*, London, New York, and Philadelphia: Falmer Press.

33. See Bates, I. (1989) "Versions of Vocationalism: An Analysis of Some Social and Political Influences on Curriculum Policy and Practice," *British Journal of Sociology of Education*, Vol. 10, pp. 215-231.

Publications by the Author
(1987–1997)

School Subjects and Curriculum Change, (Extended and Revised Edition), London, New York, and Philadelphia: Falmer Press, 1987.

International Perspectives in Curriculum History, London, Sydney, and Dover, N.H.: Croom Helm, 1987.

"Introduction." In I. F. Goodson (ed.) *International Perspectives in Curriculum History*, London, Sydney, and Wolfeboro, N.H.: Croom Helm, 1987, pp. 1–16.

"On Understanding Curriculum: The Alienation of Curriculum Theory." *Curriculum Perspectives*, Vol. 7, No. 2, 1987, pp. 41–47.

"Tomkins' *Common Countenance*: A Review." *History of Education*, Vol. 17, 1987.

The Making of Curriculum: Collected Essays, London, New York, and Philadelphia: Falmer Press, 1988.

International Perspectives in Curriculum History, London and New York: Routledge, 1988.

"Three Curricular Traditions and Their Implications." In R. Dale, R. Fergusson, and A. Robinson (eds.) *Frameworks for Teaching*, London: Hodder and Stoughton, 1988. pp. 217–219.

"Beyond the Subject Monolith." In A. Westoby (ed.) *Culture and Power in Educational Organizations*, Milton Keynes and Philadelphia: Open University Press, pp. 181–197.

"Putting Life into Educational Research." In R. Webb and R. Sherman (eds.) *Qualitative Studies in Education*, London, New York, and Philadelphia: Falmer Press, 1988, pp. 110–122.

With S. J. Ball (eds.). *Teachers Lives and Careers*, London, New York, and Philadelphia: Falmer Press, and Open University Set Book Edition, 1989.

With G. Milburn and R. J. Clark (eds.). *Reinterpreting Curriculum Research: Images and Arguments*, London, New York, and Philadelphia: Falmer Press, and London, Ontario: Althouse Press, 1989.

With S. J. Ball. "Understanding Teachers: Concepts and Contexts." In S. J. Ball and I. F. Goodson (eds.) *Teachers Lives and Careers*, London, New York, and Philadelphia: Falmer Press, and Open University Set Book Edition, 1989.

With I. Dowbiggin. "Docile Bodies: Commonalities in the History of Psychiatry and Schooling." *Qualitative Studies in Education*, Vol. 2, No. 3, 1989, pp. 203–220.

"Curriculum Reform and Curriculum Theory: A case of Historical Amnesia." *Cambridge Journal of Education*, Vol. 19, No. 2, 1989, pp. 131–141.

"Understanding/Undermining Hierarchy and Hegemony." Critical introduction to A. Hargreaves, *Curriculum and Assessment Reform*, Milton Keynes and Philadelphia: Open University Press, 1989, pp. 1–14.

With J. M. Mangan and V. A. Rhea (eds.). *Research Strategy for Computers in Education*, Interim Report #1 from the project Curriculum and Context in the Use of Computers for Classroom Learning. London, Ontario: Faculty of Education, University of Western Ontario, 1989.

With J. M. Mangan and V. A. Rhea (eds.). *Emergent Themes in Classroom Computing*, Interim Report #2 from the project Curriculum and Context in the Use of Computers for Classroom Learning. London, Ontario: Faculty of Education, University of Western Ontario, 1989.

With P. Medway (eds.). *Bringing English to Order*, London, New York, and Philadelphia: Falmer Press, 1990, pp. 272.

With P. Medway. "Introduction." In I. F. Goodson and P. Medway (eds.) *Bringing English to Order*, London, New York, and Philadelphia: Falmer Press, 1990, pp. vii–xv.

"Zur Sozialgeschichte der Schulfacher." *Bildung und Erziehung*, 1990, pp. 379–389.

"Nations at Risk." *Journal of Education Policy, Politics of Education Association Yearbook*, 1990, pp. 219–232.

"Studying Curriculum: Towards a Social Constructionist Prospective." *Journal of Curriculum Studies*, Vol. 22, No. 4, 1990, pp. 299–312.

"Subjects for Study: Research Agenda." *Journal of Curriculum and Supervision*, Vol. 5, No. 3, 1990, pp. 260–268.

"Laronplansforskning: Mot ett socialt konstruktivistiskt perspektiv." *Forskning om utbildning*, 1990, Vol. 1, pp. 4–18.

With Ian Dowbiggin. "Curriculum History: Professionalization and the Social Organization of Knowledge." *Curriculum and Teaching*, Vol. 5, Nos. 1 and 2, 1990, pp. 3–13.

"A Social History of Subjects." *Scandinavian Journal of Educational Research*, Vol. 34, No. 2, 1990, pp. 111–121.

"Social History of School Subjects." Section in *International Encyclopedia of Education*, Suppl. Vol. 2, New York: Pergamon Press, 1990, pp. 543–547.

"National Curriculum: Ideology and Identity," In *Studies in Education*, Chap. 7, London, New York, and Philadelphia: Falmer Press, 1990.

"Why Study School Subjects?" In H. Haft and S. Hopmann (eds.) *Case Studies in Curriculum Administration History*, London, New York, and Philadelphia: Falmer Press, 1990, pp. 81–90.

With I. Dowbiggin. "Commonalities in the History of School Subjects in Psychiatry." In S J. Ball (ed.) *Foucault and Education*, London: Routledge & Kegan Paul, 1990, pp. 105–192.

"Teachers' Lives." In J. Allen and J. Goetz (eds.) *Qualitative Research in Education*, 1990, Atlanta, Ga.: University of Georgia, pp. 150–160.

With C. Fliesser and A. Cole. "Induction of Community College Instructors." From the Interim Report of the project Studying Teacher Development, London, Ontario: Faculty of Education, University of Western Ontario, 1990, pp. 50–56.

With J. M. Mangan, and V. A. Rhea (eds.). *Illuminative Evaluation of Classroom Computing*, Interim Report #3 from the project Curriculum and Context in the Use of Computers for Classroom Learning. London, Ontario: Faculty of Education, University of Western Ontario, 1990.

With J. M. Mangan and V. A. Rhea (eds.). *Teacher Development and Computer Use in Schools*, Interim Report #4 from the project Curriculum and Context in the Use of Computers for Classroom Learning. London, Ontario: Faculty of Education, University of Western Ontario, 1990.

With R. Walker. *Biography, Identity and Schooling*, London, New York, and Philadelphia: Falmer Press, 1991.

With I. Dowbiggin. "Vocational Education and School Reform." *History of Education Review*, Vol. 20, No. 1, 1991, pp. 39–60.

"School Subjects: Patterns of Change." *Curriculum and Teaching*, Vol. 6, No. 1, 1991, pp. 3–11.

"La Construccion del Curriculum: Posibilidades Y Ambitos de Investigacion de la Historia del Curriculum." *Revista de Educacion on Curriculum History I*, No. 295, 1991, pp. 7–37.

With M. Apple and J. Meyer (eds.). *Sociology of Education* Special Issue on Sociology of Curriculum, 1991.

"Sponsoring the Teachers Voice." *Cambridge Journal of Education*, Vol. 21, No.1, 1991, pp. 35–45.

"Tornando-se una materia academica: padroes de explicacao e evolucao." *Teoria and Educacao* (Brazil), No. 2, 1991, pp. 230–254.

"Nations at Risk and National Curriculum." Section in *Handbook of the American Politics of Education Association*, 1991, pp. 219–232.

"Curriculum Reform and Historical Amnesia." In R. Moon (ed.) *New Curriculum-National Curriculum*, London: Hodder and Stoushton, 1991.

With J. M. Mangan (eds.). *Qualitative Studies in Educational Research: Methodologies in Transition*, RUCCUS Occasional Papers, Vol. 1, London, Ontario: University of Western Ontario, 1991.

With J. M. Mangan (eds.). *Computers, Classrooms, and Culture: Studies in the Use of Computers for Classroom Learning*, RUCCUS Occasional Papers, Vol. 2, London, Ontario: University of Western Ontario, 1991.

With J. M. Mangan. "An Alternative Paradigm for Educational Research." From the project Studying Teacher Development," London, Ontario: Faculty of Education, University of Western Ontario, 1991.

"Studying Teacher's Lives: Problems and Possibilities." From the project Studying Teacher Development, London, Ontario: Faculty of Education, University of Western Ontario, 1991.

With J. M. Mangan and V. A. Rhea (eds.). *Curriculum and Context*, Volume 1 of the Summative Report from the project Curriculum and Context in the Use of Computers for Classroom Learning. London, Ontario: Faculty of Education, University of Western Ontario, 1991.

With J. M. Mangan and V. A. Rhea (eds.). *The Use of Computers for Classroom Learning*, Volume 2 of the Summative Report from the project Curriculum and Context in the Use of Computers for Classroom Learning. London, Ontario: Faculty of Education, University of Western Ontario, 1991.

With J. M. Mangan and V. A. Rhea (eds.). *Closing the Circle: Conclusions and Recommendations*, Volume 3 of the Summative Report from the project Curriculum and Context in the Use of Computers for Classroom Learning. London, Ontario: Faculty of Education, University of Western Ontario, 1991.

With J. M. Mangan and V. A. Rhea (eds.). *Classroom Cultures and the Introduction of Computers*, Interim Report #5 from the project Curriculum and Context in the Use of Computers for Classroom Learning. London, Ontario: Faculty of Education, University of Western Ontario, 1991.

Studying Teachers' Lives, London and New York: Routledge, 1992.

"Sponsoring the Teachers Voice." In M. Fullan and A. Hargreaves (eds.) *Understanding Teacher Development*, London: Casell, and New York: Teachers College Press, 1992.

With J. M. Mangan. "Computers in Schools as Symbolic and Ideological Action: The Genealogy of the ICON." *The Curriculum Journal*, Vol. 3, No. 3, 1992, pp. 261–276.

"Studying School Subjects." *Curriculum Perspectives*, Vol. 12, No. 1, 1992.

"Studying Teachers' Lives: An Emergent Field of Inquiry." In I. F. Goodson (ed.) *Studying Teachers' Lives*, London and New York: Routledge, 1992, pp. 1–17.

"Studying Teachers' Lives: Problems and Possibilities." In I. F. Goodson (ed.) *Studying Teachers' Lives*, London and New York: Routledge, 1992, pp. 234–249.

"School Subjects: Patterns of Stability." *Education Research and Perspectives*, Vol. 19, No. 1, 1992, pp. 52-64.

"On Curriculum Form." *Sociology of Education*, Vol. 65, No. 1, 1992, pp. 66–75.

"Dar voz ao professor: As historias de vida dos professores e o seu desenvolvimento profissional." In *Vidas De Professores*, Coleccao Ciencias da Educacao, A. Novoa (ed.), Lisbon, Portugal: Porto Editora, 1992, pp. 63–78.

"'Nations at Risk' and 'National Curriculum': Ideology and Identity." In J. Lynch, C. Modgil, and S. Modgil (eds.), *Equity or Excellence? Education and Cultural Reproduction, Cultural Diversity and the Schools*, Vol. 3, London, New York, and Philadelphia: Falmer Press, 1992, pp. 199–213.

With J. M. Mangan (eds.). *History, Context, and Qualitative Methods in the Study of Education*, RUCCUS Occasional Papers, Vol. 3, London, Ontario: University of Western Ontario, 1992.

School Subjects and Curriculum Change, 3d ed., London, New York, and Philadelphia: Falmer Press, 1993.

With C. J. Anstead. "Subject Status and Curriculum Change: Commercial Education in London, Ontario, 1920-1940." *Paedagogica Historica*, Vol. 29, No. 2, 1993, pp. 459–481.

"Investigating Schooling: From the Personal to the Programmatic." *New Education*, Vol. 14, No. 1, 1993, pp. 11-20.

With C. J. Anstead. *Through the Schoolhouse Door*. Toronto: Garamond Press, 1993.

With R. P. Coulter (eds.). *Rethinking Vocationalism: Whose work/life is it?* Toronto: Our Schools/Our Selves Education Foundation, 1993.

"The Devil's Bargain." *Education Policy Analysis Archives* (electronic journal), Vol. 1, No. 3, 1993.

"Forms of Knowledge and Teacher Education." In P. Gilroy and M. Smith (eds.) *International Analyses of Teacher Education, Jet Papers 1*, Abbington, Oxfordshire: Carfax, 1993.

With C. Anstead. "Structure and Mediation: Glimpses of Everyday Life at the London Technical and Commercial High School, 1920-1940," *American Journal of Education*, Vol. 102, No. 1, 1993, pp. 55-79.

With C. Anstead. "On Explaining Curriculum Change." *The Curriculum Journal*, Vol. 4, No. 3, 1993, pp. 403-420.

John Willinsky's *The Triumph of Literature/The Fate of Literacy: English in the Secondary School Curriculum, Historical Studies in Education*, Vol. 5, No. 1, 1993, pp. 165-166.

With J. M. Mangan. "Computers in Schools as Symbolic and Ideological Action: The Genealogy of the ICON." *The Curriculum Journal*, Vol. 3, No. 3, 1993, pp 261-276.

With A. Cole. "Exploring the Teacher's Professional Knowledge." In D. McLaughlin and W. G. Tierney (eds.), *Naming Silenced Lives*, London and New York: Routledge, 1993, pp. 71-94.

Studying Curriculum: Cases and Methods, Buckingham: Open University Press/ New York: Teachers College Press/Toronto: OISE Press, 1994.

"A Genesis and Genealogy of British Curriculum Studies." *Curriculum and Teaching*, Vol. 9, No. 1, 1994, pp. 14-25.

"From Personal to Political: Developing Sociologies of Curriculum." *The Journal of Curriculum Theorizing*, Vol. 10, No. 3, 1994, pp. 9-31.

"Qualitative Research in Canadian Teacher Education: Developments in the Eye of a Vacuum," *International Journal of Qualitative Studies in Education*, Vol. 7, No. 3, 1994, pp. 227-237.

"Studying the Teacher's Life and Work," *Teaching and Teacher Education*, Vol. 10, No. 1, 1994, pp. 29-37.

With C. Fliesser. "Exchanging Gifts: Collaborative Research and Theories of Context." *Analytic Teaching*, Vol. 15, No. 2, 1994.

With A. Cole. "Teacher's Professional Knowledge." *Teacher Education Quarterly*, Vol. 21, No. 1, 1994, pp. 85-106.

The Making of Curriculum: Collected Essays, 2d ed. London, New York, and Philadelphia: Falmer Press, 1995.

Curiculo: Teoria e Historia, Petropolis, Brazil: Vozes, 1995.

Historia del Coriculum, Barcelona, Spain: Ediciones Pomares, 1995.

"The Story So Far: Personal Knowledge and the Political." *International Journal of Qualitative Studies in Education*, Vol. 8, No. 1, 1995, pp. 89–98.

"Education as a Practical Matter." *Cambridge Journal of Education*, Vol. 25, No. 2, 1995, pp. 137–148.

With C. Fliesser. "Negotiating Fair Trade: Towards Collaborative Relationships Between Researchers and Teachers in College Settings." *Peabody Journal of Education*, Vol. 70, No. 3, 1995, pp. 5–17.

"Materias Excolares y la Construccion del Curriculum: Texto y contexto." In J. G. Minguez and M. Beas (eds.) *Libro de Texto y Construccion de Materiales Curriculares*, Granada, Spain: Proyecto Sur de Ediciones S.A.L, 1995, pp. 183–199.

"A Nation at Rest: The Contexts for Change in Teacher Education in Canada." In N. K. Shimahara and I. Z. Holowinsky (eds.) *Teacher Education in Industrialized Nations*, New York and London: Garland Press, 1995, pp. 125–153.

"The Context of Cultural Inventions: Learning and Curriculum." In P. Cookson and B. Schneider (eds.) *Transforming Schools*, New York and London: Garland Press, 1995, pp. 307–327.

"Basil Bernstein and Aspects of the Sociology of the Curriculum." In P. Atkinson, B. Davies and S. Delamont (eds.) *Discourse and Reproduction*, Cresskill, N.J.: Hampton Press, 1995, pp. 121-136.

"A Genesis and Genealogy of British Curriculum Studies." In Alan Sadovnik (ed.) *Knowledge and Pedagogy: The Sociology of Basil Bernstein*, Norwood, N.J.: Ablex, 1995.

With A. Hargreaves. "Let Us Take the Lead," *Times Educational Supplement*, March 1995.

"Curriculum Contests: Environmental Studies Versus Geography." *Environmental Education Research*, Vol. 2, No. 1, 1996, pp. 71–88.

With R. Walker. "Telling Tales." In H. McEwan and K. Egan (eds.) *Narrative in Teaching, Learning, and Research*. New York: Teachers College Press, 1996.

"Studying the Teacher's Life and Work." In J. Smyth (ed.) *Critical Discourses on Teacher Development*, London: Cassell, 1996.

Index

Apple, M. 165, 182
Armstrong, M. 35
art 176
Assoc. Of Education in Citizen-
    ship 118

Ball, Benjamin 94
Ball, S.J. 53, 147, 150, 151
Baltzell, E.D. 166
Banks, O. 141, 142
Barnes, S. 184, 185, 190
Barrow, R. 23
Beachside Comprehensive 150,
    151
Beloe Committee 147
Bernstein, B 9, 26, 43, 46, 47, 50,
    51, 55, 56, 163, 168, 182
biology 52, 64, 65, 155, 156
Blyth, W.A.L. 143
botany 65
Bourdieu, P. 176, 182, 183
British Assn. For Advancement of
    Science 17, 65, 67, 189
British Social Hygiene Council 65
Brocklehust, J.B. 16
Bruner, J.S. 37
Bryan, P.W. 124
Bryce Commission 99
Bryne, E. 105, 149, 150
Bucher, R. 140

Calvin, J. 24, 39
Carnegie Task Force 181
Carson, Sean 126, 132
Certificate of Secondary Educa-
    tion (CSE) 147

cognitive maps 2, 3
College of Montaign 23, 24
comprehensive schools 9, 10 193
computers 175, 176
Connell, R.W. 182
conspiracy theory 13
Cookson, P.W. 176
Cooper, B. 52
Crowther Report 141
Cuban, L. 14
Cunningham, P. 54
curriculum 10, 11, 52
    new 113
    contests 113
    change 54
    content 50, 54, 182
    history 53, 55, 62, 63, 64, 83
    form 50, 51 & Chap. 9 & Chap.
        10
    subject centered 48, 144
    secondary school 61, 63, 65, 83

Dale, R. 49
Davies, B 46
Dawes, Richard 67, 188
Dept. Of Education & Science
        (DES) 130
disciplines 36, 39
Dodd, T. 141
Dowdeswell, W.H. 155
Durkheim, Emile 182

education,
    history 63, 144
    vocational 142–144
    philosophy of 35

Education Act (1902) UK 99
Education Act (1944) UK 28, 147, 190, 191
educational theory 61
Eggleston, J. 141, 143, 144
English 52, 117, 152
environmental studies 52, 155 & Chap. 7
Esland, G.M. 49, 50
Esquirol, Etienne 88
examination boards 28, 64, 99

Farrell, J.G. 7
Fereday, Ernest 119
Fisher, C.A. 124
Foucault, M. 84, 85, 96–98
Franklin, B. 53
French Revolution 32, 87
Friedson, Eliot 72, 86, 94
Fyson, A. 127

Garnett, Alice 102, 154
Gaskell, P.J. 53
General Certificate of Education 28
General College Entrance 147
Geographical Association 99–101, 103, 115, 117, 120, 123, 127, 129, 154
geography 52, 96–107, 154–156 & Chap. 6 & Chap. 7
Gibbons, M. 23
Giroux, H. 85
Glasgow University 25
Goldsmith's College 145, 146
Gowing, D. 103
grammar schools 10, 28, 143, 152
Green, M. 12
Gundem, B. 54

Hadlow Report 154
Halsey, A.H. 157
Hamilton, D. 23
Hanson, D. 141
Hargreaves, D. 44
Harrison, D. 32
Hirst, P.M. 36–38

history 115–117
Hobshawm, E. 18
Hodson, D. 17, 54, 189
Holmes Group 181
Honeybone, R.C. 101, 102, 114, 120
Humanities Curriculum Project 146

Industrial revolution 25, 33
Interdisciplinary Enquiry (IDE) 145
internationalism 175, 176
invented tradition, science of 18, 19

Jackson, P. 12, 44
Jameson, F. 56
Jenkins, D 30, 52

Kaestle, C. 75
Kingston University 45
Kirk, W. 115, 131
Kliebard, H.M. 53

Lacey, C. 44, 139
Lambert, R. 172
languages 152
Laurie, S.S. 62
Lawton, D. 37, 38
Layton, D. 17, 30, 31, 52, 64, 67, 121, 122, 133, 134, 140, 142, 143, 144, 154, 156, 157
local examination certificate 26
London School of Economics 45
London Institute of Education 45, 56
London University 44, 102

MacKinder, H.T. 98, 100, 105, 114, 116, 120–122, 127, 154
Magnan, Valentin 92
Mangan, M. 175, 176
Mannheim, K. 182, 188
Mardle, G. 140

Marsden, D. 44, 151
Marsh, C. 54
mathematics 52, 53, 152
McCulloch, G 52, 53
McLeish, J. 139
medicine, social history 69
Meyer, J.W. 54, 69
Ministry of Education 118
Mir, G. 23, 24
Moon, B. 53
Morel, B.A. 91, 92
Morris, Robert 148
Musgrave, P.W. 54
Musgrove, F. 49
music 16, 17, 176

National Curriculum 55, 56, 181,
    195
National Society School 188
Nicholls, A.D. 127-133
Norwood Report 26, 28, 100, 125,
    147, 149, 151, 187, 190,
    191
Nuffield Project 65, 155
Nye, R.A. 93

Offley Conference 125

Parisian Faculty of Medicine 94
Passeron, J.C. 183
payment by results 67
pedagogies 25, 104, 115, 143, 156
    discourse 46
    dominant 47
Persell, C.H. 176
Peters, R.S. 35, 37
Phenix, P.M. 36
physics, 52
Pinel, Philip 88, 90
Pitman, A.J. 183
Popkewitz, T 53
Powers, J.B. 54
Pring, R. 36
psychiatry 70–74
    knowledge, French 63
    Annales Medico
        psychologiques 89, 90

history 83, 95, 98, 107
    social history 69
    French 19th century Chapter 6
    asylum -19th century 63, 70, 76

Raising the School Leaving Age
    (ROSLA) 145
Reid, W.A. 30, 69
Research Projects 3
Revised Code 67
revisionism 61
Rothblatt, S. 31
Rothman, D. 88
Rowell, P.M. 53
Royal Geographical Society 118,
    119, 120, 124
Rudolph, F. 13

Scheck, D.C. 175
school subjects 64, 98, 107, 113,
    140, 142
    history 55, 95
    content 54, 66, 163
    origins 48, 142
    traditions 153
    social history 51, 113
    definition 153
science 67, 68, 117, 152, 156, 188,
    189, 190
    education 17, 54, 64
    social history 69
Science of Common Things, The
    67, 68
Science Masters Assoc. 65
Secondary Regulations 1904 (UK)
    27, 99
Shapin, S. 184, 185, 190
Shipman, M. 30, 146, 147
Shulman, L. 163, 182
Silver, H 64
Simon, B. 15
Smelser, N. 25
Smith, Louis 54
Smith, Adam 184
social studies 117, 118, 120
Society of Art Masters 141
Stanic, G. 53

Stenhouse, Lawrence 146
Stevens, F. 152
Strauss, A. 140
Studies in Curriculum History
        Series 53, 54
subject s)culture 139, 140
Sugarm; , B 9

Taunto Report 1868 26, 28, 187,
        191, 192
Thom; P.R. 124
Thom on, E.P. 32
Tomk s, G. 53
Trade Jnion Congress 142
tripa ite schooling 193

Uni sity Schools of Geography
        105, 120, 154
Uni rsity of Cambridge Local
        Exam. Cert. 26, 186
Ur ead, J. 122, 127
U: m, M. 166

Vulliamy, G. 16

Wakeford, J. 173
Walker, R. 46
Walker, David 101
Walker, M. 140
Waring, Mary 64
Warwick, D. 152
Watson, Foster 48, 55, 62, 155
Williams, R. 11, 50, 51, 115, 141,
        142, 144, 182
Willis, P. 183
Wise, M.J. 124
Witkin, J. 157
Wooldridge, S.W. 101, 102, 124,
        154
Woolnough, B.E. 52, 68
working-class private school 32
Wrottesley, Lord 17, 18, 189
Young, M.F.D. 12, 46, 50, 83

zoology, 65

COUNTERPOINTS

Counterpoints publishes the most compelling and imaginative books being written in education today. Grounded on the theoretical advances in criticalism, feminism and postmodernism in the last two decades of the twentieth century, Counterpoints engages the meaning of these innovations in various forms of educational expression. Committed to the proposition that theoretical literature should be accessible to a variety of audiences, the series insists that its authors avoid esoteric and jargonistic languages that transform educational scholarship into an elite discourse for the initiated. Scholarly work matters only to the degree it affects consciousness and practice at multiple sites. Counterpoints' editorial policy is based on these principles and the ability of scholars to break new ground, to open new conversations, to go where educators have never gone before.

COUNTERPOINTS